A Practical Guide to
POLICE REPORT WRITING

TOM E. KAKONIS, Ph.D.
HEAD, DEPARTMENT OF ENGLISH
FERRIS STATE COLLEGE

DONALD K. HANZEK, Ph.D.
DEPARTMENT OF ENGLISH
FERRIS STATE COLLEGE

FORMERLY EAST LANSING POLICE DEPARTMENT
AND DETROIT POLICE DEPARTMENT

Gregg Division
McGraw-Hill Book Company
New York   St. Louis   Dallas   San Francisco   Auckland   Bogotá
Düsseldorf   Johannesburg   London   Madrid   Mexico   Montreal
New Delhi   Panama   Paris   São Paulo   Singapore   Sydney   Tokyo
Toronto

Library of Congress Cataloging in Publication Data
Kakonis, Thomas E
  A practical guide to police report writing

  Includes index.
  1. Police reports. 2. Report writing. I. Hanzek,
Donald K., joint author. II. Title.
HV7936.R53K34   808'.066'363   77-21437
ISBN 0-07-033246-0

*In memory of George E. Godby, Sergeant,
East Lansing Police Department*

A PRACTICAL GUIDE TO POLICE REPORT WRITING

234567890DODO7854321098

The editors for this book were Susan H. Munger and
Alice V. Manning, the designers were Marsha Cohen and
Tracy A. Glasner, and the production supervisor was
Kathleen Morrissey. It was set in Helvetica by Black Dot,
Inc.
Printed and bound by R. R. Donnelley & Sons Company.

Contents

Preface

We have written this book for college and academy students preparing for careers in law enforcement and for officers in the field. Our purpose is to relieve officers of many of the organizational and mechanical problems of police report writing. To achieve this, we have presented a practical, orderly, systematic method for writing police reports. This system divides the report into major sections and supplementary sections. The major sections guide the officers through their presentation of an overview of the entire incident. The supplementary sections provide a convenient way to include details essential to a complete report but not necessary for an immediate grasp of the incident as a whole.

In essence, this systematic approach removes much of the organizational burden by outlining the report for an officer. As each section serves a precisely defined function, the officer can concentrate exclusively on one specific element of the report at one time. This, in turn, simplifies the writing task and reduces the chance that important material will be left out. Also, such a method often permits a standardization of language that frees the officer from many mechanical problems—grammar, punctuation, diction— that are a constant source of irritation.

We have detailed this method in Chapters 3 through 6. In these chapters each section of the report is thoroughly discussed, guidelines are provided, and models are included. The discussion of each section is accompanied by a rationale explaining both its necessity and its practicality. In addition, we have included several student reports illustrating the suggested format. And each chapter has extensive exercises designed to reinforce the student's grasp of the format.

While this discussion of format is the heart of the text, we have also included units on the role of police reports, the content of police reports, the elements of crime, and police usage and diction. The first introduces students to the importance of reports in the criminal justice system. The second treats an often neglected part of police report writing—the actual content. In this chapter we help students to understand the fine distinctions between facts, inferences, opinions, and judgments, and discuss their application to police reports. Exercises strengthen the student's awareness of these distinctions.

The last two chapters, "The Elements of Crime" and "Police Diction and Usage," serve primarily as reference sections, although the latter has numerous exercises that make it readily adaptable to classroom use. "The Elements of Crime" chapter is necessarily not exhaustive; the different phraseology and terminology used in different areas of the country make this impossible. We have, however, included the chapter to acquaint students with some of the widely accepted elements of crime and to assist civilian instructors of police report writing.

The final chapter, "Police Diction and Usage," treats in handbook form the most frequently recurring language problems in police reports. Each problem is analyzed, explained, and illustrated. Examples of faulty usage, often taken verbatim from student reports, are accompanied by corrected versions for purposes of comparison. In addition, we have included a unit on spelling. In it, the student will find the most important spelling rules along with a list of words commonly misspelled in police reports.

We gratefully acknowledge the following persons who have given us invaluable aid in writing this book: Mrs. Betty Smith, Ferris State College; Professors Robert Parsons, Terry Nerbonne, and Allan Lawson of the Department of Criminal Justice, Ferris State College; Detective Sergeant Wayne Johns and Sergeant Roger Horchner of the Michigan State Police; Lieutenant Donald Hewson of the East Lansing Police Department; and, of course, our wives, Mickie and Judy.

TOM E. KAKONIS
DONALD K. HANZEK

Chapter 1
A Rationale of
Reporting
Style

Many civilians relish the tale about the patrolman who dragged a dead horse from Kosciusko Boulevard to First Street so that he wouldn't have to contend with spelling "Kosciusko" in his report. Few officers have managed to avoid hearing it. While fictional, the story does bring up a point: many are entertained by the language problems of others. In police work, such amusement at the expense of an officer can easily have serious consequences. This can be seen in the following example of a courtroom dialogue which could easily result from the same spelling error committed by several students in their reports.

> "Now, officer, your report reads 'I raped her in a blanket and called for an ambulance.' Will you explain to the court why you attacked the defendant who had already been injured in the altercation?"
> "I did not attack the defendant, sir, I. . . ."
> "But isn't this your signature identifying you as the reporting officer?"
> "Yes, sir, it is, but. . . ."
> "And doesn't it read quite clearly 'I raped her?' That is r-a-p-e-d, is it not?"
> "Yes sir, but I meant wrapped."
> "Then it was just an error on your part?"
> "Yes sir."
> "I see. Then tell me, officer, didn't you also err . . . ?"

Veteran officers have suffered through similar courtroom scenes on countless occasions. The image of a badly embarrassed fellow officer, squirming on the stand, attempting to explain some glaring fault—spelling, diction, syntax, or omission—long endures.

Such an episode can hurt the reputation of the officer and the department. Moreover, it often has an immediate and weakening effect on the rest of the officer's testimony. A confused, embarrassed officer is more likely to make a mistake under examination, to forget pertinent material, to contradict himself or appear hesitant, thus creating an impression of uncertainty that may influence a jury's verdict. Angry over having committed such an error, the officer is more susceptible to being goaded into grosser errors: losing his temper or attempting to fence verbally with counsel. Any of these reactions could occur. And any could have a serious effect on the weight given the testimony by the court.

Making an officer look less competent in one area can seriously diminish the officer's credibility in others. After all, the old saying "If you can't try the case, try the cop" is still believed by many defense attorneys. The counsel who can discredit part of an arresting officer's testimony or create an illusion of incompetence has taken a giant step toward acquittal.

Usually, as in the above example, everyone in the court would probably know what the officer meant. But many would laugh at his discomfort. Moreover, it is not the court's responsibility to discover the officer's meaning; instead it is the officer's duty to present a clear, coherent, and accurate account that will not be misunderstood.

These accounts serve many functions. They provide line officers with invaluable information. They give planning officers the data they need to allocate resources effectively. They make an important contribution to public relations. They establish the bases for the prosecutor's actions. Additionally, as noted above, they play a critical role in the courtroom.

Alexander Pope's warning that "a little learning is a dangerous thing" does not always hold true for line officers. Police work is hazardous, and any piece of information—no matter how small—may help reduce the danger. Fortunately, modern officers are blessed with the LEIN (Law Enforcement Information Network, a computerized system for collecting and sending out information rapidly) system, which makes such data available almost instantly. In many situations field officers are no longer blind; they can often approach an auto stopped for a routine traffic violation, *knowing* that the auto has been reported stolen or that the registered owner has a record of previous arrests. But the network feeds on reports. It can only give out those data which have been secured from the field reports. Faulty reporting results when inadequate, possibly dangerous, material is given out. An incorrect license number on a stolen car report, for example, could prove disastrous.

Even seemingly routine incidents could result in injury to line officers if their information is faulty. A case in point:

An officer on the day watch took a missing persons complaint. An elderly man living with his married daughter had apparently become lost. The afternoon watch was duly apprised of the subject's name and description. Later in the evening, an officer, working alone, sighted the subject. When approached, the man suddenly lashed out with his walking stick, striking the officer in the groin.

*Before the startled officer could recover, he was struck twice more. The officer
then subdued the subject.*

What significant bit of information was this officer missing? The reporting officer,
probably without thinking, had failed to note in the report that the subject had been
confined to a mental institution for several years prior to the incident. In essence, the
assaulted officer had been victimized by his colleague.

Conversely, an officer sent out with a warrant to pick up a subject who had failed
to appear on a drunk driving charge benefited from the thorough reporting of her
colleagues. Although drunk driving is serious, the subject is usually an ordinary citizen,
and such arrests are relatively routine. Despite this, the officer read the original arrest
report before leaving the station. She learned the subject of the warrant had heaped
verbal abuse on the arresting officer and had physically resisted arrest. She also
learned that the initial charge had been resisting arrest, although this charge was later
dropped by the prosecutor. The officer, now forewarned, requested and received
assistance. Officers then effected the arrest on the warrant without difficulty. Obviously, officers should never treat any arrest lightly. But, as in this instance, the officer
armed with pertinent information has an extra edge.

A list of such examples could be extended indefinitely. Every department has its
own horror story of some disaster or near-disaster that resulted from faulty reporting.
But the point remains clear: the line officer needs all available information, and the
primary source is the field report.

Reports are directly helpful to the line officer in still another sense: they let
command officers assign personnel more effectively. Planning officers collect and
evaluate data contained in the field reports. These data allow them to identify
high-crime areas and to allocate personnel and material accordingly. For the officers in
the field, this means assistance available when and where they most need it. In
addition, command officers also use reports to justify budgetary requests for additional
personnel and equipment. To obtain these, they must demonstrate clearly that both are
required if the department is to fulfill its mission to serve and protect. Such justification
comes from the data compiled from the line officers' reports.

Those who doubt the latter point have perhaps never witnessed the sometimes
heated disputes arising from incidents which occurred on jurisdictional boundaries.
Usually, the initial argument involves line officers trying to evade a report by arguing
the incident belongs to the other department. The sequel, however, may take place
between supervisors assuming the opposite tack, for they realize how statistics can
influence a budget request. In one instance a question over the initial point of impact at
a multiple-fatal accident scene was later resolved at the command level. One agency
required statistical bolstering of its request for additional patrol officers; the other
preferred to retain a relatively unblemished traffic record. While such instances are
rare, they do occur and they further illustrate the potential effect of field reports.

On a more personal level, reports may influence an officer's career. Recognition
and promotion may hinge on the quality of an officer's reports. Frequently, high-

ranking supervisors, especially in large departments, form their impression of individual officers almost exclusively from reports. These supervisors will then lean heavily on such impressions in evaluating the officers' overall ability. They might justifiably question the qualifications of an officer who would write, as did one student, "Placing handcuffs on the suspect, he became belligerent and resisted." They may well ask: Who handcuffed the suspect? As written, the suspect handcuffed himself. In unusual circumstances the officer may require the suspect to do just that; however, this occurs only rarely. Is this one of these rare occasions, or has the reporting officer simply failed to make the meaning clear? Either way, the garbled construction does not improve the officer's stature.

Deficient report writing can do more than damage an officer's career; it can seriously detract from the department's professional image. Other departments and governmental agen ies may receive copies of the reports. And reports that are replete with misspellings, grammatical errors, and ambiguous phraseology are hardly impressive. In addition, many departments require the signatures of complainants or other reporting parties for verification of the report. Consequently, their reports are subject to immediate examination by the public. Citizens may understandably wonder if their tax money is well spent when they sign a report containing "The assult victom proceded. . . ."

In all the above instances, we have dealt with unintentional errors resulting from either negligence or a poor command of language. We must recognize that, unfortunately, not all errors fit these categories. Some are deliberate. In one instance, an officer attempting to disperse an unruly mob fired two "warning" shots into the ground. In so doing, the officer had violated departmental regulations. However, besides the usual barrage of stones, rotten eggs, and urine-filled plastic bags, the demonstration had included exploding firecrackers. Apparently the officer, aware of the violation, belatedly hoped the shots would be either unnoticed or accepted as more firecrackers being detonated, and thus omitted the firing from the report of the incident. Later, when confronted by reporters, the departmental spokesperson, on the basis of the officer's report, repeatedly denied any shots had been fired, despite the number of witnesses who declared otherwise. Ultimately the truth was revealed. The embarrassed spokesperson issued a public retraction and apology. But police credibility had already been irreparably harmed.

But good reports can be extremely helpful to public relations. Well-written reports shown to news reporters create a favorable impression of both police competence and credibility. The media people then reflect this impression in their coverage. This coverage, in turn, inspires public confidence and trust in the police. Few departments can operate effectively without both.

Moreover, police can use good reports to improve their relations with the public through various educational programs and announcements. Officers may, for example, conduct workshops suggesting specific precautions for merchants in areas with a high incidence of breaking and entering. They can advise women to be careful during an outbreak of assault or rape attempts in particular locales. They can warn parents that possible child molesters are frequenting a neighborhood. The warnings, along with a marked police presence, build public respect for the department. Often, this public awareness results in the apprehension of the criminals.

But to be effective, the officers conducting the meetings or making the announce-ments must have a thorough understanding of the problem. This understanding is derived from the field reports. Using these reports, the officers can isolate specific threats and suggest specific countermeasures. They can, for instance, ascertain that an assault suspect's preferred targets are female hospital employees—doctors, nurses, and technicians—who work uneven hours. Officers can then alert the various hospi-tals. Thus forewarned and armed with a description of the potential assailant and his customary method of operation, the prospective victims are less prone to attack.

The above illustrations demonstrate the importance of report writing to the individual officer, to the department, and to the community at large. But the assurance of justice remains the single most important function of report writing. This assurance requires that subsequent investigators and the prosecutor be made aware of all pertinent data, that the officer be capable of testifying competently, and that the court be apprised of all relevant material. Injustice could result from a breakdown in any one of these areas.

Clearly, subsequent investigators must have a complete account of the initial investigation. Without it, they are seriously handicapped, for the initial field report serves as a major source of "leads." Consequently, any errors of omission or commission could easily make the investigation ineffective. At the least, costly investigative hours would be lost in duplicating the reporting officer's activities.

The report is equally as important to the prosecutor. Any prosecution demands a thorough investigation painstakingly recorded by the reporting officer. Usually the prosecutor's initial awareness of a particular case stems from the line officer's field report. From it the prosecutor develops an overall strategy and determines which witnesses to subpoena. On occasion the prosecutor may use the report as a measure of the officer's potential effectiveness on the witness stand. This impression may then influence the prosecution's stance in any subsequent plea bargaining.

Frequently, the prosecutor's only link with the officer prior to trial may be the original field report. In capital cases prosecutors will, of course, supplement their detailed study of the report by interviewing the officer at length. But nearly all prosecutors and their assistants carry heavy case loads; they simply do not have time for careful preparation of most cases involving minor offenses. Often they do not have time for any preparation whatsoever. It is not unusual for a prosecutor to be reading a report, perhaps for the first time, while walking into the courtroom a few minutes before the trial. As this permits only a hurried conference with the officer, the prosecutor must have a clear, compact, and coherent written account. The report must provide all the necessary information in readily understandable form and language. Otherwise, the prosecutor can neither prosecute the case successfully nor properly protect the officer on the stand.

And it is on the witness stand that officers are most vulnerable. They must give detailed testimony about events which may have occurred several months prior to the trial. In this testimony they can rely on three sources:memory, notes, and the formal field report. Memory can be fickle. If officers have been involved in similar cases during the period between report and trial, they may confuse separate incidents. Informal notes have the same danger. Notes are often fragmentary and disorganized, jotted down hurriedly in an individual shorthand difficult to interpret quickly and precisely in the stress situation that often characterizes the presentation of testimony. Consequently, it is the formal report that must bear the burden, for it is here that officers can find the required information in an organized, understandable format.

But the report must be competently written. The dialogue opening this chapter illustrates only one of the many pitfalls awaiting the careless officer in court. Spelling errors, while most obvious, may be least important. They can certainly embarrass the officer. If skillfully exploited by the defense counsel, they may lead to a questioning of the officer's general competence. Other errors, though, may create critical problems of a substantial nature.

A simple comma fault (see Chapter 8, A Glossary of Police Diction and Usage), among others, could cause confusion. Consider the following excerpt from a student report:

Adam 12 stopped the Suspect vehicle at the M50 exit ramp of U.S. 27, at 1:28 a.m., officers saw the Suspect throw objects from the right front passenger window.

We have two independent statements: "Adam 12 . . . U.S. 27" and "officers . . . window." To which does the phrase "at 1:28 a.m." belong? Does the phrase indicate the time officers stopped the suspect vehicle, or does it record when the officers saw the objects thrown from the window? How much time actually elapsed between the two actions? If only three minutes, we have a possible deviation of six minutes: for if the vehicle was stopped at 1:28 a.m., the objects were thrown at 1:31 a.m.; if the objects were thrown at 1:28 a.m., the vehicle was stopped at 1:25 a.m. Confusion on this point could open other areas to dispute: the reported speed of the chase, for instance, may be called into question, as the possible elapsed time may no longer be compatible with the officer's previous testimony. Other than as a source of unneeded embarrassment to a professional police officer, the time question in this instance may prove to be of little consequence. Probably it is. But in police work, what is insignificant in ninety-nine cases may be crucial in the hundredth.

The catalog of possible errors and their ultimate consequences could be extended to some length. In Chapter 3, for example, we note how an "airtight" case was dismissed because a simple typographical error caused several witnesses to testify to the wrong date. But embarrassment and injustice are not the only outcome of inadequate reporting. Even the sentence imposed, especially in cases involving guilty pleas, may be influenced by the officer's initial report. Often, this report serves as the basis for the judge's decision. Therefore, a complete investigation is in itself not enough; a complete, comprehensive, and understandable report must follow. The officer who has written such a report is the officer who will give competent testimony, and who will provide the court with the needed information to assure justice.

In all the above we have tried to stress the importance of report writing in the criminal justice system. Obviously, we believe its role cannot be overemphasized, especially now when even greater demands are being made of line officers. Yet, despite the importance of report writing, officers must face harsh reality: they will rarely write these reports under ideal conditions. But as ideal conditions are unusual in any phase of police work, this is not an unfamiliar situation for line officers. They are accustomed to making instantaneous decisions under stress conditions in the field and then having these decisions weighed and evaluated at leisure by those sitting securely behind desks. So officers need not expect any other treatment for their reporting efforts. They will write their reports under adverse conditions, and these reports will also be scrutinized and criticized at leisure, often by people who earn their living through word usage: attorneys, magistrates, and news media personnel.

Of these restrictions in writing reports, the most severe are time and circumstance, especially time. Because there are rarely enough police officers, there is rarely enough time to do everything. Thus officers continually face the need to borrow time from one incident in order to respond to another. As most incidents require police actions that cannot be put off, the only possible way to make more time is usually to curtail or put off writing the report.

Considering the numerous responsibilities thrust upon line officers, one can readily recognize this as the only option. For any incident may require several police actions. Officers, upon arrival, may need to restore order, treat injured persons, and arrange for their transportation. In some instances, the scene must be secured for further investigation. Officers must gather physical evidence and conduct interviews. All these activities take time. And this is time that must be spent; these duties cannot be slighted. But as the elapsed time increases, so does the probability of another emergency requiring an immediate response. Consequently, to meet the new situation, officers are frequently forced to foreshorten their reports.

These circumstances recur with monotonous regularity. In metropolitan departments the voice of a harried dispatcher desperately pleading for "a car to take a run" becomes a familiar part of the line officer's life. Officers responding to the plea usually do so at the expense of their own reporting time. Officers in smaller agencies face essentially the same difficulty. With them, however, it is not that all other units are busy and unavailable; it is simply that there are no other units. The problem is apparently universal. Veteran officers in widely separated departments can attest to this phenomenon: everything happens at once. Perhaps Elbert Hubbard was really commenting on police work in his line: "Life is just one damned thing after another."

These delays, while unavoidable, compound the officer's report writing problems. Upon being dispatched to another assignment, the officer must set aside his or her notes and partially completed report. Points committed to memory must be pushed to the back of the mind, leaving the officer free to deal properly with the new problem.

Later when the officer attempts to complete the report, some of the details may no longer be clear. Some may become confused with the intervening incident or incidents. The hastily written notes may be indecipherable in spots. Memorized information may be lost or blurred. The officer may even have difficulty picking up the narrative thread of the incomplete report.

Delay can cause any or all of these problems. If the reporting incident was complex or chaotic, the effect of any postponement is heightened. In such a situation information is usually received sporadically in a disjointed manner. Therefore, pertinent details, actions, and perceptions that are acquired piecemeal come interspersed with the irrelevant. Interviews are disrupted because the officer is needed elsewhere, perhaps to direct an ambulance crew, notify other authorities, or warn bystanders away from the scene. Only later can the officer resume the interrupted questioning. As several such disruptions could occur during the course of the investigation, one can readily understand the possible adverse effect of a prolonged delay in writing the report.

Unfortunately an officer rarely escapes such disruption. Even the squadroom provides no sanctuary. The officer's partners may interrupt with comments. Desk officers may ask the officer to handle their desk duties for a few minutes. Fellow officers drift in and out at intervals for various reasons. Being a sociable lot, these officers rarely fail to disrupt with their friendly questions, joking remarks, offers of coffee, or requests for the loan of assorted equipment. Following each of these breaks, the officer is usually forced to return to the beginning of the report, reread the finished portion, try to recall the next planned entry, and then begin typing anew. As a consequence, the reporting officer finds it difficult to maintain a consistent narrative. Too often, the ultimate result is an incomplete or incoherent report.

Despite all these problems, clear, complete, and coherent reports remain essential if police are to perform efficiently. We believe the simplest, most practical method of achieving this reporting level involves a structured, formalized approach. This approach uses major headings to present a broad, chronological overview of the incident and supplementary headings to present specific details.

We will discuss each heading completely in subsequent chapters. Briefly, these formal divisions ease the officer's burden in several ways. First, they impose order. The systematically divided format gets the officer into the report quickly and relieves him or her of many difficult organizational problems. Second, recording specific details under the appropriate supplementary headings lets the officer concentrate on the overall account under the major headings. This also eliminates the need for numerous, often awkward and confusing, transitions between the general narrative and specific details. Third, this formal approach guards against omissions by having the officer focus on a single aspect of the report. In essence, the headings also act as checklists. Fourth, writing time is reduced. In the supplementary sections, for example, the officer concentrates only on putting the data into a concise form. Narrative flow is no object, for the officer has already told the story of the incident in the major units. Fifth, standardized phrases can now be used in many sections. This lets the officer write parts of the report without worrying about sentence structure, word order, or punctuation. These remain uniform; only the information changes. The officer simply inserts data pertinent to the particular situation into a preconstructed format.

In addition, readers find that this disciplined method aids comprehension. They can quickly get a grasp of the overall incident by reading the major sections. To the prosecutor, often pressed for time and laboring under a heavy case load, this can be invaluable. To the officer, testifying some months after the incident, this serves as a quick memory refresher. And the inclusion of details under appropriately headed supplementary sections lets both prosecutor and officer easily extract the exact information required in court.

In the following chapters we will illustrate this structured approach by applying it to specific situations. We believe that the officer who masters these fundamentals will find this method extremely practical. The format deals with typical police problems; consequently, it can be readily adapted to the requirements of any particular department.

Instead of including complete forms from various public agencies, we have concentrated only on the narrative portion of a report. Historically, this is where officers have had the greatest difficulty. Moreover, it is the most important part of any report. Many departments try to relieve the officers of the burden of writing the report by devising various "check-off" complaint forms. Such forms are usually more helpful to the file clerk than the line officers, for without detailed information, they remain limited. The officer who checks a box indicating the suspect vehicle in an armed robbery had a decal in the window has not greatly enlightened his fellow officers. Few cars are without window stickers of one kind or another—vehicle inspection tags, parking permits, souvenirs, etc. In a college community, the possibilities increase greatly. There are stickers for on-campus students, commuting students, handicapped students, faculty, staff, and so on. Therefore, the reporting officers must enlarge upon the checked information, if, of course, they have any other material.

Some departments help the officers supplement the checked information by providing space for written clarification. Usually, the space is limited. In a suspect's description, for example, officers will also write in the color of an article of clothing in the appropriate space. They will indicate the suspect wore a blue and white coat by inserting "blue/wht" under the heading *coat*. This is better than the simple check, yet still limited. Was it a topcoat, a car coat, a field jacket, a raincoat, or a ski coat? Was the coat predominantly blue with white trim? Or was it colored blue and white in equal proportions?

The officer in a winter resort area, for example, alert for an armed suspect preying on inebriated guests leaving after-ski parties, needs more than a "blue/white" coat. Blue and white coats in various lengths and combinations abound. On the other hand, a "blue waist-length ski jacket with dual white piping around the collar, shoulders, wrists, and waist" reduces the field considerably. Adding that the coat has a ski-area patch on the left shoulder narrows the field even more. Naming the ski area—Aspen, Kitzbühel, Vail—would be even more helpful.

A good report will contain this information if it is available. But as one can readily see, to provide for every possible occurrence in a check-off form would require a prohibitively long complaint form. The form would be self-defeating, as the time saved from writing would be consumed in reading to locate the proper box.

We do not mean to belittle the box forms. They are obviously valuable guides for much information: names, addresses, phone numbers, etc. But officers should recognize the limitations of these forms. They are aids to the narrative, not a replacement for it.

One further note:we have also incorporated units in spelling and language usage. The materials for these units were derived from student reports. The spelling list, for example, includes those words most frequently misspelled in student reports. All these words are basic to an officer's vocabulary. Our Glossary of Diction has the same source. It is not an exhaustive discussion of English grammar. Instead we merely examine the common errors committed by law enforcement students and suggest practical methods of correction.

DISCUSSION TOPICS

1. What effect can a simple reporting error have on an officer's testimony?
2. Why is it important for the prosecutor to have an easily readable account of an incident?
3. List the ways in which a good report can prevent an expensive duplication of effort.
4. How can good reports enhance the department's public image? Its professional image?
5. Comment on the different ways command officers may use a field report.
6. How can reports affect an officer's career? (Part of one detective chief's "screening" process consisted of watching officers testify.)
7. Discuss the many problems line officers encounter in report writing.
8. How can a structured approach help?

Chapter 2
The Content of
Police
Reports

The term "police reporting" is not exact. It suggests that officers need only record the observed or stated facts. This reduces the report to a chronicle. In fact, writing police reports is much more complex. It requires officers to exercise constantly some fundamental principles of any writing: perspective, selection, and organization.

PERSPECTIVE

Perspective means the vantage point from which the officer presents the findings. Customarily two such vantage points are adopted in police report writing, the first-person view and the third-person view. The former, used by many departments, is characterized by the first-person pronoun "I." The officer first identifies himself or herself by name and then presents the investigative results or observations from the viewpoint of an active participant in the incident, i.e., "I then searched the suspect and discovered a switchblade knife in his pocket."

Although the use of the first person is not incorrect, at least two objections can be made to its use in police report writing: it can confuse the reader, and it may cause the writer to unconsciously slant information. Confusion results because the reader continually has to reidentify the reporting officer. This may seem simple, but it is often complicated by the involvement of several officers in the incident. In addition, should the reporting officer be in a two-person unit, use of the plural "we" will further add to the reader's difficulty. The reader must now keep in mind which of the officers is the "I" and which two—of several possibly involved—are the "we." The reader, often a prosecutor or supervisor pressed for time, needs no such distractions. He or she should be free to concentrate on the incident itself.

The second objection to using the first person is the possibility of slanting the information. Although one can hardly escape slanting when relating an account involving one's own activities, in police reports such slanting must be reduced to a minimum. But the use of the first person frequently does the opposite. It heightens the officer's sense of involvement and reinforces, although unconsciously, the tendency to present observations in a personal light.

Both of the above problems can be made less serious if the third-person vantage point is used. From this perspective the reader gets what is essentially a "camera-eye" view of the incident. The reporting officer, though an active participant, continually refers to himself or herself and other officers by name. The officer presents all activities as if viewed by a camera covering the incident. This vantage point forces the officer to observe and report his or her own conduct more objectively, thus giving the reader a clearer account of the entire incident. Moreover, naming the officers concerned removes from the reader the burden of constantly rechecking to determine which officer was involved in a particular aspect of the incident.

To maintain objectivity in this perspective, the reporting officer uses third-person pronouns (he, she) in referring to himself or herself. But the officer should use them sparingly and only *when the pronoun clearly refers to the officer.* For example, the officer may report: "Officer Lear activated all emergency equipment. He then informed Dispatch." There is no ambiguity in this pronoun; the "he" in the second sentence clearly refers to Officer Lear in the first sentence.

While complete objectivity is difficult, if not impossible, to attain, the third-person vantage point is more likely to achieve the desired effect than the first-person. It lets the reader view and evaluate without the intrusion of the subjective "I." This does not, of course, mean the officer can never use the first-person pronoun in a report. But such usage should be restricted to direct quotations with the speaker clearly identified. For instance, the officer could record: "Officer Lear then stated, 'I am placing you under arrest for felonious assault.'" Here, to avoid any ambiguity the reporting officer has noted the exact words. But the "I" is readily understood as meaning the reporting officer and because it is in a direct quotation, it does not interfere with the objective presentation.

SELECTIVITY

Selectivity is equally important. Officers cannot include every detail and every word. To do so would be absurd. It would swell every report to unmanageable and impracticable dimensions. Officers must decide what is worth including and what is not. Irrelevant details and remarks must be discarded if the officer is to write a coherent report rather than present a disjointed narrative filled with inconsequential material. But there is no need for officers to make these decisions arbitrarily. They are trained to make such distinctions in their investigations. They have only to apply the same criteria to the report.

For example, officers investigating a B&E discover a set of muddy footprints leading from the point of entry into the building's interior. Officers should use the decreasing amounts of mud deposited on the floor to trace the burglar's progress through the building. They should examine each print to find the ones most clearly showing the size of the shoes and any markings on them. These can be photographed, measured, and cast. They should then scrutinize the other complete and partial prints to see if any bear some distinguishing feature, perhaps a partial brand name, not found on the others. They may even select prints from various rooms to help establish the suspect's presence there; these, too, can be photographed. But recording the exact dimensions of every muddy print would be too time-consuming and of little additional value. Most of the material would be unnecessary. Such an account could read:

Officer LEE discovered a set of muddy footprints leading from the broken window into the interior of the house. Commencing with the print nearest the window, officers counted seventeen (17) complete prints and nine (9) partial. The prints indicated that the Suspect walked from the point of entry through the kitchen into the dining room, then into the living room.

Beginning with the point nearest the point of entry, the measurements of each print are as follows:

No. 1 Left shoe print. Size 11-12, 14 inches long, $3^1/_2$ inches wide at base of toe, $3^1/_4$ inches wide at heel, no instep gap. Vertically ribbed pattern on sole. A partial brand name C--SP visible on heel. Print found 7 inches from doorsill. Measurements, casts, and photographs by Officer LEE.

No. 2 Right shoe print. Description same as above. Found 9 inches from doorsill.

No. 3 Left shoe print. Description same as No. 1 above. Found 36 inches from baseboard.

(And so forth for twenty-six footprints.)

At this stage the frustrated reader, numbed by the mass of details, would probably have difficulty recalling the point of entry and the suspect's progress through the house. The reader would be forced to check the report from the beginning once more to ascertain the most important information.

First, as we shall discuss later, the details of the measurements, casts, and photographs can be put in a supplementary section. In the narrative, officers need only indicate that these actions were performed and that the results are available. Second, even in the supplementary section, a complete description—including casts, measurements, and photographs—of each and every print would be a bit too much. Even if the departmental budget can absorb the cost of the paper, the expenditures for plaster and film might get out of hand, especially if such extravagances were practiced at every scene. Twenty-six casts and photographs of the same shoe prints are rarely necessary.

The same reasoning holds true for officers conducting interviews. A complainant or witness may make various remarks that have no bearing on the case in point. An assault victim, for example, may say, "I don't know what my wife will say when she sees my black eye. She'll probably yell like hell because my glasses are broken." These and similar comments have little or no bearing on the investigation. It would be foolish for the officer to act as a tape recorder and dutifully write down every word. Unless the victim is making a formal deposition, the officer must strip away the nonessentials and through a judicious combining of direct quotations and paraphrased statements relate the victim's story clearly, accurately, and concisely. To do this the officer must be selective about what to include in the report. The narrative must be phrased carefully to give a faithful, correct account of the victim's statement, free from distortion.

The possibilities of including unneeded details are virtually limitless, ranging from word-for-word transcriptions of radio traffic to a minute account of every step taken by each officer involved. A simple request for assistance during a chase becomes:

Officer GARCIA notified Dispatch via radio that Scout 9-6 was in pursuit of a 1975 dark-green over light-green Chevrolet Club Coupe, Michigan 1975 registration XLT 999, northbound on Canterbury at Broadway. Two occupants in the vehicle. Vehicle involved in hit-and-run accident at Canterbury and Poplar. Officer GARCIA requested assistance in halting Suspect vehicle.

Unquestionably, this is the information that would be relayed to the dispatcher. Common sense dictates that the dispatcher must have a description of the suspect vehicle, know the direction and the purpose of the chase, and know the unit involved. But all this information, while part of the radio message, will appear elsewhere in the report. It will also be recorded on a radio log or tape. To include it in the narrative part of the report would be unduly repetitious. If later asked about the radio message, the officer can respond without checking either the log or the tape, for *standard police procedure* would require the above information in the message. Therefore, the inclusion of the word-for-word message is unnecessary. On the above, officers could simply report:

> While pursuing Suspect vehicle north on Canterbury at Broadway, officers advised Dispatch and requested assistance.

This is clear and compact. Details not needed at this point have been omitted. But it still incorporates a partial description of the chase and specifies at which point the call was made.

Officers may also include unnecessary details relating to their own actions. They may give an exhaustive account minutely detailing their activities: where they parked the patrol car; which officer got out on which side; how they got to the doorway; who knocked; who was on the left side of the doorway and who on the right; and so on. Once in a while, every officer will encounter an incident which requires this attention to detail. It may be an armed robbery in progress with a subsequent exchange of gunfire. In such an incident, command officers may demand a precise, point-by-point, position-by-position account of each officer's actions. But in most instances, it is neither necessary nor practicable. Officers are trained to approach the scene carefully. They are trained to exercise certain precautionary measures. These actions should be automatic; they are standard police procedure. Therefore, it is hardly necessary for the officers to include these steps in their report. On the stand later, they can always relate accurately what they did, for these responses are ingrained.

But selection is more than simply removing extraneous information or avoiding repetition. Not only must officers discover and report the *facts*, but they are frequently required to make *inferences* based on these facts. In the report writing process this requirement makes it imperative that the reporting officer be able to distinguish between *facts* and *inferences* and that the officer label each clearly for the reader. The reader must never be confused on this issue: to interpret *inference* as *fact* would hamper further investigation and needlessly endanger the prosecutor's efforts.

What is the distinction between *fact* and *inference*? And how does each enter into police report writing?

Facts. *Facts* can be *verified*. Typically in police reports, facts are composed of physical evidence, statements, and investigative actions. A weapon found on an assault suspect is physical evidence. A wrecking bar at the scene of a B&E is physical evidence. The fingerprints on the bar are physical evidence. Tire tracks at the scene of a hit-and-run accident are physical evidence, as are the properly documented photographs and casts of the tracks. The list could be extended indefinitely. But all have the common characteristic of *substantiality*. They are perceptible through the physical senses. Attorneys may argue over their admissibility, debate their relevance, or question their origin; however, their *existence* remains *undisputed*.

Interviews are another kind of factual reporting. Investigating officers, as noted above, continually face the problem of writing down verbal exchanges. Such interviews, if accurately reproduced and properly attributed, are *facts*: they can be verified. The reporting officers can, except in unusual circumstances, substantiate that the particular statement was made. The statement itself may be *false*; however, the *fact* that the person gave it is not in question. Usually confirmation can be received from other witnesses, other officers, or electronic devices. But officers must be careful to attribute such statements properly; otherwise, a reader may accept the *content* of the statement as true, when indeed the statement was a falsehood. In such instances, it is the reporting officer's responsibility to indicate clearly that he or she is merely reporting what the person said, not vouching for the truth of the statement.

Investigative actions are also factual in nature. Officers must include the investigative steps carried out in each incident. These steps—such as dusting for fingerprints, making cast impressions of tire tracks or footprints, measuring pry marks, photographing the scene, interviewing potential witnesses, and so on—can be verified, usually through results obtained, witnesses, or physical evidence. For example, whether or not an officer interviewed a prospective witness near the scene of an incident can be ascertained simply by contacting the witness.

When officers adhere strictly to the facts, they encounter little difficulty. Unfortunately, despite Sgt. Friday's oft-quoted "Just give me the facts, Ma'am," police reports need more. A factual report of a B&E would note that the rear door was open; that the lock was broken; that there was a crowbar on the floor; that there was a set of footprints with the toes pointing toward the interior of the building; and that the victim reported various items missing from different rooms. But if the officers merely recorded this information, they would leave the reader with an incomplete account. The reader, who was not physically present at the scene, would be forced to put all the details together into a coherent hypothesis.

Inferences. Formulating a hypothesis is not the reader's function; it is the officer's. Police officers are trained to investigate thoroughly and then to give a reasoned account of what *probably* transpired. In so doing they are making *inferences: statements about the unknown based upon what is known*, i.e., the facts or physical evidence, interviews, and the investigative results.

Examples of *inferential* or *deductive* reasoning are familiar to all readers of detective stories. Perhaps Sir Arthur Conan Doyle's famed creation Sherlock Holmes best illustrates this kind of reasoning. In "The Blue Carbuncle," for instance, Holmes, in a conversation with Dr. Watson, applies this method to draw a picture of the unknown owner of a lost hat:

> *"What can you gather from this old battered felt?"*
> *"Here is my lens. You know my methods. What can you gather yourself as to the individuality of the man who has worn this article?"*
> *I took the tattered object in my hands and turned it over rather ruefully. It was a very ordinary black hat of the usual round shape, hard and much the*

worse for wear. The lining had been of red silk, but was a good deal discoloured. There was no maker's name; but, as Holmes had remarked, the initials "H.B." were scrawled upon one side. It was pierced in the brim for a hat-securer, but the elastic was missing. For the rest, it was cracked, exceedingly dusty, and spotted in several places, although there seemed to have been some attempt to hide the discoloured patches by smearing them with ink.

"I can see nothing," said I, handing it back to my friend.

"On the contrary, Watson, you can see everything. You fail, however, to reason from what you see. You are too timid in drawing your inferences."

"Then, pray tell me what it is that you can infer from this hat?"

He picked it up and gazed at it in the peculiar introspective fashion which was characteristic of him. "It is perhaps less suggestive than it might have been," he remarked, "and yet there are a few inferences which are very distinct, and a few others which represent at least a strong balance of probability. That the man was highly intellectual is of course obvious upon the face of it, and also that he was fairly well-to-do within the last three years, although he has now fallen upon evil days. He had foresight, but has less now than formerly, pointing to a moral retrogression, which, when taken with the decline of his fortunes, seems to indicate some evil influence, probably drink, at work upon him. This may account also for the obvious fact that his wife has ceased to love him."

"My dear Holmes!"

"He has, however, retained some degree of self-respect," he continued, disregarding my remonstrance. "He is a man who leads a sedentary life, goes out little, is out of training entirely, is middle-aged, has grizzled hair which he has had cut within the last few days, and which he anoints with lime-cream. These are the more patent facts which are to be deduced from his hat. Also, by the way, that it is extremely improbable that he has gas laid on in his house."

"You are certainly joking, Holmes."

"Not in the least. Is it possible that even now, when I give you these results, you are unable to see how they are attained?"

"I have no doubt that I am very stupid, but I must confess that I am unable to follow you. For example, how did you deduce that this man was intellectual?"

For answer Holmes clapped the hat upon his head. It came right over the forehead and settled upon the bridge of his nose. "It is a question of cubic capacity," said he; "a man with so large a brain must have something in it."

"The decline of his fortunes, then?"

"This hat is three years old. These flat brims curled at the edges came in then. It is a hat of the very best quality. Look at the band of ribbed silk and the excellent lining. If this man could afford to buy so expensive a hat three years ago, and has had no hat since, then he has assuredly gone down in the world."

"Well, that is clear enough, certainly. But how about the foresight and the moral retrogression?"

Sherlock Holmes laughed. "Here is the foresight," said he, putting his finger upon the little disc and loop of the hat-securer. "They are never sold upon hats. If this man ordered one, it is a sign of a certain amount of foresight, since he went out of his way to take this precaution against the wind. But since we see that he has broken the elastic and has not troubled to replace it, it is obvious that he has less foresight now than formerly, which is a distinct proof of a weakening nature. On the other hand, he has endeavoured to conceal some of these stains upon the felt by daubing them with ink, which is a sign that he has not entirely lost his self-respect."

"Your reasoning is certainly plausible."

"The further points, that he is middle-aged, that his hair is grizzled, that it has been recently cut, and that he uses lime-cream, are all to be gathered from a close examination of the lower part of the lining. The lens discloses a large number of hair-ends, clean cut by the scissors of the barber. They all appear to be adhesive, and there is a distinct odour of lime-cream. This dust, you will observe, is not the gritty, gray dust of the street but the fluffy brown dust of the house, showing that it has been hung up indoors most of the time; while the marks of moisture upon the inside are proof positive that the wearer perspired very freely, and could therefore, hardly be in the best of training."

"But his wife—you said that she had ceased to love him."

"This hat has not been brushed for weeks. When I see you, my dear Watson, with a week's accumulation of dust upon your hat, and when your wife allows you to go out in such a state, I shall fear that you also have been unfortunate enough to lose your wife's affection."

"But he might be a bachelor."

"Nay, he was bringing home a goose as a peace-offering to his wife. Remember the card upon the bird's leg."

"You have an answer to everything. But how on earth do you deduce that the gas is not laid on in his house?"

"One tallow stain, or even two, might come by chance; but when I see no less than five, I think that there can be little doubt that the individual must be brought into frequent contact with burning tallow—walks upstairs at night probably with his hat in one hand and a guttering candle in the other. Anyhow, he never got tallow-stains from a gas-jet. Are you satisfied?"

Line officers need not possess the powers of the legendary Holmes; however, they must often utilize the same deductive process in order to reconstruct all or part of an incident. From the dimension of pry marks on a door, officers can *infer* that the marks were probably made by a screwdriver. From the tread marks at the scene, they may *infer* that the suspect drove a small foreign car. From the absence of any sign of forcible entry at a larceny, they may *infer* the perpetrator had a key or was adept at picking locks.

The officers may be wrong in every instance. Instead of a screwdriver, it may develop the burglar used a flat metal rod. The tire tracks may turn out to have been made by a small American car with foreign tires. The absence of evidence indicating forcible entry may be attributable to the supposed victim's staging the entire incident and making a false report.

All of this does not mean that officers should not make inferences. They must. And most of the time the deductions of professional police officers will be correct. But they must also recognize that they may be wrong. That is why it is imperative that the officers recognize that *they are making an inference* and *not recording a fact*. The officers' awareness of the distinction will enable them to label each inference properly so as not to mislead the reader. Each inference should be carefully prefaced to mark it as such. For instance, in an open B&E, an officer should not flatly state: "The Suspect gained entry by breaking the window in the rear door with a brick. He then reached inside and unlocked the door." Instead, after a careful investigation noting all the facts, the officer should report: "*Based on the evidence,* it *appears* that . . ."; or "Based on the above, officers *believe*. . . ." In each of the latter examples, the reader is given a considered hypothesis by the trained officers who were present at the scene. The account is clearly designated as *inferential*. The officers, on the basis of the known evidence, are giving their view of how the incident probably occurred. They may be wrong; but the reader has been duly advised that the reconstruction was *inferential* and *not factual*. Consequently, subsequent investigators are still free to reevaluate the data should logical discrepancies appear in the original hypothesis.

Opinions.   In addition to the *facts* which must be included and the *inferences* which may be included, officers should be familiar with *opinions* and *judgments*, which should *never* be included in police reports. *Opinions* are *personal beliefs* with *no substantial evidential basis*, i.e., the so-called gut-feeling reactions. The lack of solid evidential support distinguishes *opinions* from *inferences*.

For example, in a rural area some haystacks are burned. While investigation revealed the fires were set deliberately, no clues existed as to the arsonist's identity. However, the investigating officers, familiar with the neighborhood, listed a local troublemaker as the likely suspect, and the investigation focused on him. In their opinion, he had set the fires, even though there was no physical evidence pointing to him, there were no witnesses placing him at the scene, and he had no known motivation to set the fires. Although he had been in continual difficulty with the authorities, his encounters involved drunk and disorderly disturbances, not arson. The officers discounted all the above and pursued their "gut feeling," based only on the grounds that the suspect was a troublemaker. Many hours were spent attempting to prove this theory before the truth evolved. A witness, previously not interviewed because of the officer's certainty, came forth and identified the arsonists: some vindictive hunters who had been chased from the victim's farm.

Opinions such as the one above have no place in police reports. They blind the investigators. They result in unwarranted harassment of innocent persons. And frequently they permit the guilty to avoid capture. *Inferences* are acceptable and often necessary; *opinions* are neither.

Judgments.   *Judgments* also have no place in police work. By *judgments* we mean expressions of *approval* or *disapproval.* These judgments may occur overtly in the form of flat declarations or covertly in the slanting of information. A reporting officer, for instance, aware that a witness's statement was false, may write: "Witness is a liar." Such a declaration involves two assumptions: first, the witness *knew* the truth, and, second the witness *deliberately* misstated it. Neither assumption may be correct.

For example, a witness near the scene of a shooting incident may report that she had heard *four* shots. Investigating officers, however, found only *three* expended rounds. Asserting that the witness is a liar not only is unjust to the witness, but may also be a disservice to subsequent investigators who will tend to disregard other pertinent testimony the witness may offer. The witness may simply have been mistaken; she honestly believed she had heard *four* shots and so reported. The officers would do well to record their investigative results, take the witness's statement, and note the discrepancy without editorial comment.

In the same vein, veteran officers could extend example after example of witnesses who gave faulty information not through an absence of integrity but rather from incorrect perceptions. It is the fortunate investigator who, at an armed robbery, receives the same description of the perpetrator and weapon from each witness present. Such descriptions often range from a "tall, Negro male, rather thin, carrying a revolver" to a "medium height, white male, heavy-set, carrying an automatic." Usually upon apprehending the suspect, the officers discover no one witness was completely accurate; the suspect turns out to be a combination of the various descriptions.

Consequently, officers must refrain from such open expressions of approval or disapproval. After all, to call a witness a liar is to imply that the witness consistently and deliberately gives false information.

Judgments that are not expressed openly, however, provide greater difficulty in police reports. Officers should constantly guard against using "loaded" language that indicates approval or disapproval and may, as a consequence, influence the reader's evaluation of the report. Too often, for example, police reports characterize people with long hair, wearing patched and faded blue jeans and soiled sneakers as "hippies" or "hippie-type individuals." On the witness stand these reporting officers may encounter some difficulty in defining these terms satisfactorily. Moreover, such expressions, with their implied disapproval, may provide the defense attorney with the means to discredit the officers' testimony.

Even apparently harmless adverbs may reflect a judgment on the part of the reporting officer. The officer who writes, "The complainant *lamely* stated 'I thought I had locked the door,'" has made a judgment. The adverb *lamely* implies that the officer questions the validity of the statement or finds it inadequate. Either reflects disapproval. The officer has, perhaps unintentionally, influenced the reader's perception of the incident.

In summary, then, *facts* can be *verified*. They are the bases of police reports. Facts alone, however, are often inadequate, as they may present the reader with a disjointed, incoherent mass of detail. To place this mass of detail into an overall context readily understandable to the reader, the officers must frequently resort to clearly identified *inferences*: statements about the *unknown based on what is known*. But officers should exclude their *opinions, personal beliefs* based on *unsubstantiated evidence*, and *judgments, expressions* of *approval* or *disapproval*.

ORGANIZATION

After conducting the investigation and gathering evidence, the police officer must organize the report. The specific details of organization will be discussed later. However, there are four general guidelines: first, officers should begin with their initial involvement in the incident; second, they should proceed in chronological order as much as is practicable; third, they should relegate specific details unnecessary for the overall understanding of the incident to appropriately named supplementary sections; fourth, they should write in the past tense since the event has already taken place.

The first point is both simple and obvious. Many officers, however, plunge right into the middle of the action. Then they have difficulty incorporating their initial involvement into the report. In a later chapter, we have specified a standardized opening designed to eliminate the problem. The second point is also obvious. Proceeding in a chronological sequence gives order to the material of the report and ensures against omissions.

The third point—putting the specific details in the supplementary sections—aids both the reporting officer and the reader. The officer is freed from the burden of the continual transitions required when moving from specific details to the general flow of the narrative. The reader benefits from an uninterrupted overall presentation of the incident. Moreover, the officer is less likely to omit important details if he or she does not have to write complete sentences and maintain a smooth narrative flow in the supplementary section. The reporting officer can, instead, concentrate on one particular aspect of the report, i.e., evidence, free from distraction. By the same token, the reader who needs this information—often a prosecutor pressed for time—can quickly find it in a neatly labeled, compact form.

The fourth point is perhaps only stylistic, but it does help the officer maintain chronological perspective. The officer writes the report *after* the incident, and so it would be easier to write it in the past tense.

In short, officers are urged to adopt the advice of the king in *Alice's Adventures in Wonderland*:

"Begin at the beginning," the King said, gravely,
"and go on till you come to the end; then stop."

APPLICATIONS

Classify the italicized material that follows as fact, inference, opinion, or judgment. Since some passages may be classified as more than one of the above, explain your answers.

EXAMPLE:

Victim's body was slumped over the steering wheel of an orange 1976 Porsche Targo. . . . Victim was clad in a blue, one-piece "Bogner" ski suit. Victim was not wearing shoes; however, a pair of Hanson Exhibition ski boots was on the seat beside her. Boots are a lady's size 6 and apparently belong to the Victim. . . . Victim had no identification. . . . Officers believe victim may be registered in one of the exclusive ski lodges in the area.

This is an *inference*. The Porsche, the ski outfit, and the boots are *facts*, the *known*. A Porsche costs several thousand dollars; Bogner ski outfits are extremely expensive; and Hanson Exhibition boots retail at well over $200. Therefore, officers can deduce the victim was a guest at an exclusive ski lodge, not at a dormitory requiring clients to furnish their own sleeping bags.

1. We *suspect John ORMOND committed this burglary.* He lives in the same area, and he has been in a lot of trouble. Last month he was arrested near the burglary scene for reckless driving.
2. Suspect is a *hippy type* with long hair and patched jeans. . . .
3. Officers received the *usual* response from the witness; she said she saw nothing.
4. "The defendant is a *mental case*."
   "Is he an inmate in a mental institution?"
   "No, but *he acted nuts*."
   "What did he do?"
   "He went *off his rocker*."
5. When questioned by officers, the witness answered *reluctantly*.
6. Complainant reported someone broke into his home over the weekend. . . . Complainant stated his new, console-model color television set was stolen. . . . Officers were at above address the previous week on a family disturbance report. Officers did not observe any television set at that time. Complainant is also currently unemployed. *Officers believe complainant has filed a false report.*
7. Re: An assault in a tavern parking lot.
   Victims state the two assailants left in a blue Dodge van and give officers the registration number. Barmaid states the two suspects left the bar fifteen minutes before the victims left. Officers find reported suspects in an Opel coupe. Neither suspect is the registered owner of the van. Neither suspect is marked; their clothes are clean. *Officers believe suspects either were involved in the incident or know more than they will admit.*
8. Charlie is a *good* cop. He would never accept a bribe.
9. Re: Hit-and-run accident where apprehended suspect was driving a green Chevrolet.
   Witness stated, "I saw this blue Ford hit the man in the crosswalk and continue on without stopping."

10. Witness and the suspect lived in the same *rattrap.*
11. Re: Evidence.
    One (1) shotgun: "Ted Williams" brand, 20 gauge, top loading, single shot, wooden stock, engraved receiver, 28-inch barrel, Serial No. 17382. Found under blanket in trunk of Suspect's auto by Officer LEAR. Evidence Tag No. 13.
12. While officers were interviewing the Complainant, the Witness *sneaked* out of the room. Officers had to go to her home to interview her.
13. Re: Disturbance at a business establishment.
    Complainant clenched his fist and shouted at officers and Mr. Jerome Giles, proprietor of the store. Complainant, *clearly a black-power advocate,* accused officers of prejudicial conduct.
14. Complainant reported someone broke into his wine cellar and stole several bottles of wine. . . . Officers discovered the glass broken from the cellar window. The dust had been rubbed from the window casing. . . . Clean areas on the dusty wine racks indicate where bottles had stood. *Based on the above, officers believe suspect(s) entered by breaking the glass from the cellar window some time between. . . . Suspect(s) then removed several bottles of wine and left through the same window.*
15. Re: Street disturbance.
    Suspect, *showing off for the crowd,* shouted obscenities at the officers and refused to move on.

Chapter 3
The Arrest Report:
Major Headings

Arrest Reports vary by departments. Many use a report form specifically designed for arrests, regardless of the incident. Other departments require two separate reports: one for the particular offense and another for the arrest. Still others have only one departmental report form for all offenses, including those resulting in arrests. No matter what kind of report a department requires, officers will find the format in this chapter useful. Since it deals with the information required in all arrests, it can easily be used by any department.

Many of the headings in this arrest format will also appear in other types of reports. They have been included here for two reasons: first, and most obviously, officers may need any or all in a particular Arrest Report; second, officers should become familiar with them as soon as possible. Subsequent chapters concerning other reports will then reinforce the officers' awareness of the function and usefulness of each section.

In the Arrest Report format, officers should use the following major headings:

Initial Information	The officers' immediate involvement
Investigation	The narrative account of events leading to the arrest
Arrest	Circumstances surrounding the formal arrest
Disposition	Circumstances surrounding the transporting, booking, and lodging of the arrestee

The report may also contain these supplementary headings: Evidence, Injured Person(s), Notifications Made, Exceptional Occurrences, and Additional Information.

THE ARREST REPORT: MAJOR HEADINGS

The Initial Information Section.   The first part of any report is the Initial Information section. In it the officers report how they first became involved in the incident. Although there are many ways officers can become involved in an incident, certain data are always present and always required in police reports. However, many officers fail either to include these data or to blend them smoothly into the report. To avoid both errors, officers should follow a set format for including the required data. In a good set format,

> No essential details are left out
>
> Data are presented clearly and in the same order in each report
>
> The same general phrasing and punctuation can be used for each report
>
> The Initial Information section will lead smoothly into the body of the report

The list below achieves these goals. In addition, officers using this formulaic introduction will find that it quickly becomes automatic. Regardless of the nature of the incident, they always have a standard opening. They merely insert the data as indicated in this sequence:

> Time of initial involvement
> Day of the week
> Month, day, year
> Names of reporting officers
> Duty assignment
> Officers' location
> Source of information
> Location and reported nature of the incident

For example, officers dispatched by radio to investigate a reported breaking and entering in progress would begin their report:

INITIAL INFORMATION

At 1920 hrs., Wednesday, May 5, 1976, Officers COHEN and REGAN (Sct. 9-4), northbound in the 2100 block of Lancaster, received a radio run: 1313 Perry, B&E in progress.

This opening is clean and efficient. The information contained is essential, and it appears in a set, logical pattern, which can be easily duplicated in any report.

RATIONALE:

This patterning does more than provide the reader with the essential information immediately. It also helps to get the officer into the narrative without confusion. This is important; for police officers, like nearly everyone else, may be intimidated by blank paper. Often the simple act of beginning creates a sense of assurance that enables a writer to move smoothly through the entire paper. Using a standardized approach lets officers begin with just such a sense of assurance. The false starts and erasures that can shake officers' confidence are no longer problems, for the officers know exactly how they will begin the report. This is helpful not only to the officers. False starts and erasures do little to help the department's image, nor do they inspire much confidence on the part of the citizen filing the complaint.

Although clearly helpful, this formulaic introduction would be of little value if the information contained were not relevant. But it is relevant. This information is necessary in all police reports. Consequently it is common sense that a set order of presentation be adopted to avoid errors of omission or interpretation.

The following point-by-point discussion will illustrate the importance of each item included in the Initial Information section.

Officers should begin with the time of their initial involvement. Since reports must be arranged as nearly as possibly in chronological order, this opening seems logical and forms a basis for the rest of the report. In addition, it avoids the pitfalls found in the time-honored beginning: "At the above time and date." There may be several times and dates above, and the time and date of the reporting officers' involvement may not correspond to any of them. This can be readily seen in the following sequence of events:

An assault occurred at 11:30 p.m., Monday, June 16.
The victim reported the assault to the police desk officer, via telephone, at 11:55 p.m.
No units were available to respond immediately.
At 12:10 a.m., Tuesday, June 17, the responding officers received this information and investigated.

The box section of most report forms will indicate the *time* and *date* of the *incident* (11:30 p.m., Monday, June 16) and the *time* and *date reported* to police (11:55 p.m., Monday, June 16). But the *responding officers* were not advised of the incident until *12:10 a.m., Tuesday, June 17*—a different time, a different day, and a different date than either of the "above" times and dates.

Is this difference in time insignificant? Perhaps. However, if subsequent investigation reveals that the assailant had returned and renewed the assault on the victim at some time between 11:55 p.m. (time reported to police) and 12:10 a.m. (time officers received call), it would be important for the responding officers to note the *precise* time they were dispatched to investigate.

Officers cannot always rely on the dispatcher to record this information accurately for them. In many departments the phones, the desk, and the radio are manned by a single officer. That officer may become so involved in various activities—answering phones, talking to a complainant at the desk, handling radio traffic from another unit—that he or she simply forgets to record the time officers were dispatched. Later, while entering the information on the station log or radio log, the dispatcher guesses at the actual time. It is not unusual for a responding officer's request for "time of run" to elicit a "Hell, I was just going to ask you."

Officers who remain unconvinced should review the confusion surrounding the time of the police involvement in the murders of actress Sharon Tate and four others. In this case the prosecutor encountered a bewildering jumble of conflicting testimony. The Los Angeles Police Station log records that units were dispatched to investigate at *9:14 a.m.*; but the reporting party insisted he had first called at *8:33 a.m.* Moreover, the first officer at the scene set his arrival time at *9:05 a.m.*, nearly *ten* minutes *before* he was officially dispatched. The second officer to arrive set his arrival time at between *9:15 a.m.* and *9:25 a.m.* The third officer arrived *after* the other two; yet he gave his arrival time as *8:40 a.m.* With five bodies the investigators have enough problems without trying to sort out who got where when.

The next items, the day of the week and the date, have already been partially discussed. But including the day of the week serves other valuable functions. First, it allows an officer to make reasoned inferences about other matters or conditions—such as the amount of vehicular or pedestrian traffic in an area or the number of shoppers in a store—that were not regarded as important at the time of the report. Second, it provides a cross-reference ensuring against errors which may result from sloppy penmanship, inaccurate typing, or faulty transcription. This is especially important in agencies using the "one-write" system of handwritten reports.

In the example below, several officers in a metropolitan department failed to note the day of the week in their report. Officers can judge the consequences of this omission.

> *A two-officer radio car was dispatched to investigate a reported assault. Two other units, each manned by two officers, assisted. Upon arrival at the scene, officers discovered that the assailant, now quietly sitting in an armchair, had struck his victim from behind with a heavy piece of concrete, cutting off the victim's ear and shattering his collarbone.*
>
> *While ambulance attendants removed the victim, the assailant remained quietly seated. Suddenly he lunged from his chair and attacked the nearest officer. Officers subdued the assailant, but, in so doing, inflicted injuries requiring his hospitalization.*
>
> *During the trial several weeks later, the assailant's attorney asked each prosecution witness, including the six officers, only one question: "This alleged incident occurred on July 17?"* Each witness, who had already concurred with this information as presented by the prosecutor, responded affirmatively.*

*Date and time are fictitious although the numerical sequence of days is accurate.

> *The defense called one witness, the defendant, and again asked only one question: "Where were you on July 17?"*
> *Defendant answered, "In jail."*
> *Verdict: Case dismissed.*
> *Six officers and assorted civilian witnesses had all testified that the incident had taken place on a day that the defendant had spent entirely in jail. He had been serving a fifteen-day sentence and had not been released until July 18.*

What had happened? A clerk preparing the formal indictment from the officer's handwritten report had copied July *19* as July *17*. Since no day of the week had been specified in the original report, all witnesses mistakenly testified the incident had occurred on *Friday*, July *17*, when it had actually taken place on *Sunday*, July *19*.

The officers were embarrassed; the prosecution was indignant; the judge was irate; the departmental brass was livid; but the assailant was elated and the press members were ecstatic. The embarrassment was avoidable. Had the reporting officers noted the day of the week, a cross-reference would have been available to prevent the errors in testimony.

It was an unusual occurrence, but police officers quickly find that the unusual becomes almost commonplace.

The next segment basically provides a service to the reader by naming the responding officers. This saves a busy prosecutor from having to search through boxes of information or pages of narrative trying to discover who the "undersigned" or "above" officers really are. Knowing the officers involved, the reader can readily follow each officer's actions. In addition, it avoids confusion if other officers later become involved in the incident. And it quickly establishes the third-person perspective we recommend that officers use to maintain an objective position.

The officers' duty assignment may or may not be included here. If space is provided for this information on the face of the report, the information need not be added here. If not, there are good reasons for its insertion at this point. First, knowing the duty assignment can refresh the officer's memory during a court appearance. Second, various interpretations of an officer's actions can result from the officer's familiarity or unfamiliarity with a specific area. Either can be reasonably substantiated if the duty assignment is known. Third, commendation or censure may depend on which officer was "in charge" in a given situation. In many departments this fine distinction is based on normal duty assignments, not seniority. The officer regularly assigned to the unit is in command; seniority is a factor only when both officers are in their regularly assigned units or both are on temporary assignment.

The next item in the Initial Information section indicates where the officers were when they became aware of the incident. Failure to record this creates problems for both the officer and the department. If, as noted above, the time that elapses between the officers' receipt of a run and their arrival at the scene becomes important, officers would do well to note their location so that they can account for this time. Frequently such justification becomes necessary.

The following account suggests the importance of this information. A shop owner called the police to report sounds of movement in his shop, which was closed for the night. After waiting for what seemed like too long a time, the shopkeeper decided to investigate himself. Fortunately, the burglar had already fled. However, had the shopkeeper met an armed prowler and ended either in the hospital or in the morgue, people would undoubtedly have asked some leading questions, foremost among them: Why did it take so long for the police to respond that the shop owner felt he had to take action himself?

If the officer's report included his or her *location* upon receiving the call, as well as the time, the department spokesperson could answer. The spokesperson could even use the occasion to point out that the department is badly understaffed and overextended, resulting in such tragedies as this. This might even produce media and community support rather than censure. And remember that having more police officers is not an unimportant consideration to the officers in the street. The more help available, the better.

If, however, the officer's initial report did not contain this information, explanation would become difficult. Attempts to explain the officer's tardiness on the basis of distance traveled would seem as if they were made up after the fact to excuse police negligence.

The final segments of the Initial Information section indicate how the officers were made aware of the incident, the location of the incident, and the reported nature of the incident. All influence the officers' actions. Officers who are stopped on the street by a citizen reporting an incident will use an approach different from the one they would use if they received a radio call about the same incident. The location of the incident, near or far, will influence the officers' method of procedure. And the reported nature of the incident may be all-important: officers will respond differently to a B&E in progress than to a simple B&E complaint. Furthermore, upon arrival the officers frequently discover a situation so different from the reported incident that the initial information may be forgotten if they don't write it down; seemingly harmless "family trouble" runs, for instance, sometimes turn out to be cuttings or shootings involving neighbors. Officers who have not recorded the original run may later find themselves hard-pressed to explain their actions.

Placing this information at the end of the unit gives the officers an easy transition into the next part of the report. It also allows the officers to write more than one or two sentences, if necessary, without interrupting the continuity of the report. Since the necessary details have been given, officers can now move smoothly and naturally into the succeeding section of the narrative.

The examples below show how easily this approach can be used in a variety of situations.

Incidents stemming from officers' observations:

At 1630 hrs., Sunday, July 11, 1976, Officers COHEN and

REGAN (Sct. 9-4), northbound on Woodward at Webb, observed Suspect vehicle, westbound on Webb, run the red light at Woodward.

. . . . noticed the glass broken from the front (south) door of Falstaff's Pharmacy, 1313 Perry.

. . . . observed Suspect apparently "casing" shops; Suspect was walking in and out of alcove entranceways without entering the shops. He also appeared to ignore window displays and to be looking inside the shops.

Note: Officers are urged not to use the traditional phrase "acting in a suspicious manner" in such an incident, unless, of course, the officer *describes the manner specifically.* Otherwise, an officer may be subjected to some severe and embarrassing cross-examination while trying to define "suspicious manner" to the satisfaction of the court.

Incidents stemming directly from citizen:

. . . were stopped by Edward LANCASTER (address above), who reported a "floating crap game" at 1710 E. Grand.

. . . were hailed by an unidentified woman, who reported several men were attacking another man in the alley at the rear of 2110 Mercado.

Note: Some officers would use the phrase "unidentified citizen" or "unknown subject" instead of "unidentified woman." This can complicate further investigation if it becomes necessary to locate the reporting party. Investigators would be unable to determine even the sex of the person being sought without first calling the reporting officer. If there is a lengthy time lapse, even this may not do. Therefore, we recommend that officers at least specify the sex of the reporting party. In some circumstances, officers would do well to include a description in the Additional Information section.

THE INVESTIGATION SECTION

The Investigation section is the core of the Arrest Report, for it is here that the reporting officer will "tell the story" of the incident, ending in the arrest of the suspect(s). Since the narrative will vary widely from report to report, depending, of course, on the incident itself, the prescriptive approach used for the Initial Information section is not workable. However, there are general guidelines to help the officers.

First, they should present their investigation in a chronological sequence. They have already noted the time of the initial involvement; now they need only to continue, using that time as the base.

If anything unusual or worthy of attention occurred while the officers were en route to the scene, they should note it immediately in the Investigation section. For example, officers dispatched to a B&E early in the morning, when traffic is light, may pass a vehicle coming from the general area of the incident. There may or may not be a relationship. However, officers should note the information, for the occupants, even though not involved in the B&E, may later provide detectives with helpful leads. In such an instance, the officer could begin the Investigation section as follows:

INVESTIGATION

At 0320 hrs., while en route to the scene, officers observed a pickup truck (Ref: <u>Additional Information.</u>) with two occupants eastbound on Hall at Main.

At this point the pickup truck will probably be of little interest to the detective reading the report. Therefore, the officer does not have to slow the reader's progress by writing a detailed description of the pickup here. Instead, the officer should merely indicate that the information is available, in this instance in the Additional Information section. Should later investigation reveal that the apprehended suspect had accomplices, the information would require a follow-up. Or investigators may seek the occupants of the pickup as possible witnesses. In either instance the necessary data would be readily available.

If nothing unusual has attracted the officers' attention on the way to the scene, then logically the Investigation section can begin with the officers' arrival. And officers should make it a habit always to note the time of their arrival at the scene and to incorporate this information in the report. Doing so helps establish the outside time limits of the events for investigators later, and this is often necessary for a successful investigation.

Some situations will require special positioning of the unit and the officers upon arrival at the scene. If this is the case, officers should indicate these positions in the report. For example, officers responding to a B&E would require the placement of car and officers to provide effective surveillance of the scene. Officers could then begin the Investigation section:

INVESTIGATION

Upon arrival at the scene (0325 hrs.), officers parked the unit at the rear of 1313 Perry. Officer COHEN took a position at the northeast corner of the building while Officer REGAN stationed himself at the southwest corner.

Usually such precise positioning is not required. Indeed, it is often impossible. Only on television do police officers always find a convenient and strategically located parking place. Moreover, in most instances it would be unnecessary, as well as a disservice, to force the reader to wade through such irrelevant detail as in this report of a family disturbance call:

Officers arrived at the scene at 4:30 p.m. and parked the patrol car in front of 1710 Comus. Officers locked the patrol car and walked to the front door. Officers knocked on the front door, and it was opened by the Victim, later identified as Priscilla W. MONK. As Mrs. MONK opened the door, she invited officers in. Mrs. MONK opened the door and stepped to one side. . . .

This account is wordy and full of unnecessary details. Officers could simply record this as follows:

Upon arrival at the above address (1630 hrs.), officers identified themselves and were admitted by the Victim, Mrs.
Priscilla MONK.

This version contains fewer than one-third the number of words in the original. Yet it gives the same basic information and more, for in this account the officers have also identified themselves to the victim, an important consideration in this day of "mistaken identities."

Next, officers should survey the scene briefly upon arrival and note significant points in their report. Often first impressions can be helpful in re-creating the original scene, for during the course of an investigation various objects can be removed or misplaced, either purposely or accidentally. Witnesses and occasionally even victims may give accounts that either conflict with the officers' first impressions or later distort the officers' impressions.

An incident that occurred in a large campus community illustrates the importance of making this quick survey and including it in the report. In the incident officers responded to an "assist injured persons" call at a fraternity house. They found two injured men seated on a sofa in the lounge, one holding a blood-soaked towel to his forehead, the other with a towel wrapped around his right hand. Both men gave officers the same version of the incident: the man with the head injury had slipped in the parking lot and cut his forehead on a car bumper; the other had gone to his assistance, also slipped, and cut his hand on broken glass in the parking lot. Several witnesses corroborated these statements.

Careless officers would have probably accepted this version—with the proverbial grain of salt, perhaps. But the responding officers had made a quick survey of the physical scene while moving forward to assist the injured persons. Despite the obviously heavy bleeding, they saw no evidence of blood either in the entryway from the parking lot or in the hallway leading to the lounge. Nor was there blood on the sofa. Officers did note, however, that an easy chair across the room had a large dark stain, later found to be blood with some dark-brown glass fragments intermixed. There was a large stain on the floor in front of the chair. And a book on a nearby table was also stained.

In spite of the account given by everyone present, officers checked the entire parking lot after giving first aid and sending the injured to the hospital in an ambulance. They found no traces of blood in the parking lot. All this information was duly noted in the report.

Two days later, the man with the injured head went to the prosecutor and changed his story. He now declared that he had been seated in the armchair, reading, when the second man (injured hand) had entered. The second man, without provocation, then broke a beer bottle on the end table and struck the complainant in the face with the jagged end of the bottle. The complainant had evidently told the original story because he was afraid that if he told the truth, his fraternity brothers would be hostile.

Because the officers had refused to accept without reservation an account that was apparently at odds with the physical evidence, they had included the results of their investigation in the report. Consequently, rather than washing her hands of the matter and condemning the victim for having lied in the first place, the prosecutor was prepared to cope with this abrupt turn of events.

Once the officers have reconstructed the physical scene, they only have to record their actions and the actions of others involved in proper sequence. These actions depend on the nature of the incident, the people involved, and the situation faced by the officers. If the actions are described in chronological order, reporting them should not be difficult.

Some problem may result when the officers are engaged in separate activities at the same moment. When this occurs, one officer's activities and observations can be presented first, and then the other officer's, with a statement indicating the activities were simultaneous.

For example, officers may pursue a stolen auto containing two suspects. Suspects abandon the auto and flee on foot in opposite directions. Officers split, one going after each suspect. Both suspects are then apprehended. In the report officers could first detail the chase and apprehension of one suspect and then merely begin the account of the second suspect's apprehension in the following manner:

> While Officer SMITH, driving the patrol car, pursued Suspect No. 1 (CARSON, the driver), Officer ORTIZ, on foot, pursued Suspect No. 2 (RODERIGO, the passenger) north on Milton from Chaucer.

Another general guideline for officers to follow in the Investigation section has already been mentioned (see page 31): placing some of the details in the appropriate supplementary sections. Many details are essential for the complete report but are not needed for an overall understanding of the incident. In fact, including them often obstructs the reader's progress and creates confusion. Moreover, reporting officers find it difficult to write up an incident clearly when faced with the mechanical problems of incorporating a mass of details. Therefore, we suggest officers put into this section only those details necessary for a clear, concise, and coherent account of the incident.

Among the details that can be placed in other sections are lengthy descriptions of vehicles. When only one vehicle is involved in an incident, the prosecutor, hurrying through the report, is rarely concerned about the specific description. In most cases, whether the vehicle is a Ford or a Cadillac is probably of little importance for the prosecutor is trying to achieve an overall grasp of the incident. The vehicle description would only distract and disrupt this effort. Therefore, the reporting officers need only assure the prosecutor that the information is readily available in the report.

For example, officers, having received complete descriptions of a suspect and his vehicle, are assigned to a roadblock. The Investigation section of their report could read:

Upon arrival at blockade point (0700 hrs.), officers positioned patrol cars across roadway and stationed themselves behind the units. At approximately 0710 hrs., officers saw Suspect vehicle (Ref.: <u>Evidence</u>) approaching the checkpoint from the south.

Or it could read:

Upon arrival at blockade point (0700 hrs.), officers positioned patrol car across roadway and stationed themselves behind the units. At approximately 0710 hrs., officers saw Suspect vehicle, a 1974 Dodge sedan, white over blue, Michigan 1974 registration XLT 796, registered owner Samuel Boswell, 1752 Grey's Inn Avenue, approach the checkpoint from the south.

Clearly, the prosecutor would prefer the first example. At this point it is only necessary to know what happened. The long description provided in the second version is not wanted, nor is it needed. The first tells where the information is should the prosecutor require it for an examination of the officer on the stand.

Obviously, if two or more vehicles are involved, the officers must provide the reader with enough information to avoid confusion. One way is to identify them by make and to specify a number: for example, Ford (Veh. No. 1). Or officers could reverse the order: Vehicle No. 1 (Ford). If both vehicles are the same make, then officers can add the color to help distinguish between them. But even in these circumstances the complete description is rarely required in this section.

Other details which may be presented under supplementary headings include such points as precise description of injuries and the exact amount of force officers may have used in making an arrest. Officers can note in the Investigation section who was injured and relate the extent of injury in the Injured Persons section. In case force has been used, officers do not have to include a blow-by-blow version in the Investigation section. They must certainly note that force was used and why, but the detailed account can be placed in an Exceptional Occurrences section.

Some common sense paragraphing guidelines should also help officers. Although paragraphing is important, it is also a source of frustration for many officers, who vaguely recall discussions of "topic sentences" and "different modes of paragraph development" from their high school or college English classes.

This sense of frustration is unnecessary. Officers are not writing compositions for an English class. Consequently, they do not need to concern themselves unduly with either "topic sentences" or "modes of development." Instead, they should follow two practical guidelines: *appearance* and *natural breaks* in the flow of the narrative.

Appearance means the visual image of the report that the reader gets. And in police reports, short paragraphs look best. At the same time, the paragraphs should be of different lengths. Several consecutive paragraphs that contain nearly the exact same number of words can alienate a reader as quickly as a page-long, unbroken series of sentences.

Therefore, we recommend that reporting officers use appearance as a guiding principle in paragraphing. They should try to write brief paragraphs of differing lengths. A quick glance will let the officer know how well he or she is succeeding. If there are a series of short paragraphs, the officer can make the next paragraph longer. If a paragraph seems to be growing too long, the officer can simply stop at the end of a sentence.

While this guideline seems arbitrary, it is *practicable* in police reporting, because two basic principles of paragraphing are part of the very nature of a police report: *unity*—the focusing on a single point—and *coherence*—the smooth linking of various elements. A police report has unity because it deals with a single incident, regardless of how complex that incident is. And the report has coherence because the incident is reported in chronological order. As a result, officers have considerable freedom in varying the appearance of their reports. The officers can interrupt the narrative to create paragraphs of the desired length *without disrupting* the reader's concentration.

If officers combine this sense of appearance with the natural breaks in the narrative, they will strengthen their reports. These natural breaks occur in nearly all incidents. The investigation usually breaks down into several distinct parts, however closely related in space, time, or activity. Reporting officers can use these parts as a basis for paragraphing. For example, officers respond to a "B&E in progress" call and apprehend a suspect in the building. Their Investigation section could be divided as follows:

Paragraph 1:   Responding officers' arrival and preliminary assessment of the situation
Paragraph 2:   Positioning of unit and responding officers

Paragraph 3: Arrival of assisting officers and coordination of approach, including any attempts to "flush" suspect from building
Paragraph 4: Entry and search of premises
Paragraph 5: Circumstances surrounding the actual apprehension of the suspect

These paragraphs form blocks of closely associated activities. Probably they will be of varying lengths, none too long. However, if a particular situation results in paragraphs of monotonously uniform length, the officer should not be afraid to combine two paragraphs or divide one into separate paragraphs. In the above outline, for instance, paragraphs 1 and 2 could easily be combined, as could 3 and 4. Paragraph 5 could probably be divided into two, or perhaps even three, separate paragraphs, depending upon the circumstances of the arrest. The officers could make these changes without affecting the reader's understanding of the incident.

RATIONALE:

If officers follow the above guidelines, they will have little difficulty in writing reports that project a clean, professional image. Other elaborate paragraphing techniques are unnecessary, indeed, often undesirable, since most police officers have little time to spend on such niceties. Bosses believe the officer's place is on the street; therefore, the officer should try to follow these principles—appearance and natural breaks in the narrative—and to avoid the two undesirable extremes: a monotonous series of one-sentence paragraphs and a one-paragraph report.

Both extremes have a bad effect on readers. The first presents information in an apparently unorganized and disjointed manner. The report is probably unified since it focuses on a single incident. It is probably coherent since it is chronologically ordered. However, the initial effect will be one of disunity and incoherence. And readers may well question how carefully the reported investigation has been conducted. In addition, readers will have difficulty in rechecking various points. Since there is no distinct grouping of information, they must search through several sentences in order to find information they want.

The other extreme—one long, uninterrupted mass of words—occurs with greater frequency and is equally undesirable. Its appearance causes the readers to wonder if they will ever absorb all the information. Often they don't. They may easily miss a significant point by accidentally skipping entire lines of the narrative. Upon discovering this, if they do, the readers must either backtrack to find the overlooked data or begin rereading the entire paragraph. The result is the same, a loss of continuity.

Another major problem with a paragraph of this type lies in the difficulty of locating specific information. Readers, especially prosecutors, may wish to make notes on certain key points. When the material they need is buried in the middle of a page-long paragraph, they face a difficult, time-consuming task.

Therefore, we repeat: Let appearance *and the* natural units *in the narrative guide your paragraphing.*

THE ARREST SECTION

The Arrest section is another major heading in the Arrest Report. In this section, officers should note *all the circumstances concerning the actual arrest*, beginning with the point of formal arrest. This section will include:

Time of arrest
Charge *at time of arrest*
Search of suspect's person
Admonishment
Subsequent or related investigation

An Arrest section reporting the apprehension of a suspect in a B&E, for example, may read as follows:

At 0420 hrs., May 13, 1975, officers placed Suspect Ida J. WILLIAMS under arrest on a charge of Breaking and Entering (NT). Officer YOUNG searched the Suspect and discovered a switchblade knife.

Officer JOHNSON then read the Suspect her rights from the departmental Miranda warning card. Officers YOUNG and SCHMIDT witnessed the reading.

Suspect stated she understood her rights and refused to make any statement. She was then transported in Scout 9-4 to the Gotham City Jail by Officers SCHMIDT and WAGNER.

Officers YOUNG and JOHNSON continued their investigation. (Include the details of the subsequent investigation, that is, photographs, fingerprints, collecting of evidence, interviews with witnesses, etc.)

Any complicating factors in the arrest—resistance to arrest, for instance—would be included at the appropriate chronological point, as would a brief account of the means used to overcome such resistance. Or should the suspect attempt to escape, this, too, along with officers' actions to prevent the escape, logically belongs in this section.

One further note: Here, as in the Investigation section, the reporting officer may need to include interviews with complainants, victims, or witnesses. We suggest that the interviews be incorporated with appropriate *subheadings under* the *major headings.* This will let the reader place these interviews in proper perspective as essential parts of the overall narrative, not separate elements. It also avoids the disruptions caused by too many major headings.

RATIONALE

Noting the time of arrest is a precautionary measure. It may well avoid later embarrassing problems in such concerns as probable cause. Informing suspects of the charge simply assures them of their legal rights. The charge may be changed later. However, the initial charge is important. The question may become: Precisely on what grounds was the arrest made? If so, the grounds had better substantiate the initial charge. A case in point:

Officers working the midnight watch were caught up in a wave of complaints involving quick-change artists at various service stations. Several attendants gave detailed descriptions of the perpetrators and their auto, which had out-of-state license plates. While en route to the station after taking the fourth report, officers discovered the suspects' auto parked outside a tavern. Before officers could take any action, the suspects, visibly intoxicated, left the bar.

The officers could not arrest the suspects for their quick-change activities: at each gas station, the amount of money obtained by trickery had been less than $20, thus constituting only a misdemeanor. A warrant would be necessary to arrest them on this charge. But the officers had not had time to get a warrant; moreover, at 2:30 a.m., Sunday, warrants are not easy to get. Yet the suspects were about to slip away.

The officers could, however, arrest and hold them on Common Drunk charges. Warrants could then be issued on the Larceny by Trick offense. The officers followed this course, and the suspects were later tried and convicted for their quick-change operations.

The decision by the officers to charge the suspects initially as common drunks avoided three equally objectionable alternatives. First, the suspects did not go free by leaving the state before warrants could be issued. Second, long, costly extradition proceedings were not required for what was essentially a series of minor offenses. Third, and perhaps the most important, officers were not liable for false arrest as they had grounds for the initial charge.

While the search of the suspect's person is automatic upon arrest, many officers forget to point out which officer performed it. The result is often confusion on the witness stand. The confusion then turns into a legal headache for the prosecutor. How does the prosecutor introduce evidence found during the search when the arresting officers are uncertain about who actually found the evidence? The situation can easily be avoided by simply noting such information on the report. The results of the search should also be noted here. Any evidence found must be recorded, but it need not be described in detail; that can be done in the Evidence section. For example, officers could write: "Officer BROWN searched Suspect and uncovered one bayonet and two revolvers (Ref.: Evidence)." The prosecutor now knows the suspect was armed at the time of apprehension and how the suspect was armed. Including complete descriptions of the weapons and precisely where on the suspect's person they were found would only cause the prosecutor to lose the thread of the narrative. When needed, the details are instantly accessible in the Evidence section.

Investigation after the formal arrest should also appear in this section. Placing it at the end makes it easily available and keeps it in chronological order. Although it is part of the investigative process, it logically belongs in this section—for consciously or unconsciously, once an arrest has been made, the focus of an investigation alters. Officers are now intent on gathering the necessary evidence to build an adequate case against the arrestee. This may result in errors in further investigation. Officers, confident that they have arrested the right person, may fail to ask the proper questions to get the whole story; or they may unconsciously guide a witness or complainant. For example, in an assault case where the arrested suspect was wearing a black ski jacket, the officers may ask: "Was the assailant wearing a black ski jacket?" rather than: "Was the assailant wearing a coat?" A confused witness, nervous in the presence of the police, can be easily influenced by such suggestions and actually believe he did see an assailant in a black ski jacket when, in fact, he had merely seen a shadowy figure. As a result, subsequent investigators, relying on the witness's statement may overlook other possibilities. And the prosecutor may receive an unwelcome surprise in court when a shrewd defense attorney begins cross-examination. Including the investigative results here clearly shows this change in the focus of the investigation, and this may be helpful to investigation later. While the officers should still pursue the investigation objectively, there can be little doubt that the emphasis has now shifted.

Also, any efforts on the part of the suspect to resist or evade arrest should be included in this section. Such attempts could occur at any point. Some arrestees react docilely to everything; others react violently. Some remain passive until being searched; then they suddenly lash out. At whatever point these actions occur, officers should include them in the report.

THE DISPOSITION SECTION

Our next major section, headed Disposition, will usually be brief. In it the arresting officer should clearly show the chain of responsibility for the prisoner leading to and including booking. This unit will normally contain

Names of transporting officers
Time of transit (departure from scene of arrest, arrival at jail)
Booking location
Time of booking
Booking charge (include the specific code violation)
Booking officer
Officer advising booking (where applicable)

EXAMPLE

At 0410 hrs. Officers LEAR and REGAN transported Suspect to the Gotham City Jail. Time of arrival: 0420 hrs.

At 0420 hrs. Suspect OTTO was booked for UDAA (M-0001) by Officer Oscar WASHINGTON.

Booking advised by Lt. Peter J. FRENCH.

RATIONALE:

It is important to identify the officers responsible for the prisoner at any given time. During transportation, the prisoner may try to dispose of overlooked evidence or weapons. He may try to injure or kill himself. He may later complain of having been maltreated while en route to the jail. These and other possibilities make it a necessity for the reporting officers to clearly show who had responsibility for the prisoner. If the arresting officers transported him, they should so note; if assisting officers performed this duty, they should be named.

The items that are reported next indicate precisely when and where the line officers were relieved of custody and by whom.

The booking charge is a formality; however, even here, the charge may differ from the initial one. Some departments do not formally book a suspect until the booking is authorized by a command officer. In such instances the name of the officer advising the booking should be noted.

As discussed in the Arrest section above, suspects may create difficulties at any time. If they do so while being booked, their actions logically belong at the appropriate chronological point in this unit, for prisoners are the line officer's responsibility until booking is formally completed.

APPLICATIONS

Exercise 1

Write the Initial Information section using the given information. In this, as well as all other exercises, supply any necessary details not given.

EXAMPLE:

You are one of two officers in a radio car. You are driving north in the 1800 block of Harold Street when you receive a radio message to investigate a reported assault. The assault had taken place at 1066 William Boulevard. The message was received at 8:57 p.m., August 14, 1976, a Saturday.

INITIAL INFORMATION

At 2057 hrs., Saturday, August 14, 1976, Officers WRIGHT and GARCIA (Sct. 9-4), northbound in the 1800 block of Harold, received a radio run: 1066 William, assault.

(a) You are in a two-officer radio unit cruising south on Voltaire Boulevard at Candide Street. It is a Monday morning, July 26, 1976. At 11:20 a.m. you receive a radio run to investigate a reported armed robbery in progress at Griffith's Emporium, 21 Hughes Plaza.

(b) You are walking a beat in a business district. While walking east in the 1800 block of Milton Street, you see a man grab a woman's purse in front of 1830 Milton, knocking her to the ground. The man then runs east on Milton to Dryden, then north on Dryden. The incident occurred at 3:20 p.m., December 16, 1976, a Thursday.

(c) Assume you are in a two-officer radio car. At eight o'clock on a Saturday evening, August 21, 1976, you are driving east in the alley paralleling Herbert Street and between the 1200 blocks of Herbert and Herrick. A woman flags you down. She reports that there is a woman lying in the roadway in the 600 block of Byron Street.

(d) You are working alone in a radio car. At 7:30 a.m., Thursday, June 17, 1976, you see a 1976, red over white, Buick hardtop, westbound on Chidiock Avenue, run the red light at Tichbourne Street. You are driving south on Tichbourne Street at the time. The Buick has current Michigan license plates XXX 013.

(e) You are alone in Car 13, working in a small department. On a Sunday morning, June 6, 1976, at ten o'clock, the following radio traffic occurs:

"Sidney to Car 13."

"Car 13 to Sidney: Go ahead."

"Sidney to Car 13: Yeah, Sam. Do you want to go to 597 Augustine—you know that's the big white house on the corner of Augustine and Gregory—and see the lady there? The lady says she saw two kids monkeying around a car parked in front. She thinks they may have swiped something."

"Car 13 to Sidney: Okay, did you get any description?"

"Sidney to Car 13: No, she just said she saw the kids monkeying around with the car and then hung up."

"Car 13: Okay, I'll be out there."

Exercise 2

Complete the Investigation, Arrest, and Disposition sections of the report begun in Exercise 1. Use the given information for each section as a guide. To help you we have continued our example from Exercise 1.

EXAMPLE:

Information: Incorporate the following information into the Investigation section.

Officers arrive at the scene.

They observe the suspect striking the prone victim with an ashtray.

One officer orders suspect to drop the ashtray.

Suspect drops the ashtray.

One officer checks the victim while the other covers the suspect.

One officer calls for an ambulance and then gives first aid to the bleeding, unconscious victim. (Note: Details of the injury and treatment would appear in the Injured Persons section.)

Victim does not regain consciousness prior to arrival of ambulance.

INVESTIGATION

Upon arrival at the scene (2100 hrs.), officers observed the Victim lying on his back on the front porch. Suspect was straddling the Victim's stomach and striking him repeatedly with an ashtray. Officer Garcia ran to the porch and ordered the Suspect to drop the ashtray. Suspect looked at Officer Garcia, dropped the ashtray, and stood with his hands in the air. Officer Wright checked the Victim and found him unconscious. Victim was also bleeding heavily from several cuts on his head (Ref.: Injured Persons). Wright radioed for an ambulance, applied compresses to Victim's wounds, and treated him for shock. Victim did not regain consciousness. Since Suspect refused to make any statements or answer any questions, officers are unable to determine the motive for the attack.

Information: Incorporate the following information into the Arrest section.

One officer places suspect under arrest for Assault and Battery.

One officer searches and handcuffs suspect.

One officer gives suspect his rights.

Suspect refuses to make any statements.

One officer secures the ashtray for evidence. (Note: Complete description of the ashtray would be placed in the Evidence section.)

One officer checks neighboring residents for possible witnesses, with negative results. (Note: The names and addresses of those contacted can be listed in the Additional Information section. Since no results were obtained, the reader doesn't need such information at this point.)

ARREST

At 2140 hrs. Officer Wright placed the Suspect under arrest for Assault and Battery. Wright searched and handcuffed the Suspect. Wright then read the Suspect his rights, using the departmental Miranda card; reading was witnessed by Officer Garcia. Suspect acknowledged the warning and refused to make any statement or answer any questions. Officer Wright then escorted Suspect to Scout 9-4.

Officer Garcia placed the ashtray in a manila envelope (Ref.: Evidence). Garcia then interviewed neighbors (Ref.: Additional Information) but found no witnesses to the incident.

Information: Incorporate the following information into the Disposition section.

Officers transport suspect to jail.

Officers book suspect for Assault and Battery.

DISPOSITION

At 2210 hrs. Officers Wright and Garcia transported Suspect to the Bunyan City Jail, arriving at 2220 hrs.

At 2225 hrs. Suspect, Vincent C. Jacobs, was booked on a charge of Assault and Battery (01-013) by Sgt. Pierre Smith. Sgt. Smith again read the Suspect his rights; Suspect again declined to make any statements.

The information below will help you complete each section of the report begun in Exercise 1*a*.

Information: Incorporate the following information into the Investigation section.

You arrive at the scene at 11:23 a.m.

You drop your partner in the alley at the rear of Griffith's Emporium, and you drive to the front.

You park the unit in front of an adjacent building and proceed on foot.

When you reach the front door, you see a man in the store running toward you. He is waving a knife and carrying a paper bag.

You level your service revolver at him and order him to halt and drop the knife. He does so.

Your partner enters from the rear of the store.

The store owner, Frederick Paul Griffith, tells you the paper bag contains money the suspect took from him at knife-point.

You check the bag and discover it is filled with currency.

You recover the knife and arrest the suspect.

Information: Incorporate the following into your Arrest section.

At 11:28 a.m. you arrest the suspect for Armed Robbery.

You search and handcuff the suspect.

You read the suspect his rights.

You secure the evidence (knife, bag, and money).

You request transportation for your prisoner.

You interview the proprietor, who had been alone in the store when the suspect entered.

Information: Include the following information in your Disposition section.

Identity of the transporting officers

Location of booking and time of arrival

Charge and time of booking

Booking officer

Exercise 3

Using the given information as a guide, complete the Investigation, Arrest, and Disposition sections of the report begun in Exercise 1b.

Information: Incorporate the following information into your Investigation section.

You check the victim to determine if she has been injured.

Victim assures you that she is unhurt.

You leave her to pursue the suspect.

You follow the suspect—who fails to obey your commands to halt—east on Milton and then north on Dryden.

You overtake the suspect in front of 1688 Dryden.

As you approach the suspect, he throws the stolen purse at you and then attacks.

After a brief struggle, you control the suspect and place him under arrest.

Information: Incorporate the following information into your Arrest section.

At 3:25 p.m., without further difficulty, you arrest the suspect for Larceny from a Person.

You search and handcuff the suspect.

You give the suspect his rights.

You recover the stolen purse and preserve it as evidence.

You request transportation for your prisoner.

You interview the victim, and request that she go to the station to verify ownership and contents of the purse.

Information: Include the following information in your Disposition section.

Identity of the officers transporting your prisoner

Booking location and time of arrival

Booking charge and time of booking

Booking officer

Exercise 4

Select one of the other incidents in Exercise 1. Supplying your own information, write the Investigation, Arrest, and Disposition sections for that incident.

Chapter 4
The Arrest Report:
Supplementary
Headings

There are several specific headings possible in an Arrest Report. Among the most common are:

Evidence
Injured Person(s)
Exceptional Occurrences
Notification
Additional Information

Any, all, or none may be needed in a specific incident. Their order of presentation is not important, although the above order seems the most logical. Nor should officers limit themselves to just these supplementary sections. Officers are encouraged to develop their own headings as required to suit the case in point. But they should be selective. Far too many police reports present a ragged account because the reporting officer used too many headings, resulting in reports which seem made up entirely of "Additionals" and "Interviews." Too many supplementary sections can be as troublesome for the reader as none. They must serve specific functions: to record specific details that would only get in the way of the narrative or to present data that can be quickly and easily extracted.

In the following pages we will discuss the headings most frequently required. We believe the information included in each section is essential, but we do not insist on either the inclusion of *all* the material in a particular unit or the order of presentation. We recognize that officers may have to change, add, or omit material because of the regulations of the department, the demands of time, or the nature of the incident. Therefore, we have set down several examples suggesting patterns officers can use to treat the most frequently occurring problems.

One further point: Complete sentences are not required in these units. The purpose of each unit is to provide as much specific detail as possible as concisely as possible. Narrative flow is not important. The officer has already written the overall narrative account of the incident. Now the officer must pull together into neat, correctly labeled packages the details referred to but left out of the narrative. Consequently, the quantity of necessary detail, not the "smooth flow" of the narrative, is the main thing.

THE EVIDENCE SECTION

Officers must maintain a precise chain of evidence. Putting an Evidence unit in the report will help make sure that this is done. Under Evidence, officers should:

Give the disposition of the evidence
List the items of evidence (including quantities)
Describe each item in detail
Specify the exact location discovered
Name the officer finding the evidence
Indicate how the evidence was marked for identification
Note the evidence tag number

When many pieces of evidence are present, officers can use the "cataloging" method to avoid unnecessarily repeating information. Several of these pieces will probably be handled in the same manner: packaged, tagged, and turned over to an evidence officer, for example. In such circumstances, officers can write a covering statement that includes this information and relates it to a "catalog" that comes either before or after the statement. The technique is illustrated in the examples below.

EVIDENCE

Officer LEWIS placed the following evidence in separate, uncontaminated envelopes, sealed the envelopes, and initialed the seals ERL:

Four (4) cigarettes, gray paper, hand-rolled, tapered tips, approximately 3 inches in length and 1/4 inch in diameter, containing a green powder suspected of being marijuana. Found in Suspect's left front shirt pocket by Officer LEWIS. Evidence Tag. No. EL 133.

Two (2) cigarettes: Description same as above. Found under right front passenger seat of Suspect's auto by Officer ROBERTS. Evidence Tag No EL 134.

> Evidence turned over to Sgt. Carl JACKSON, Crime Lab, at 1410 hrs., June 16, 1976, to be tested for controlled substances.

RATIONALE:

Handling evidence, like writing reports, is best done using a standardized procedure. But procedures often differ. Some departments have strict procedural guidelines. If officers in such a department comply with these rules, they will not need to fear embarrassment during a later court appearance. Other departments have no established procedures, and the officers must do their best to make one up each time. Frequently, this results in the officers' using a different method for each case. Consequently, the officers may be hard-pressed later while in court to recall exactly what they did with a given piece of evidence.

In small departments, for example, it is not unusual to find the chief's office doubling as an evidence room, with the chief's desk serving as a "safe." An officer who has used the lower right-hand drawer of the "safe" on one occasion and the upper left on another may understandably have some difficulty recalling information about specific evidence. One can readily see the importance of recording in detail exactly how the evidence in each case was handled.

Writing down an exact description helps avoid later errors in identifying the evidence, for too many unexpected things can happen. The police crime laboratory technician may accidentally switch containers. Evidence tags may become detached, lost, or unreadable as the result of a coffee spill. Officers rushing to court may grab the wrong envelope off the shelf in the evidence room. And, unfortunately, evidence tampering is not unknown. Accurate descriptions form the only practicable safeguard against such occurrences.

To maintain a proper chain of evidence, officers must state exactly where the evidence was found and by whom. The prosecutor, to introduce the evidence, must have this information. But too often, officers simply note that the evidence was found "on the Suspect." Not only does this hamper the prosecutor's efforts, but also the defense attorney will insist on learning where on the suspect it was found and who found it. Needless to say, the arresting officers' failure to remember these items will hardly help the case.

Below are additional examples of ways to handle evidence:

EVIDENCE

The following evidence was handled in accordance with departmental procedures and turned over to Evidence Officer George GLOUCESTER at 1720 hrs., July 27, 1976:

One (1) crowbar: "Hercules" brand, gray steel, 2 feet long, initials ERL etched on tapered end by Officer LEWIS. Found approximately 7 feet northeast of rear door to 133 Smith by Officer LEWIS. Evidence Tag No. EL76.

One (1) plaster mold: Impression of footprint found 6 inches from the outer edge of door stoop by Officer TANAKA. Print shows a checkered pattern on sole. Partial brand name visible: "---ount." Mold made and initialed ERL by Officer LEWIS. Evidence Tag No. EL77.

Attached to report:

Four (4) photographs: Taken of pry mark impressions on rear door frame of 133 Smith by Officer TANAKA.

Four (4) photographs: Taken of footprint described above by Officer TANAKA.

EVIDENCE

Officer TANAKA tagged the following recovered items, impounded as evidence, and locked them in the gun cabinet in the office of the Chief of Police at 3:10 a.m., July 14, 1976:

One (1) shotgun: "Remington," 12 gauge, model 109, pump, Serial No. 13333. Tag No. T-1.

One (1) rifle: "Winchester," 30-30 caliber, model 74, lever action, Serial No. 33133. Tag No. T-2.

One (1) rifle: "Marlin Glenfield," 22 caliber, model 70, semi automatic, Serial No. 33331. Tag No. T-3.

Above items found in the trunk of Suspect's auto by Officer TANAKA.

Suspect's auto, a 1974 Dodge Charger Sport Coupe, red over white, Michigan 1973 registration XLT 999, towed to the Gotham City Garage by Lon LANCASTER of Gotham Shell Service.

EVIDENCE

One (1) "fifth" of "Calvert's" whiskey, approximately half full. Found open on front seat beside Suspect by Officer TANAKA. Sealed, tagged (No. T-4), and placed in evidence locker in the squad room at 0420 hrs., October 31, 1976, by Officer TANAKA.

THE INJURED PERSON(S) SECTION

The Injured Person(s) section lets the reporting officer describe the extent of the injuries sustained by persons involved in the incident. As in the Evidence section, including such detailed information in the narrative would simply hinder the reader's progress as well as create difficulties for the reporting officer.

In this section of the report, the reporting officer can point out precisely who was injured, the nature and the extent of the injuries, the person(s) giving treatment, the nature of the treatment, and where treatment was given. The officer should also note, of course, how the injured persons were transported.

A typical Injured Person(s) section could read as follows:

INJURED PERSON

Suspect transported to Receiving Hospital Emergency by Scout 904 (MURPHY and KING) at 1720 hrs. Suspect treated for a diagonal cut (1) approximately 1/2 inch above his left eye by Dr. FISCHER. The cut, approximately 3 inches long and 1/4 inch deep, required nine (9) stitches and bandages. Suspect released from Emergency at 1741 hrs.

If there are several injured persons, the cataloging technique should again prove helpful. In a Felonious Driving offense, for instance, officers may have many injured persons, including the suspect. Officers could use the following format to show where the injured persons were sent for treatment.

INJURED PERSONS

The following injured were transported as designated below.

To Receiving Hospital Emergency by Mercy Ambulance (Attendants: YORK and GLOUCESTER) at 1510 hrs.:

RODRIGUEZ, Oswald J. w/m, 36, 1812 Inverness Avenue.
TX: 999-9999. Treated for broken right arm and multiple facial cuts by Dr. DUNCAN. Arm set in cast; cuts cleaned and disinfected. Released at 1630 hrs.

PARKER, Clara C. w/f, 34, 1055 Hastings Street.
TX: 999-1111. Treated for fractured ribs and shock by Dr. FRANK. Internal injuries suspected. Details of treatment unavailable. Held for further observation.

To St. Cuthbert's Hospital Emergency by Fire Rescue Squad 17-1 (Sgts. KLEIN and ABEL) at 1515 hrs.:

GOLDSTEIN, Denise L. w/f, 29, 1215 Charter Street.
TX: 111-9911. Treated for cut approximately 2 inches below the knee in front of left leg by Dr. MacDUFF. The cut, approximately 4 inches long and 1/2 inch deep, required 29 stitches and bandaging. Released at 1700 hrs.

Officers should have previously indicated (in the Investigation section) how the injuries were received and where the persons were when they were injured. If the officers have not done so, they should include the information here. If the personal data (age, address, phone) appear elsewhere, on the face of the report, for example, then it should be omitted here. Often, however, the box spaces on the face of the report are either too small or too few, making it necessary for the officer to put the information somewhere else. This is a convenient place.

RATIONALE:

First, and quite simply, it is the officer's business to record accurately all the available information on injuries received in the incident being investigated.

Second, prosecutors need this information to help decide the formal charge. They would probably question a felonious driving charge where the victim suffered only superficial abrasions. On the other hand, if there are several serious injuries, as in the above example, the decision may well be to press just such a charge, for prosecutors are well aware that the appearance presented by the victims will undoubtedly affect the court.

Third, prosecutors rarely enjoy being surprised in court, especially by the sudden appearance of a defendant wrapped in bandages and seated in a wheelchair when the official report read "Suspect suffered minor injuries." The suspect may have. But defendants, as well as others, have been known to break out suddenly in a rash of afflictions not present at the time of the incident. In such instances officers had better have ready a complete description of the "minor injuries." If not, the authors, to list just two people, would not look forward to discussing the case with the prosecutor later.

We have also recommended that officers note who transported the injured persons. Until properly relieved, the reporting officers are responsible for the welfare of the injured. It is important then that they know who relieved them of the responsibility and when. It may be as important as maintaining a tight chain of evidence, for several unpleasant possibilities may emerge later. For example, people transported by ambulance arrive at the hospital with injuries much more severe than was apparent at the scene. Or they arrive and have to wait, temporarily becoming "lost" among the many Saturday night casualties in the emergency center. Complications set in. Accusations are made, often much later. Now the question becomes: Who is responsible? Or perhaps an injured person later insists his or her injuries were made worse by careless or incompetent treatment by the police. In such an instance the ambulance attendants may be able to attest to the quality of the officer's aid.

In any of these cases, the reputation of the officers and the department may well depend on whether or not the officers recorded who transported the injured, who treated them, and what was the extent of injury.

THE EXCEPTIONAL OCCURRENCES SECTION

The Exceptional Occurrences section serves two purposes: to make the reader aware of unusual circumstances, and to provide a detailed account of the occurrence. In this unit, officers should record *anything* unusual that happened during the incident. If a suspect resisted arrest, for example, the precise nature of the resistance and the amount and type of force used to overcome it should be described here. If a suspect attempted to escape, this too should be noted here. A suspect's verbal abuse of arresting officers or threats to them also belong in this section. In short, any exceptional behavior worthy of special attention belongs under this heading. The subduing of a belligerent suspect, for example, may read as follows:

EXCEPTIONAL OCCURRENCES

When asked to step from his auto, the Suspect opened the door and slammed it against Officer GRIFFIN, knocking him to the ground. Suspect then leaped from the auto onto GRIFFIN. Using his fist, the Suspect struck GRIFFIN in the face several times before being subdued by Officer SAN-CHEZ. SANCHEZ pulled the Suspect from Officer GRIFFIN and struck the Suspect in the midsection with the butt end of the nightstick. SANCHEZ next pushed the Suspect flat on the ground, face down, and handcuffed him.

Officer SANCHEZ then gave first aid to Officer GRIFFIN, who was bleeding heavily from the mouth and nose.

Suspect remained belligerent while being placed in the patrol unit and cursed the officers during transport to jail. (Give examples of some of the curses; not all, however, are necessary. In many cases to include all of them would require several additional pages.)

Bashfulness is not a requirement for police work. Officers should record exactly what the suspect said. If the suspect called them "lousy, blue-coated bastards," they should put it down.

RATIONALE:

As with the other supplementary headings, this section allows the officers to record specific details which would clutter the narrative. But they are important details. The account of the old Texas Ranger's report on the shooting of a suspect—"He missed; I didn't"—may be amusing, but it is not applicable to modern police work. Courts, media, and the public want assurance that police are acting with restraint. If force is exerted, they want to know why. They also want to know how much so that they can decide whether or not it was excessive. Consequently, using a separate section for this type of information lets the officers explain in detail. It also lets the reader judge this exceptional aspect of the case without distraction.

Moreover, the heading itself signals the prosecutor that special attention is required. The prosecutor is aware that complications exist and can now concentrate on them, evaluate them, and plan accordingly. The prosecutor also knows enough to ask the officers specific questions and get specific answers, not vague generalizations. He or she can ask exactly what profanity was used and get it word for word, and few prosecutors are unaware of the effect that such word-for-word testimony has on juries.

THE NOTIFICATIONS MADE SECTION

The Notifications Made section gives officers a convenient method of recording the various notifications often required. The officers should record all notifications made regarding the incident. A separate unit for these notifications also serves as a checklist for the officers. They can quickly see if they have overlooked notifying someone since they must list all notifications here. The number of notifications will, of course, depend on the incident. In a narcotics-related homicide, officers may have to notify a command officer, the homicide bureau, the narcotics bureau, the crime laboratory, and perhaps the victim's next of kin. In a drunk driving arrest, on the other hand, officers may only have to notify the Breathalyzer operator and someone to pick up the arrestee's auto.

Regardless of the number of notifications, officers should include the following information:

Officers making the notification
Person(s) notified
Title/position of person(s) notified
Time of notification
Response required, if any

A Notifications Made section that consists of a simple notification could read:

NOTIFICATIONS MADE

At 1630 hrs., Officer BROOKS notified Det. Sgt. Richard ROSENCRANTZ, Narcotics Bureau. Sent copy of report at his request.

If several notifications are made, we once more suggest the cataloging technique. To avoid confusion, we also suggest that officers list the notifications in the order made. For example:

NOTIFICATIONS MADE

By Officer BROOKS:
    KENNEDY, Otto P.   Sergeant, Homicide Bureau. 1610 hrs.
    NEWMAN, Samuel T.   Detective, Narcotics Bureau. 1615 hrs.
    ZIMMERMAN, John L.   Technician, Crime Laboratory. 1617 hrs.

By Officer COLLINS:
    SPLINT, Oscar R.   Victim's father. Home address: 1400 Chaucer Lane, Gotham City. TX: 123-1234. Stated he would meet detectives at St. Cuthbert's Hospital. 1612 hrs.

RATIONALE:

Using a separate unit for all notifications guards against "failure to notify" charges. In essence, the unit gives the officers a checklist. While writing the final report, the officers can quickly see whether or not they have failed to notify someone. The same reasoning holds for the readers. They can quickly see which notifications were made and, as a result, determine whether the list is complete.

Recording the names of persons notified protects the reporting officer. Occasionally, unpleasant repercussions can result from a failure to do so. A case in point:

Officers arrested a suspect on a narcotics charge. They impounded the suspect's vehicle and ordered a "hold" on it for the narcotics detectives. One arresting officer duly informed the narcotics bureau but failed to identify the person notified. Apparently the notification became lost, misplaced, or forgotten by the narcotics officer. As a result, the suspect's auto was not searched before being released. Subsequent investigation revealed that more narcotics had been hidden in the taillight housing of the suspect's auto. When, to use the old saying, "everything hit the fan," all narcotics personnel disclaimed any knowledge of a request to search the auto. The reporting officer, who had failed to identify the person notified, could only insist that he had "told somebody over there." (The officer also failed to indicate in the report that a "hold" had been placed on the vehicle; otherwise, narcotics officers may still have been alerted in time.)

Getting the name of the person notified and recording it takes little time. Often, as can be seen from the above case, it can be time well spent.

THE ADDITIONAL INFORMATION SECTION

In the Additional Information section officers can give information not previously reported. Details that are not immediately pertinent but that may later be helpful can be placed here. Or the unit may be used for details that do not logically fit under any of the other supplementary headings. The possibilities are many, among them:

The names and assignments of assisting officers
What assisting officers can testify to
Disposition of property not impounded
Possible witnesses or informants not interviewed
Suggested similarities to modus operandi in other incidents
Officers' inferences

The following example illustrates how unrelated elements can be presented:

ADDITIONAL INFORMATION

Assisting Officers, Charles COMUS and Laurence JONES (Sct. 9-8), can testify to Suspect's resisting arrest, the search of the Suspect, and the Suspect's receiving his rights.

Suspect's vehicle, a 1973 Chevrolet Bel-Air sedan, black over white, Michigan 1973 registration ZBT 777, towed to Gotham Shell Service (Operator: Horace HIGGINS). No hold on vehicle.

Occupants of a 1971 Ford Torino coach, blue over green, Michigan 1973 registration FSC 421, may have witnessed Suspect's attacking Officer LEAR. Secretary of State's Office lists owner as Michael MONK, 597 Augustine, Gotham City. Officers were unable to contact.

RATIONALE:

Many details are either necessary or helpful, but including them in the narrative would only slow the reader's progress. Yet they do not merit individual headings. This unit is a convenient catchall for such information. In the above example, for instance, the prosecutor probably knows that the reporting officers received some assistance, and may even recall the names of the assisting officers. But in order to find out what they can testify to, the prosecutor must reread the report. Even then the prosecutor must make inferences based on when the assisting officers arrived. Providing this information in a separate section lets the prosecutor determine with a minimum of difficulty whether or not he needs to subpoena these officers.

Also in the above example, the description of the suspect's vehicle and its disposition would only clutter the narrative. It was not impounded; therefore, it does not belong in the Evidence section. Since there is no other place for it, the logical move is to include it here. The value of the last item in the example may prove to be limited. The prosecutor may decide that the civilian witnesses are not needed. Or when contacted, the occupants may either declare they saw nothing or refuse to make a statement altogether. But the opposite may occur. The prosecutor may decide that civilian witnesses would be helpful, and the occupants' testimony may prove to be of substantial value to the officers.

Including inferences in this section requires discretion by the officers. However, a large part of police work is making inferences, the "educated" guesses based on existing evidence. Officers sometimes have no other logical place for these inferences: they cannot establish a direct connection between the case in point and some other incident although there are data that suggest a possible link. A carefully phrased inferential statement based on these data can be effectively placed in the Additional Information section. The following account shows the potential value of these inferences.

Officers observed an auto parked in a no stopping zone. As they approached, the driver of the auto, seeing the patrol car, accelerated in an attempt to elude officers. The lone suspect continued straight for a few blocks and then turned into a side street, colliding with another vehicle. The driver of this vehicle was severely injured. While one officer remained at the scene of the collision, requested ambulances, and aided the victim, the other officer, on foot, pursued the suspect, who had abandoned the wrecked car. Suspect was caught.

After completing their duties at the scene, officers were notified that the suspect had been driving a stolen auto. Officers then reasoned

The auto was stolen

People in stolen autos do not deliberately risk attracting attention

This car was parked in a no stopping zone—clearly not an inconspicuous place

Therefore, suspect must have had some purpose in parking there.

As a result the officers returned to the area where the car was first noticed and interviewed shopkeepers. Officers found that detectives had already taken an Armed Robbery Report at a shop a few doors away from where the car was first seen. The holdup had occurred at approximately the same time as the chase and the accident. With this information, officers further reasoned that a possible connection existed between the suspect in the stolen auto and the robbery suspects. They added this inference as a supplementary section to their report on the UDAA/Felonious Driving arrest.

Thus alerted by the officers, detectives questioned the driver of the stolen car. He disclaimed any knowledge of the holdup, and no link was ever proved. However, detectives methodically investigated his acquaintances. Among these acquaintances, detectives found suspects later identified as the holdup men.

The armed robbery was not part of the officers' report. Had they not interviewed the shopkeepers, they could have even remained ignorant of the robbery, for the detectives were on a different radio frequency and the officers were occupied at the accident when the alert was broadcast.

EXAMPLES OF ARREST REPORTS

We have included below several arrest reports written by students in the law enforcement program at Ferris State College. Some are reports of simulated incidents that were given as classroom exercises; others are reports of situations the students faced during their field internship with various police agencies. In either instance, the basis of each report was an actual incident.

Readers should note the overall clarity and precision these students have achieved through using the prescribed format. The students first give the reader a clear, total view of each incident, without unnecessary detail. They then provide the details in separate, readily accessible units.

1

INITIAL INFORMATION

At 10:30 a.m., Saturday, November 27, 1975, Officers MESSER and ZGORSKI (Unit 401), northbound on Saginaw at Seventh, observed the Suspect vehicle (Ref.: <u>Evidence</u>), traveling west on Seventh, fail to stop for a stop sign.

INVESTIGATION

Officer MESSER turned west onto Seventh in pursuit and attempted to halt Suspect vehicle by sounding the horn. When the driver of the Suspect vehicle ignored this, MESSER turned on the lights and siren. When the driver of the Suspect vehicle saw the patrol unit beside him at Lewis, he

---

turned his head, looked at the officers for several seconds, and then accelerated.

Officer ZGORSKI immediately informed Dispatch and requested assistance. At 10:34 a.m., Dispatch reported that Unit 405 was en route.

At 10:35 a.m., Unit 405 (Officers FLORES and BASS) pulled in front of Suspect vehicle on Seventh at Weeping. Suspect vehicle then stopped behind Unit 405 on Seventh, approximately 100 yards west of Weeping. Officers MESSER and ZGORSKI parked behind the Suspect vehicle. As Officers MESSER and ZGORSKI, on foot, approached the Suspect vehicle, they observed the driver (the only occupant) throw some short, pencil-shaped objects from the front passenger window into a dry ditch. When Officers FLORES and BASS arrived at the Suspect vehicle to assist, ZGORSKI searched the area where the thrown objects had apparently landed. He immediately found six cigarettes believed to contain marijuana.

ARREST

Officer MESSER advised Suspect that he was under arrest for Possession of Narcotics and told him to get out of the car. Suspect complied. As Suspect left his vehicle, the officers noticed that he was dressed in a U.S. Army uniform.

At this time Suspect said, "Ya really think you're gonna arrest me, eh?" Officer MESSER said "Yes" and reached for her handcuffs. Officer MESSER told Suspect to turn around and interlace his fingers behind his neck. Instead, Suspect pushed her aside with his hands and tried to run past the officers. Officer MESSER grabbed his shirt collar. At the same instant, Officer BASS stuck his foot out into Suspect's path. Suspect tripped, fell backward, landed on his left hip and left elbow, and slid 2 feet across the pavement, scraping some skin from his arm. No other injuries were visible, and Suspect complained of no other discomfort when Officer MESSER questioned him.

Officer MESSER handcuffed Suspect (identified as Kim Steve COOPER). Officer ZGORSKI then searched Suspect and discovered six more cigarettes similar to those found in the ditch. At 10:55 a.m., Officer ZGORSKI read Suspect his rights from a Miranda card. Suspect said that he understood these rights and refused to make any statements concerning the offense. He did volunteer that he was presently in the U.S. Army on a three-day pass from the Warren Army Base.

Officers FLORES and BASS remained with the Suspect's vehicle pending its impoundment at the police garage.

DISPOSITION

At 11:00 a.m., Officers MESSER and ZGORSKI transported Suspect to Little Creek Community Hospital where he was treated for minor injuries.

At 11:45 a.m., Officers MESSER and ZGORSKI transported Suspect from the hospital to Little Creek County Jail. Suspect (Kim Steve COOPER) was booked at 11:50 a.m. by Sheriff's Deputy William P. JACOBS on a charge of Possession of Narcotics (13-1313). JACOBS again informed COOPER of his Miranda rights. COOPER acknowledged these but still made no statements.

EVIDENCE

Officer MESSER placed the following evidence in separate, uncontaminated envelopes, sealed the envelopes, and initialed the seals GM:

Six (6) cigarettes: hand-rolled, tapered ends, brown paper, approximately $2\frac{1}{2}$ inches in length and $\frac{1}{4}$ inch in diameter, containing a green substance suspected to be marijuana. Found in Suspect's right front pants pocket by Officer ZGORSKI: Evidence Tag No. LC-1.

Six (6) cigarettes: Description same as above. Found in the dry ditch in front of 1763 Seventh by Officer ZGORSKI. Believed thrown from auto by the Suspect. Evidence Tag

No. LC-2. Evidence turned over to Sgt. Daniel V. RINGER, Narcotics Bureau, at 12:15 p.m., November 27, 1975.

Suspect's auto, a red, two-door, 1969 Ford XL, Michigan 1975 registration XXX 080, towed to the Police Garage by Prell's Wrecker Service (Driver: John PRELL). Escorted by Officers FLORES and BASS. Hold placed on vehicle for narcotics detectives.

INJURED PERSON

Suspect received abrasions on his lower left forearm and left elbow. At 11:15 a.m., Dr. Jonathan HICKS of the Little Creek Community Hospital disinfected the scraped area and wrapped it in sterile gauze. Dr. HICKS released COOPER to officers at 11:35 a.m.

NOTIFICATION MADE

By Officer MESSER:

Sgt. Daniel V. RINGER, Narcotics Bureau. 11:05 a.m.

Sgt. Jay D. DRIVER, Shift Commander, 8th MP Detachment, Little Creek, Michigan. Advised that Spec. Kim Steve COOPER, 13th Service Co., 13th Regt., Warren Army Base, Warren, Wyoming, was being held for violation of Controlled Substance Act. 12:20 p.m.

EXCEPTIONAL OCCURRENCES

When Officer MESSER was about to handcuff Suspect during the arrest, Suspect pushed her aside and tried to flee. Suspect was immediately apprehended and subdued (Ref.: Arrest).

ADDITIONAL INFORMATION

Officers FLORES and BASS can testify to the following:

Suspect had six marijuana cigarettes on his person.

Suspect attempted to resist arrest, resulting in his suffering minor injuries.

Security was maintained over Suspect's vehicle.

STATUS

Open.

Signed:

Ginny C. MESSER

COMMENT:

Ginny has followed the suggested opening precisely. As a result, the reader now possesses a good deal of information: the time, the day, the date, the names of the officers, and their location. More important, the reader also knows exactly how the officers became involved even though the final report concerns a totally different offense.

Her Investigation section gives a concise description of the chase. She has omitted unnecessary details. Her request for assistance, for example, is brief for she recognizes that a word-for-word account of the radio message would serve no purpose. Yet she provides the essential details to the reader. Ginny clearly indicates each officer's actions as necessary in the natural, chronological order of occurrence. She has carefully documented the position of cars and officers. As a result there is no confusion about who witnessed the objects being thrown from the window. Had she been less precise, a busy prosecutor could assume that all four officers saw the objects being thrown. This assumption could easily cause problems, since a defense attorney might well question such a stroke of fortune for the prosecution's case.

Ginny's Arrest section is rather long because she has included the details of the suspect's resistance. She could have simply noted here that resistance was offered and overcome and then included the detailed account in the Exceptional Occurrences section. This would make it easier for the reader to understand the overall incident. After getting the total view, the reader could then examine the details as presented in a separate, unified package.

Ginny shows her customary good sense in the Evidence section. In the field, she *separated* the items of evidence; in her report, she documented the separation. She recognized that the cigarettes found on the suspect would have more value as evidence than those found on the ground. The cigarettes found on the ground provide sufficient *probable cause* to justify the search; however, getting them admitted in court is another matter entirely. Her forethought prevents a defense attorney's clouding the issue by mixing the cigarettes and requesting her to identify which were found on the suspect's person.

2

INITIAL INFORMATION

At 3:20 p.m., Friday, December 17, 1976, Officer PARK (Beat 12), walking south on Osage at Rose, observed Suspect walk into the alcove of Casca's Clothing Store. Suspect apparently ignored the window displays, looked in the door, turned around, and went back to the sidewalk. He repeated this procedure at each store on the 1100 block of Osage Street until he reached Silver Avenue. Officer noticed the Suspect was wearing an army overcoat that was several sizes too large for him. Suspect crossed Osage Street and went in the Osage Street entrance of Falstaff's Emporium. At this time (3:24 p.m.), officer used the call box at the corner of Osage and Silver to make her routine call. Officer then followed the Suspect into Falstaff's.

INVESTIGATION

At 3:26 p.m., Officer PARK entered the store and asked a clerk (Alice PEABODY) to call the store detective. After pointing out the Suspect to Store Detective SOBEL (3:28 p.m.), Officer PARK went to the corner of Osage and Locust, which enabled her to observe Falstaff's only two customer exits.

The Suspect left the store via the Locust Street exit (3:39 p.m.) and walked past Officer PARK. At this time, the officer observed the Suspect's coat fly open, revealing an army blanket pocket, sewn onto the inner lining, filled with various articles of clothing wrapped in what appeared to be the manufacturer's original plastic packaging.

ARREST

Officer PARK requested the Suspect to accompany her into Falstaff's. Upon Suspect's compliance, the Officer summoned the store detective. When the Suspect could furnish no proof of purchase as requested by the store detective, Officer PARK placed Suspect under arrest and read him his Miranda warnings. A search of the Suspect revealed various articles of clothing in only the above-mentioned pocket. Identification of the Suspect was made at this time.

At 3:53 p.m., Officer PARK called headquarters, requesting a car to take Suspect to the city jail.

DISPOSITION

At 4:12 p.m., Sgt. NOBLE advised the booking of Suspect, F. Scott ANDERSON, at the city jail. Suspect was charged with Larceny from a Building (00013).

EVIDENCE

Suspect's size forty-two (42) green army overcoat, with an army blanket sewn onto the lining of the left front panel, was tagged and placed in the Evidence Room by Officer PARK at 4:22 p.m. Evidence Tag No. 4443.

The following items, all with price tags intact and attached, were found in the "booster" pocket of Suspect's overcoat by Officer PARK. Officer PARK tagged and placed the items in the Evidence Room at 4:22 p.m.

One (1) ski jacket: "White Stag" ladies size nine (9), yellow, waist length, unwrapped. Evidence Tag No. 4444. $27.00

Two (2) ski pants: "Bogner," ladies size nine (9), yellow with narrow blue stripe on outer leg, in plastic wrappers. Value $110.00 each. Evidence Tag Nos. 4445, 4446.
$220.00

Two (2) negligees: "California," ladies size nine (9), yellow, in plastic wrappers. Value $21.00 each. Evidence Tag Nos. 4447, 4448. $42.00

                                                    Total Value $289.00

ADDITIONAL INFORMATION

Store Detective SOBEL can testify to the following:

The Suspect received his Miranda warnings before being questioned by Officer PARK.

The above-stated items were found during a search of the Suspect by Officer PARK.

There was no store record showing the purchase of the above items on the day in question.

Signed:

Michelle PARK

COMMENT:

In the Initial Information section Michelle has described the suspect's actions that drew her attention. She has *not* used the vague "suspicious-looking" or "acted suspiciously," both of which could create problems in a later court appearance. The formulaic opening pattern she followed let her expand at the end of the section and relate all the circumstances that aroused her suspicion. This sequence also enables her to make a smooth transition into the Investigation section.

In this opening section and the first part of the Investigation section, Michelle reports the sequence of events that resulted in the suspect's arrest. Technically, the actual arrest incident didn't really begin until the suspect left the store; yet Michelle's background material gives the reader an overall view. The reader does not have to question why she happened to be stationed where she could observe the suspect leave the store; the reader, instead, has been given exactly the same information on which Michelle proceeded at each step.

Students should also note how Michelle has carefully reported that the suspect's "booster" pocket was clearly visible. Her doing so at this point lets a command officer or prosecutor continue reading without having to worry about illegal search charges. The officer can also recognize later the exact grounds upon which she based each of her actions, should a later court case require this information.

The remainder of Michelle's report is also well done. She could have waited to verify the actual theft (the booster pocket establishes reasonable grounds), but the wisest policy is always to get the arrestee off the street and out of the public view as quickly as possible. Taking him in to the store detective accomplishes this. It also provides her with ready assistance while awaiting the arrival of transporting officers.

Not one to waste time, she took this opportunity to confirm that the goods had not been purchased.

Michelle's only mistake is her failure to record the names of the transporting officers. Normally, the arresting officer would accompany the transporting officers in this instance; consequently, her omission is minor. But as such an omission could be critical in other cases, we suggest officers get into the habit of including these names.

3

INITIAL INFORMATION

At 1410 hrs., Sunday, August 15, 1976, Officers GOLAT and McDONOUGH (Sct. 23-1), northbound in the alley connecting the 1300 blocks of Charles and Bank, observed a reportedly stolen auto with two occupants parked in the east-west alley behind 1330 Bank Street.

INVESTIGATION

As officers approached, Suspect vehicle began to flee and failed to make a safety stop at the alley's east exit at Jane Street. Officers then turned on emergency lights and siren while advising Dispatch of the pursuit. Suspect vehicle proceeded south on Jane, failed to stop for the stop sign at the corner of Jane and Charles, then continued west on Charles for one block. Suspect vehicle entered the intersection of Charles and Grand against the red light and stopped in the middle of the intersection, blocking the left westbound lane of Charles.

As Suspects abandoned the vehicle and fled on foot, officers parked patrol car behind the vehicle and requested backup officers for control of the intersection. Officer GOLAT then pursued the Suspect driver on foot across the two eastbound lanes of Charles but lost sight of her between the houses at 1280 and 1290 Charles Street. Officer GOLAT then returned to the intersection, broadcast a description of the escaped Suspect, secured the stolen vehicle for evidence, placed backup officers (Sct. 23-2) for traffic control, and requested a wrecker to tow the stolen vehicle from the scene.

While Officer GOLAT was taking the above action, Officer McDONOUGH pursued the Suspect passenger on foot east on the westbound lanes of Charles, north on the alley connecting Charles and Bank, and then west on the alley connecting Grand and Jane. Suspect then ran from the alley between the houses of 1330 and 1320 Bank where he was overtaken by Officer McDONOUGH.

ARREST

At 1420 hrs., Officer McDONOUGH informed the Suspect, Michael Earl WALLACE, that he was under arrest for Auto Theft. When the officer attempted to handcuff him, the Suspect resisted arrest and was injured as Officer McDONOUGH subdued him.

Officer McDONOUGH then searched the Suspect and read him his Miranda rights from the department Miranda card. The reading was witnessed by Officer GOLAT, who had just arrived at the scene of the arrest. The Suspect refused to make any statements and was escorted to the patrol car by officers.

DISPOSITION

At 1430 hrs. Officers GOLAT and McDONOUGH transported the prisoner to the St. Joseph Hospital prison ward, arriving at 1440 hrs. Prisoner, Michael Earl WALLACE, was then booked into the prison ward by Booking Officer James E. CLANAHAN (#718) under the charges of Taking Possession of and Driving Away a Motor Vehicle (750.413) and Assault and Battery (750.81).

EVIDENCE

Recovered auto, a 1974 Chevrolet Impala, white/red, two-door sedan, Michigan license #DZJ 591, VIN #C5P68H152096, was towed to the Central City Garage by Middleton's Towing (Driver: Mike MIDDLETON). Escorted by Scout 23-2 (Officers BIANCHI and SHOLKE). Hold placed on vehicle for detectives.

INJURIES

Suspect, Michael Earl WALLACE, sustained a 3-inch-long horizontal cut over his right eye. Suspect was treated in the prison ward of St. Joseph Hospital by Dr. Wilhiem Z. ZEE. Treatment consisted of 14 stitches.

EXCEPTIONAL OCCURRENCES

When Officer McDONOUGH placed handcuffs on the Suspect's left wrist, the Suspect swung with his right arm, striking Officer McDONOUGH in the face with his fist. The officer countered by jerking on the handcuffs, causing Suspect to lose his balance and fall to the ground, striking his forehead on the pavement. Suspect gave no further resistance.

NOTIFICATIONS MADE

By Officer GOLAT:

Mrs. Sara Jane MOORE, 2110 Beastie Boulevard, Detroit, Michigan, TX 776-9756, owner of recovered vehicle. Told that she could pick up her auto at the Central City Garage at 0900 hrs., 8/16/76. 1530 hrs.

By Officer McDONOUGH:

Sgt. Russell J. KANERVA, Identification Section. Requested a latent prints check on recovered vehicle. 1530 hrs.

ADDITIONAL INFORMATION

Assisting Officers Michael BIANCHI and John SHOLKE (Sct. 23-2) controlled traffic at Grand and Charles and maintained chain of custody on the impounded vehicle.

STATUS

Open

                                  Signed:

                                  Kenneth C. GOLAT

COMMENT:

Ken organizes the Investigation section well. The suspects' running in different directions results in different activities by each officer. Faced with the need to record separate chases that took place at the same time, Ken chose to describe the unsuccessful one first. This let him include essential information—broadcasting a description, securing the stolen vehicle, and directing traffic—without interrupting the natural flow of the narrative. It is now easy for him to go on: he simply notes that the second chase occurred at the same time as the other actions. The capture of the suspect then leads naturally without interruption into the Arrest section.

APPLICATIONS

Exercise 1

Use the given information to write an Evidence section. Supply any details needed.

(a) Information: You have arrested a suspect for Possession of Stolen Property. In the van he was driving at the time of arrest, you found several stolen television sets, radios, and tape recorders. You have identified all the recovered items and stored them in the evidence room. The suspect's van was impounded at the police garage.

(b) Information: You have arrested a suspect for Auto Theft. Suspect was driving the stolen auto at time of arrest. You impound the auto at the police garage, pending release to the owner.

(c) Information: Working alone in a small community, you arrest some juveniles for Illegal Possession of Liquor. A search of the car uncovers several sealed cans of beer and two opened, partially empty bottles of whiskey.

(d) Information: You have arrested a suspect for Breaking and Entering. You have recovered the tool used (a crowbar) to gain entrance. You have also photographed and measured the prymarks on the door and jamb at the point of entry. Your search of the suspect uncovered a switchblade hidden inside her left sock.

Exercise 2

Using the stated information, write an Injured Persons section. Supply details as needed.

(*a*) Information: While making an arrest, you have injured the suspect. Suspect has lacerations on his forehead requiring medical attention. You transport the suspect.

(*b*) Information: The victim in a cutting incident has been taken to the hospital by ambulance. She has severe cuts on the chest and throat and will remain in the hospital.

(*c*) Information: You have several injured victims in a felonious driving incident. The victims were in two separate vehicles when the incident occurred. They were taken to two different hospitals by ambulance.

(*d*) Information: While effecting an arrest on a warrant, you are attacked by the suspect's German Shepherd dog. You suffer several deep cuts on the forearm, caused by the dog's teeth.

Exercise 3

Using the information given, write a Notifications Made section. Supply details as needed:

(*a*) Information: Having apprehended a juvenile driving a stolen auto, you notify the juvenile bureau, the arrestee's parents, and the car owner.

(*b*) Information: You have arrested several persons in an old residence on narcotics charges. The residence is clearly in violation of city health and housing codes. You notify the narcotics bureau, the public health department, and the city building inspector.

(*c*) Information: You are searching for a burglary suspect who has taken refuge in a suburban garage. While searching, your partner is bitten by a raccoon, which then escapes. You must now notify public health officials and the animal control officer.

Exercise 4

Use the given information to write Exceptional Occurrences sections. Supply details as necessary.

(*a*) Information: When you apprehended the suspect, he resisted by attacking you with a length of metal pipe. You and your partner were forced to use your nightsticks to ward off the blows and subdue the suspect.

(*b*) Information: You have arrested an influential citizen for drunk driving. She curses at you and your partner, and also threatens to use her influence against you.

(*c*) Information: You have entered a home to make an arrest on a warrant. As you prepare to leave with the suspect in custody, his wife suddenly flies into a rage. She shouts obscenities at you and your partner and throws various objects (vases, books, etc.) on the floor.

Exercise 5

Write Additional Information sections based on the given information. Supply details as needed.

(*a*) Information: As part of your investigation following an Assault arrest, you interview residents in adjoining apartments to locate possible witnesses. Your interviews produce no results. List those interviewed.

(*b*) Information: You have requested assistance to effect an arrest. The backup officers arrive in time to witness the suspect's resistance and the force exerted by you and your partner to overcome the resistance. Assisting officers also witness the search and reading of the rights. These officers then supervise the towing away of the suspect's vehicle (no hold placed on the vehicle).

(*c*) Information: You arrest a suspect in the act of breaking and entering. You hear another person running from the scene, but you are unable to see the person. There is no physical evidence to indicate an accomplice. Moreover, the arrested suspect refuses to talk. However, you recall that two weeks ago you had filled field interview cards on the arrested suspect and a companion.

Exercise 6

Write a complete report on the incident described below. Supply your own details as needed, i.e., direct quotations, descriptions, and names. Generally follow the indicated outline; however, use only essential details under the major headings. Put others in the proper supplementary sections.

Initial Information
It is March 12, 1976, a Friday. You are in a two-person radio car driving west on Perry Street at Mason Street. At 2:15 p.m. you receive a radio message sending you to 1313 Moloch Street to investigate a reported family disturbance.

Investigation

Upon arrival you knock on the front door, which connects the living quarters with a front porch. The door is opened inward by the complainant, a Mrs. Patricia Samuels. You note that she has facial injuries. Mrs. Samuels smiles, reports her husband has been beating her, and invites you in.

As your partner enters, Mrs. Samuels swings the door open wider and steps away from it. A shotgun blast sounds from inside the house. Several pellets strike the door. Some strike your partner in the hand and arm; some remain embedded in the flesh; others bounce onto the floor. (You later discover the shotgun was loaded with home-reloaded fine bird shot.)

You and your partner continue into the house and see a man with a shotgun seated in a rocking chair under the archway joining the front room (where you are) and a dining room. The man is about 15 feet away. He still has the shotgun pointed at the door and is attempting to eject the spent shell.

Arrest

You tell the man he is under arrest and order him to drop the shotgun; instead he swings at your partner with the shotgun butt. You disarm him, injuring him in the process.

After you have handcuffed the suspect, Mr. Turk Samuels, his wife suddenly goes berserk and attacks your partner with a small table. You disarm her without further injury to anyone.

You attempt to question Mr. Samuels but receive no understandable response. Mrs. Samuels then tells you that her husband is a mental patient on leave from an institution. Mrs. Samuels denies any knowledge of her husband's having a shotgun or planning to use it. She further excuses her attack on the officers as a momentary loss of control at seeing her husband injured. You gather any necessary evidence: the shotgun, pellets from the door, expended and live rounds from the weapon, and the pellets which struck your partner.

Disposition

You transport Mr. Samuels to the hospital and put him in the prison ward. No charges are brought against Mrs. Samuels at this time.

Evidence

List all evidence recovered.

Injured Persons

List the extent of injuries and the treatment given to both the suspect and your partner. Note that Mrs. Samuels will seek her own treatment.

Notifications Made

Notify the institution that gave the suspect his leave.

Exceptional Occurrences

Note that your partner was struck by shotgun pellets. Describe how you disarmed the suspect. Describe how you disarmed Mrs. Samuels.

For comparison purposes, we have included Ginny Messer's report on the same incident.

INITIAL INFORMATION

At 2:15 p.m., Friday, March 12, 1976, Officers MESSER and SCHMITT (Unit 313), westbound on Perry at Mason, received a radio run: "1313 Moloch Street, family trouble."

INVESTIGATION

Upon arrival at the above address (2:22 p.m.), officers walked up onto the open-air front porch (north side of house). Officer MESSER stood to the right of the front door and Officer SCHMITT to its left. MESSER knocked on the door and identified herself and her partner as police officers.

The front door was opened several seconds later by a woman who introduced herself as Mrs. Patricia SAMUELS. The door opened inward so that Mrs. SAMUELS was standing at the free end of the door inside the house. Officers noted the following injuries to Mrs. SAMUELS' head and face: a $1/2$ inch cut on the right side of her lower lip, which was swollen and bleeding; a swollen left eye, almost closed; and several small contusions on the left side of her face.

Mrs. SAMUELS said that she was glad that the officers had arrived so quickly. Officer MESSER then asked Mrs. SAMUELS for permission to enter the house. Mrs. SAMUELS smiled and said, "I'm sorry to have to bother you, Officers. Tell my husband to stop beating me. Please, do come in."

As Officer SCHMITT entered, Mrs. SAMUELS, in one motion, pushed the door open 2 feet wider and stepped back and to the right into the living room. While Officer SCHMITT was walking past the free end of the door, a shotgun blast sounded from the eastern side of the house. Most of the small pellets from the shell either remained embedded in the front door or bounced off the door and fell to the floor. Four pellets struck Officer SCHMITT's left hand and remained embedded in his flesh. Other pellets struck Officer SCHMITT's left arm, putting three pellet-sized holes in the officer's long-sleeved shirt.

Officer MESSER joined her partner inside the house. Officers spotted a man sitting in a rocking chair in the archway between the living room (north end of the house) and the dining room (southeast corner of house). The man was 15 feet away and still pointing a shotgun at the front door while attempting to eject the expended shell.

Both officers drew their weapons and pointed them at the Suspect.

ARREST

Officer SCHMITT told the Suspect that he was under arrest for Assault with Intent to Commit Murder. Officer MESSER told the Suspect to put his shotgun on the floor and then to stand up and put his hands behind his head. Instead, the Suspect stood up and jabbed the shotgun butt at Officer SCHMITT. Officer SCHMITT grabbed the stock of the shotgun and pushed it upward to avoid injury. During this upward swing, the butt struck the Suspect's two front teeth, breaking off half of each one. After breaking the Suspect's teeth, the butt swung further upward and struck his nose from below, forcing his head backward. The Suspect released his grip on the shotgun, which then fell to the floor. Officer MESSER handcuffed the Suspect and read him his rights from a Miranda card (at 2:26 p.m.). The Suspect said that he understood his rights and would make statements.

As soon as the Suspect was handcuffed, his nose started bleeding and swelling. When Mrs. SAMUELS looked at the Suspect's face, she said, ''You've hurt him.'' She knocked a lamp off a small, three-legged end table that was at the west end of the living room. Mrs. SAMUELS then picked up the end table, ran across the living room, and started swinging the end table at Officer SCHMITT. Officer MESSER approached Mrs. SAMUELS from the rear and pulled both of her arms sharply backward at the elbows. The end table fell to the floor, and Mrs. SAMUELS started crying.

While Officer MESSER was trying to calm Mrs. SAMUELS, Officer SCHMITT inspected his shotgun injuries and found the four pellets still embedded in his left hand. Officer SCHMITT raised his sleeve and found no pellet penetration, only red marks where three pellets had struck and bounced off.

At 2:32 p.m.,Officer SCHMITT tried to question Mr. SAMUELS but could get no rational answers from him. Mrs. SAMUELS then told officers that her husband was a mental patient on a weekend pass from the Alpena Asylum. Mrs. SAMUELS added that she "just went crazy" when she saw her husband hurt. Officer MESSER asked Mrs. SAMUELS why she let the officers enter the house knowing that her husband had a shotgun pointed at them. Mrs. SAMUELS denied having any knowledge of her husband's shotgun or his plans to use it.

At 2:40 p.m. Officers MESSER and SCHMITT took the shotgun and several pellets from the door as evidence.

DISPOSITION

Officers transported Mr. SAMUELS to City General Hospital, arriving at 2:45 p.m. Mr. SAMUELS was taken to the prison ward where he was booked at 2:55 p.m. by Officer Ben STONE on a charge of Assault with Intent to Commit Murder (13-0013). Mrs. SAMUELS stayed at home and was not charged at this time.

EVIDENCE

Officer MESSER properly identified the following items and placed them in the Evidence Room at 3:20 p.m.:

One (1) shotgun: 20 gauge, pump action, "Accu-brand." Marked GCM on the right side of frame with a metal stylus. Evidence Tag No. 3-313.

Two (2) shotgun shells: 20 gauge, loaded, green, "Accu-brand," hand loaded with #8 birdshot. Removed from above shotgun by Officer MESSER. Initialed GCM and packaged. Evidence Tag No. 3-314.

Four (4) pellets: #8 bird shot extracted from the front door of 1313 Moloch by Officer MESSER. Packaged, sealed, and tagged. Evidence Tag No. 3-315.

Four (4) pellets: #8 bird shot extracted from Officer SCHMITT's left hand by Dr. HAYES. Packaged, sealed, and tagged. Evidence Tag No. 3-316.

One (1) shotgun shell: "Accu-brand," 20 gauge, expended. Removed from above shotgun by Officer MESSER. Initialed GCM and packaged. Evidence Tag No. 3-317.

INJURED PERSONS

Mrs. Patricia W. SAMUELS' injuries were sustained before the officers arrived. Mrs. SAMUELS said that she would visit her family doctor later (Dr. John B. GROSS, Medical Arts Clinic).

Suspect, Turk SAMUELS, suffered a broken nose and two broken front teeth. He was treated for the broken nose in the prison ward of City General Hospital at 3:30 p.m. by Dr. Joseph B. HAYES, who reset the nose with surgical tape. Dental care was not given.

At 3:05 p.m., Officer William L. SCHMITT was treated by Dr. HAYES at City General Hospital for a shotgun wound. Four small-shot pellets were removed from Officer SCHMITT's left hand, which was then disinfected and wrapped in sterile gauze. (The pellets had penetrated the skin tissue about $1/4$ inch. One was lodged in the ring finger above the knuckle, one was in the middle finger above the knuckle, and two were located near the center of the hand.)

NOTIFICATIONS MADE

By Officer MESSER:

Mr. SAMUELS' psychiatrist, Dr. Carl J. LEONI, Jr., Alpena Asylum, Alpena, Michigan. 4:30 p.m.

EXCEPTIONAL OCCURRENCES

While entering the house at 1313 Moloch Street to settle a family dispute, Officer SCHMITT was injured when a shotgun was fired by Suspect (Ref.: Investigation).

Suspect received facial injuries while resisting arrest and assaulting Officer SCHMITT (Ref.: Arrest).

When Patricia W. SAMUELS, Suspect's wife, saw the extent of her husband's injuries, she became irrational and assaulted Officer SCHMITT (Ref.: Arrest).

STATUS

Open, pending psychiatric examination of Suspect.

Signed:

Ginny C. MESSER

COMMENT:

Usually officers need not painstakingly record their position when knocking on a door. However, the shot fired changes the situation. It is now important to establish everyone's exact location. While officers routinely identify themselves, the officer's being struck here demands that such identification be noted in the report. Thus, there can be no question on this point later. Ginny has also described Mrs. Samuels' appearance upon answering the door. This prevents any suggestion that she incurred the injuries during the struggle.

Again Ginny has chosen to include the details of each struggle in the narrative section. Although, as usual, Ginny's account is well written, we still suggest officers leave these details to the Exceptional Occurrences section. This would considerably shorten the Arrest section without detracting from the reader's grasp of the incident.

Exercise 7

Use the given information to write a complete Arrest Report. Supply any details necessary.

At 11:15 p.m., October 29, a Monday, you are in a two-officer radio car going west on I 99 at Vernon Road, a rural area. You see the headlights of an approaching vehicle weaving across both eastbound lanes of the divided highway. You cross the median at an emergency crossing strip and follow the suspect vehicle.

You follow the suspect vehicle for approximately 1 mile. During this time the vehicle continues to weave from lane to lane, twice going completely off the roadway on the right and once having both left wheels on the median.

You move alongside the suspect vehicle and signal the driver to pull to the shoulder of the highway. The driver apparently ignores your signals, for he turns slightly to the left, nearly striking the patrol car. You then activate your speaker and order him to the side of the road. He complies, but in so doing he nearly drives into a drainage ditch located 50 feet from the right edge of the paved surface.

Upon approaching the vehicle, you smell a strong odor of liquor, apparently coming from the suspect vehicle. You ask the driver for his operator's license and vehicle registration. The driver fumbles in his breast pocket and drops his wallet on the floor. You immediately order him from the car with both hands on the top of his head. He steps from the car, but stumbles and nearly falls.

You again ask for his identification. After two unsuccessful attempts, he takes out his license from the recovered wallet. The license identifies him as Porter P. Peto, DOB 1–2–24, 1313 Gadskill Drive, Page, Michigan. You then give him the field sobriety test, which he fails.

You place him under arrest for Driving under the Influence of Liquor. Peto makes no statement other than to say he only had "two beers" and to ask for "a break."

You request a wrecker and then transport Peto to the station. At the station, you read him the implied consent form. At 11:45 p.m. and 12:00 midnight, Sgt. Quinn Quickly gives two Breathalyzer tests. Results are 0.19 and 0.21, respectively.

You book Peto.

Exercise 8

Write the Arrest Report for the following incident. Supply any needed details.

You are in a two-officer radio unit in a suburban community. At 9:30 p.m., April 5, 1976, a Thursday, you see a pickup truck parked beside Lancaster's Lawn and Garden Center, 1370 Mortimer Road. The truck has a metal cap over the box area; its lights are out, but you detect exhaust gases escaping from the tailpipe.

You request a LEIN run on the pickup with negative results. You advise Dispatch and park the patrol car. You and your partner separate and approach on foot. Two apparently new lawnmowers in the pickup can be seen through the cab's rear window. You check the building and find it locked, but you then hear voices outside the building at the rear. Behind the building is an unroofed, fenced enclosure. The gate to the enclosure is unlocked. You and your partner then see two men in the enclosed area trying to start a garden tractor.

You confront the two men. One tells you that they are employees "working late." You ask for and receive their identification. Your partner calls Dispatch for a LEIN check and also asks that the owner of Lancaster's be contacted.

Dispatch returns negative results from the LEIN run but reports that neither man is employed at the store. Dispatch also informs you that the owner is on his way.

The owner arrives and confirms that the lawnmowers in the pickup were taken from the enclosure. He furnishes you the invoice with corresponding numbers to verify identification. The owner further states the gate had been locked with a chain and padlock. You find both in the cab of the pickup. The chain had apparently been sawed through with a hacksaw. You also find a hacksaw on the floor of the pickup.

You place the men under arrest, gather the evidence, arrange for towing the truck, and leave the owner to secure the enclosure.

Chapter 5
Incidents against
Property

Television police officers lead an exciting existence. High-speed chases with all their accompanying effects—flashing lights, screaming sirens, screeching tires—highlight each tour of duty. Arrests for minor offenses are frequent and often effected with a casual ease. Major arrests are common. Even ordinary incidents included to give a touch of reality usually reflect, at the least, a degree of glamour, whimsical humor, or irony.

But real officers face a less exciting prospect. On some tours of duty, they, too, will become involved in high-speed chases; and sometimes they, too, will encounter glamorous or eccentric people or make arrests. But, more likely, their tours will consist of uneventful, routine patrol interrupted every now and then by events that demand patient and tactful peace officers, not heroes. The real officers will settle family quarrels and quiet various disturbances—noisy parties, complaints of loud radios or barking dogs, etc. They will deal with neighborhood disputes ranging from arguments over a parking space to violent differences over boundary lines. They will transport people and material. They will escort vehicles, direct traffic, guide strangers, and perform dozens of other duties. They will also investigate larcenies and burglaries.

The last duty leads to the point at issue, for the others usually require no reports. Larceny and burglary complaints do. Moreover, as with the other activities above, they make up the "bread and butter" part of the officers' lives. And the facts are that for every high-speed chase report, officers will take several larceny complaints; that for every Arrest Report, they will write several Burglary Reports. Since property theft is a major police problem, officers may as well face the simple fact: they will write Larceny and Burglary Reports with monotonous regularity. Therefore, it seems logical that they should adopt a standard format that will help them perform this duty.

A good standard format should follow, as closely as possible, the natural order of events. Briefly stated, in a typical situation involving a Larceny or Burglary Report, the natural order conforms to the following sequence. Upon arrival at the scene, the investigating officer will be met by the complainant and will be given a brief description of the incident. After that, the officer will conduct a physical investigation of the scene. Then he or she will request any assistance necessary and available. Next the officer will conduct an in-depth interview of the complainant. The officer will identify the whereabouts of the complainant at the time of the occurrence, establish the time limits, determine what is missing, and obtain any possible leads. If these leads materialize, the officer, depending on whether or not assistance is available, will investigate further. With minor variations these steps make up the usual course of such investigations.

Ideally, the report should conform to this pattern. This will make the officer's job easier by helping to keep the presentation in chronological order, thus eliminating confusion and guarding against the omission of necessary details. To meet these requirements, we suggest the following format:

Initial Information
Investigation
    Physical Investigation
    Interview with Complainant(s)
    Interview with Witness(es)
    Further Investigation
Reconstruction

After these major headings, the reporting officer will add supplementary headings as required. In addition to those suggested in Chapter 3, the officer will need a Missing Property unit. Again, we urge officers to create their own supplementary headings wherever appropriate.

THE INITIAL INFORMATION SECTION

Once again, the first unit of *every* report is the Initial Information section. Officers may follow exactly the same format given in Chapter 3. In fact, we suggest they do so. The more the writer uses the formulaic opening, the more automatic it will become. As this happens, the officer's mind becomes freer to concentrate on other aspects of the report.

However, the nature of Larceny and Burglary Reports does allow for some simplification. Officers need not include their location upon receiving the call. The information is rarely needed in such complaints because there is generally no immediate danger to citizens and so time of response is a less important factor. Frequently, these incidents will have occurred days or even months before the police were notified. Homes burglarized while the residents were away for several months provide one example. Also, some victims fail to notify the police immediately. Rather, they hesitate. They finally inform their insurance agents, and only upon being told a police report is required by the insurance company do they notify the police. Few departments would recommend a "Code three" response to incidents of this nature.

Actually, in practice, the opposite is true. In many departments officers dispatched to take known Larceny and Burglary Reports are still regarded as being "in service." They may very well be diverted to handle an emergency, thus postponing their report. While no department deliberately slights a citizen by not responding immediately to a legitimate complaint, sometimes these delays cannot be avoided. Certainly a personal injury accident, an armed robbery in progress, or an emergency blood run must take precedence over a Larceny Report, regardless of the money involved. Given these circumstances, an exact accounting for time is rarely necessary. Moreover, the officer doing the report always operates from the perspective of time. He writes *after* the investigation. If there are special circumstances indicating the need for a strict accounting of time, he will know it when writing the report.

Whether or not the savings in time and space are worthwhile, students may judge by examining the two versions below. One includes the officers' location upon receiving the run; the other does not.

INITIAL INFORMATION

At 1130 hrs., Tuesday, June 22, 1976, Officers LEAR and REGAN (Scout 9-4), eastbound on Tempest at Caliban, received a radio run: 1812 Verona, larceny.

INITIAL INFORMATION

At 1130 hrs., Tuesday, June 22, 1976, Officers LEAR and REGAN received a radio run: 1812 Verona, larceny.

Either account would do. Both serve two purposes: to present pertinent data and to stimulate writing. In departments that require the complainant's signature on the completed report, the second purpose becomes especially important. In many cases, the complainant, depressed over the loss of valuables and concerned about the insurance company's possible reactions, becomes annoyed at the police, whom he may consider accountable—however vaguely. The officer who begins a report crisply, using the above prescribed language, projects an air of professional competence which relieves that anger and restores confidence in the police.

THE INVESTIGATION SECTION

As we have noted, the Investigation unit should follow as nearly as possible the chronological sequence of the officer's investigation. Therefore, we suggest the reporting officer use these guidelines:

Begin with arrival at the scene.

Give a brief account of the incident as told by the reporting party or complainant.

Record the results of the physical investigation.

Write up, under appropriate subheadings, the substance of in-depth interviews with the complainant(s) and witness(es).

Describe subsequent investigative actions.

Usually, upon arrival, the responding officer will need a brief account of the specific incident. The radio operator may have simply dispatched her to "meet a man" or "see a woman" at the specified address. As such calls could be anything from a citizen's complaining of juvenile trespasses to another's demanding an investigation of a flying saucer reportedly circling the area, the officer often arrives with no real knowledge of the nature of the complaint. Even if previously told, he or she will still need specific information about the particular incident.

The officer should put this account in the report immediately after noting time of arrival. Doing so achieves several desirable purposes. First, it maintains chronological order. Second, it serves as a check for the officer's evaluation of his or her own investigation; later, if need be, the officer can determine precisely on what information she or he had proceeded. Third, it informs the reader, who can now judge the officer's actions from a similar point. An officer following these recommendations would begin a typical Investigation section of an Incident against Property Report in the following manner:

INVESTIGATION

Upon arrival at the above address (1430 hrs.), officers identified themselves and were admitted by the Complainant, Mrs. Felicia FALSTAFF. Complainant stated that someone had entered her home during her absence and stolen several appliances and miscellaneous items.

The initial interview with the complainant should be very limited. Proper police work demands that officers conduct an objective investigation. Holding an extensive interview with the complainant before the physical investigation may interfere with this objectivity. An officer's empathy with the complainant, for example, may influence the course of the investigation. Instead of being objective, the officers could find themselves, even without meaning to, looking for facts that will support the complainant's account.

The opposite also occurs. Being human, the officer may take a quick dislike to the complainant. This, too, can result in a distorted investigation. The officer may either give the investigation too little attention or spend too much time and effort trying to disprove the complainant's story.

Both courses are objectionable. All complaining citizens are entitled to an investigation conducted by open-minded police officers. Such officers first search for the physical evidence without any preconceived ideas to support or to refute. They then evaluate the facts *impersonally*, for personal attitudes can only interfere. Moreover, officers armed with the results of the physical investigation are less likely to leave out pertinent questions during subsequent interviews. They are now simply better prepared for the task. For all these reasons, we suggest officers perform the physical investigation first. Correspondingly, to maintain chronological order, the next item in the Investigation section should reflect the officers' actions—the officers should record the steps taken and the facts obtained.

Following the physical investigation, the officers will usually interview the complainant and any witnesses at length. These interviews should be placed in the Investigation section under appropriate subheadings. Using subheadings prevents confusion. It clearly signals that the interviews are an integral part of the total investigation, not separate elements. Frequently, officers seem to separate these interviews from the investigation by using major headings. This can confuse a reader, who is then forced to pick up the narrative thread that had apparently ended. Subheadings help avoid many of these abrupt, distracting major transitions. Yet they still let the reporting officer concentrate on a single area of the report, and the reader still has a unified, compact account of the interviews.

Officers should try to keep these interview segments concise. Paraphrasing will help. Unfortunately, many officers use a question and answer technique and rely almost completely on direct quotations. This usually results in wordiness, because most answers are full of material that has nothing to do with the incident. Also, such reporting may be inaccurate. Direct quotation must be *exact*. Any time officers enclose a statement in quotation marks they are indicating to the reader that the *precise words* have been recorded. Without a tape recorder, achieving such precision is not only difficult, it is painfully slow. Using this technique, for example, an officer could finish with the following account:

Interview with Complainant: Officer LEAR asked the Complainant when she was last in the house prior to the burglary.

Complainant replied, "I left home about ten o'clock this morning. I got into my own car and went to the beauty shop because I had an appointment to have my hair done. After that, at just about noon, I went for lunch at Pericles Pizza Palace—they always have good submarine sandwiches there. Then I did some shopping downtown. I guess I got home at about three o'clock or so. That's when I saw the back door was unlocked. I then saw that my Amana Radar Range was gone. So was my toaster, Mixmaster, and new coffee pot. That's when I called you." Officer LEAR then asked if she had seen any strangers or suspicious-looking persons hanging around lately. The Complainant stated, "No, I haven't noticed anyone new around." Officer LEAR then asked her if she had any idea who might have stolen the items. Complainant stated, "No, I don't know anybody who would do such a thing." Officer LEAR then asked if she was sure she had locked the house before leaving. Complainant said she was certain "because I always lock the door before I go out."

One can quickly see that the possibilities for error in grammar, substance, or punctuation are great in such a procedure.

By paraphrasing, the reporting officer would write up the same interview as follows:

Interview with Complainant: After completing a check of the premises, Officer LEAR interviewed the Complainant. Complainant stated she had left her home by auto at approximately 10:00 a.m., this date, for a hair appointment and some shopping. Complainant was certain the house was locked at that time. Upon her return at approximately 3:00 p.m., this date, she discovered the rear door unlocked and several appliances missing. Complainant could suggest no possible suspects.

Clearly, the officer would be better off not using the first approach and just summarizing the important points of the interview. But in unusual circumstances the first approach may be better. If, for example, the physical evidence is at odds with the complainant's statement, the officer may decide that an exact deposition is necessary. In this and similar unusual situations the officer can take a formal statement on separate pages and attach it to the report. In the Investigation section he or she can then include a summary of this statement and inform the reader where the complete, detailed account is available. This gives later investigators and the prosecutor a concise account that does not disrupt their understanding of the complete incident; yet any detailed information they may need is readily at hand.

As previously noted (Chapter 3), the reporting officer can also reduce the number of words in the Investigation section by omitting details that can be presented more effectively elsewhere. Among these are descriptions of evidence and stolen property. These descriptions should be placed under the appropriate supplementary headings. In the above account, for instance, the reader does not need to know at this point that the appliances stolen included a Norelco twelve-cup, filter-drip, automatic coffeemaker with a black and chrome heating base, chrome handle, and a brown plastic filter, having a retail value of $39.95. Removing these details from the narrative eliminates transitional problems and lets the reporting officer concentrate on developing the total incident. Also, with this technique the reader is not forced to go through a mass of details while trying to get an overall view of the incident.

After writing up these interviews, the reporting officer should note any further investigative action taken. Frequently, more investigation will be required either to follow leads obtained, to complete the physical investigation previously begun, or to promote better public relations. The first is self-evident: the complainant or witnesses may furnish information—perhaps the names of possible suspects or eyewitnesses—that requires immediate action. The other two points, although separate, have the same purpose—they extend courtesies to the complainant and witnesses. By postponing such activities as photographing, making cast impressions, and lifting fingerprints until after the interview, the officer reduces the time that the complainant and witnesses must be away from their normal activities. Obviously, officers should follow this practice only when such a delay will not affect the physical evidence.Officers should not, for example, put off collecting blood samples where a burglar had apparently cut himself entering the premises. Any delay in analysis could make the samples useless. On the other hand, as long as the officer takes elementary precautions to protect the scene, there is no problem with delaying taking photographs of broken windows or pry-bar impressions on a door frame. When practicable, therefore, postponing some activities costs nothing and greatly strengthens the department's public relations.

Occasionally, should time permit, this same consideration may lead officers to follow a course they already know to be fruitless. In one case, at the complainant's insistence, officers attempted "to lift" fingerprints from a bathtub near the point of entry of a breaking and entering in spite of the following: First, everything indicated the burglar had worn gloves. Second, it was extremely unlikely that the burglar had touched the bathtub. Third, the incident had occurred in an unheated house during a period of subfreezing weather; even if the burglar had removed his gloves and had touched the bathtub, the odds against his leaving detectable prints would be astronomical. No usable prints were obtained, but the complainant's regard for the police measurably increased. Again, the officers must use common sense. Often, there will be no time for such niceties. If not, they must simply explain the facts, and this may not be easy, since the public is accustomed to all sorts of miracles being performed every day by police technicians on various television programs.

These same programs also influence student officers and rookies, who mistakenly assume that an unlimited wealth of technical talent is instantaneously available regardless of the incident. In most agencies this assistance, while it may exist, is necessarily reserved for the more serious offenses. Larcenies, burglaries, and other offenses against property only infrequently receive such attention. Usually, the burden of all preliminary investigation in these cases falls on the responding officers.

Although they vary in importance, any of the above circumstances could lead to investigation after the interviews. Therefore, the reporting officer should logically insert these actions at the end of the Investigation section.

The above format for the Investigation section should simplify the officer's reporting duties. The chronological ordering corresponds to the customary sequence of the investigation itself; it is a natural rather than an artificial structuring. Some changes in the format may sometimes be necessary, but the deviation will probably be slight and easy to understand. Officers working in pairs, for example, may divide investigative responsibilities; one will conduct the physical investigation while the other interviews those persons involved. In such an instance the reporting officer should still record the physical search first and then indicate at the beginning of the interview section that the actions occurred simultaneously. Such an account could read:

INVESTIGATION

Upon arrival at the scene (1130 hrs.), officers were admitted by the Complainant, Miss Vickie VOLTAIRE. Complainant reported someone had broken into her home and stolen a cookie jar containing miscellaneous coins from her kitchen cupboard. Officer BARTON made a physical search of the premises. He found that the rear east door had apparently been forced open. Pry marks were visible on both door and jamb. No other physical evidence was found.

Officer BARTON then measured and photographed the pry marks on both door and jamb (Ref.: Evidence). BARTON unsuccessfully attempted to lift prints from the rear door

> knobs, the kitchen cabinets and cupboards, and the kitchen table.
>
> Interview with Complainant: While Officer BARTON conducted the physical investigation, Officer MULLINS interviewed the Complainant in her living room. Complainant stated. . . .

Other variations can be handled in a similar way. If for some reason the responding officers interviewed the complainant first, they can simply change the order to correspond with the changed sequence of investigation.

By using the prescribed reporting format and by following the suggestions given in Chapters 2 and 3, officers can eliminate many difficulties in writing the Investigation unit.

THE RECONSTRUCTION SECTION

In the Reconstruction section the officer should present a reasoned account of what *probably* occurred. It must be an *inferential* statement based only on the officer's assessment of the physical evidence and information derived from any interviews held. It should include:

Apparent method of entry or operation

Possible time of occurrence (usually the establishment of outside limits rather than a specific time)

Evident nature of the incident

Possible suspects (if any)

Properly written, the unit will provide the reader with a concise, coherent, workable hypothesis, formulated by the officers at the scene. The various investigative results must be drawn together by someone; usually that someone is the responding line officer. After all, the line officer obtained these results in the first place. It was the line officer who performed the physical investigation and spoke to the parties involved. Consequently, it is the line officer's responsibility to put the data together and reconstruct the incident.

To reconstruct an incident, the officer must make *inferences*: statements about the unknown based on the known. Since there is always a possibility of error, the officer should avoid confusion by carefully identifying all inferences. The Reconstruction section, for example, may begin as follows:

RECONSTRUCTION

Based on the above, officers believe. . . .

The words *based on the above*, let the reader know that what is to follow stems from the stated information at this point. Subsequent investigation, of course, may unearth evidence disproving the officer's thesis. Sometimes it will. But the officer can hardly be held accountable for information not yet uncovered.

However, most of the time further investigation will support the police officer's theory, provided the theory is restricted to logical inferences. Should the officer include *opinion* or *judgment*, however, some unpleasant consequences may occur. Following is an incident in which the officers ignored these rules but were spared such unpleasantness through sheer good fortune:

Officers working the day watch were dispatched to a small shop specializing in men's wear. Upon arrival, they were informed by the lone clerk that someone had broken in and stolen several suits from the storeroom at the rear of the shop. Officers discovered the rear door had apparently been pried open, breaking the lock. The heavily traveled, paved alley at the rear yielded nothing. Nor did the carpeted storeroom. The clerk reported he had locked the shop at 9:30 p.m., the previous day. He had entered through the front door, which was still locked upon his arrival, at 9:00 a.m., reporting date. Shortly thereafter, he discovered the theft. There were two additional factors: the building had been found unlocked by officers twice during the preceding month; on the second occasion the owner, disgruntled at being awakened, had threatened to fire the clerk if it happened again.

Using this information, the officers flatly declared in their report that the clerk had failed to secure the building, resulting in someone's entering and removing the clothing. They then went on to state that in order to avoid being fired he had staged the apparent B&E as a cover for his negligence. The insurance representative notified the shop owner of the officer's suspicions and refused to cover the loss; the owner immediately dismissed the clerk. The clerk then filed a civil suit against the officers.

Fortunately, at least for the officers, later events substantiated their theory. A man arrested for a traffic violation shortly thereafter was wearing one of the stolen suits of clothing. Under questioning, he admitted that he had been passing by the shop, had seen the rear door open, and had taken the opportunity to steal the clothing. If this arrest had not occurred, the officers would have found themselves in an untenable position.

This risk was ill-advised. Their Reconstruction was not inferential; it was *opinionated*. After all, because the clerk had been careless does not imply that he was a liar.

Nor does it logically follow that he would deliberately stage an incident and make a false police report. By explicitly stating this opinion, however, the officers could easily have been guilty of damaging the reputation of an innocent person. In this instance, even though their guess was correct, only a chance event prevented a civil suit and possible disciplinary action.

The risk was also needless. The officers could simply have talked to the detectives about their suspicions, or the officers could have suggested their suspicions in the report without an outright declaration. They could have presented an acceptable reconstruction:

RECONSTRUCTION

Based on the above, officers believe Suspect(s) entered the building between 9:30 p.m. . . . . and 9:00 a.m., this date, by forcing open the rear (south) door with a flat instrument, possibly a wrecking bar. Suspect(s) apparently then removed several suits (Ref.: <u>Missing Property</u>), using the same door to exit.

With the given information, this is a reasonable *inference*. Then the officers could have recorded in an Additional Information section the dates on which the shop had been found unlocked and the fact of the owner's threat. This information would alert investigators to the possibility of a false report; yet it would jeopardize neither the officers nor the citizen.

THE SUPPLEMENTARY SECTIONS

Most of the supplementary sections have already been discussed in connection with the Arrest Report (Chapter 4). Some—Evidence, Notifications Made, and Additional Information—will be used frequently in Offenses against Property Reports. Others—Injured Persons and Exceptional Occurrences—will not. While the content may differ from that of an Arrest Report, the method of presentation is unchanged. Therefore, further discussion here is unnecessary. Officers have only to refer to the appropriate section in Chapter 4 or to the student examples at the end of the chapter.

But offenses against property may require an additional heading: Missing Property. In this unit the reporting officer records in compact form the available information about all items missing. Here the officers should:

Specify the quantities missing
Identify the type of property
Describe the property
List any identification numbers

Note the location from which the property is missing
Include the estimated value (unit and total)

As with the Evidence section, officers will find cataloging useful when dealing with several pieces of property. For example, a burglary resulting in the loss of several articles of clothing could be recorded:

MISSING PROPERTY

Complainant reported the following articles missing from her bedroom closet:

One (1) pantsuit: "Bobbie Brooks" brand, size 12, light-green flared pants with white stitching on the legs, dark-green Western-style jacket with white stitching around collar and pockets.   Value $100.00

One (1) tennis outfit: "Jantzen" brand, size 12, white shorts with narrow blue stripes on legs, white sleeveless top with blue piping around collar.   Value $75.00

One (1) jumpsuit: "Michigan" brand, size 12, dark blue with short sleeves.   Value $40.00

Two (2) blouses: "Superior" brand, both size 12, one white sleeveless with ruffled collar, the other blue, short-sleeved, Peter Pan collar.@ $20.00 each. Value $40.00

Total Value $255.00

All values are those given by the Complainant.

Sometimes officers have difficulty assigning values to missing items. To overcome this, many departments have developed set policies. These policies range from accepting the complainant's assessment to having the officers make the estimate. Some departments require both; they then use only the officer's figures for reporting purposes. While these figures are necessary to measure the financial impact of crime, officers should remember that they are only approximations. Each officer will, of course, follow departmental procedure. But in the absence of an established policy, we suggest that officers simply accept any *reasonable* value given by the complainant. However, as in the above example, the *officer should clearly identify the complainant as the source*.

Our reasoning is simple. Officers are not insurance adjustors; nor are they necessarily cost experts in fields ranging from women's clothing to industrial machinery. Moreover, it seems pointless for an officer to further antagonize an already upset complainant by lowering the value of lost property. Perhaps a five-year-old color television set is really worth $400 to a complainant who doesn't have the $400 to replace it. *Evaluating* the property is the insurance agent's job; *recovering* it is the officer's.

EXAMPLES OF INCIDENTS AGAINST PROPERTY REPORTS

Following are more reports written by students in the law enforcement program at Ferris State College. Again these reports are based on simulated incidents or stem from incidents that occurred during the students' internships. All are based on incidents that actually occurred.

1

INITIAL INFORMATION

At 4:10 p.m., Wednesday, May 19, 1976, Officers SPEARS and HART, while on patrol, received a radio run: "See the woman, 101 Chaucer Street, Apartment 13."

INVESTIGATION

Upon arrival at the above address (4:30 p.m.), the officers were met at the door by the Complainant, Mrs. Gordon MILTON. She told the officers that someone had stolen several articles of her clothing from the bedroom closet of the apartment while she and her husband were away on vacation.

Officer HART examined the apartment, which was located on the second floor of the building and overlooked a courtyard. He discovered that all the windows were still locked from the inside. Mrs. MILTON told HART that the door, which was the only one to the apartment, had been locked when she and her husband had returned home. HART noted there were no pry marks, nor was there any evidence of a forced entry on any of the windows or the door.

Interview with Complainant: Mrs. MILTON told Officer SPEARS that she and her husband had left on vacation for Vail, Colorado, at 10:00 a.m., Saturday, May 1, 1976. They returned on May 19, at 3:00 p.m. She began to unpack; while placing clothes in the bedroom closet, she discovered that several articles of her summer clothing were missing. As far as she and her husband could tell, nothing else in the apartment had been touched.

Mrs. MILTON added that she had asked the apartment manager, Ms. Esmerelda DONNE, who lived in Apartment 1, to keep an eye on the apartment while the MILTONS were away. Mrs. MILTON further stated that DONNE had previously admired several articles of Mrs. MILTON'S clothing. One outfit that DONNE had particularly admired, a red sleeveless dress, was among those articles missing.

Mrs. MILTON added that she and DONNE were approximately of the same size and build.

SPEARS asked Mrs. MILTON if she knew anything about DONNE'S background. Mrs. MILTON replied that she did not.

Further Investigation: While Officer SPEARS catalogued the missing items, Officer HART went to Apartment 1 and was met at the door by Mr. Harold ELIOT. ELIOT said that DONNE had been fired as apartment manager on May 11 because of "too many complaints by tenants that she was going into unoccupied apartments." ELIOT stated that he was the new apartment manager and that DONNE had left no forwarding address with him. ELIOT further stated that Isaac VOMISA, 211 W. Manana Drive, owned the apartment complex, and would have any forwarding address.

When asked if he knew anything that might help to locate DONNE, ELIOT said that he knew nothing of her background, but that he could give a description of her car (Ref.: <u>Additional Information</u>).

HART asked which apartments on the second floor were occupied from May 1 through May 11. ELIOT said only two, Apartments 12 and 14, and those people still lived there.

Officer HART then rejoined Officer SPEARS in Complainant's apartment.

HART went to Apartment 12, occupied by Mr. Glenn SHAW. SHAW said he had seen DONNE enter Apartment 13 on Sunday, May 9, but he did not see her leave the apartment.

Meanwhile, SPEARS went to Apartment 14, occupied by Mr. and Mrs. Arte MILLER. The MILLERS said they had seen DONNE enter Apartment 13 on either the 3d or 4th of May, but they could not remember the exact date. They did not see her leave the apartment.

Officer SPEARS attempted to telephone Mr. VOMISA but received only a recorded message that "Mr. Vomisa would be in at eight o'clock Monday morning. Please call then."

RECONSTRUCTION

Based on the above information, it appears that Ms. Esmerelda DONNE, using her passkey, may have entered the MILTON apartment some time between 10:00 a.m., May 1, 1976, and 3:00 p.m., May 19, 1976. She then removed several articles of clothing belonging to Mrs. MILTON.

STOLEN PROPERTY

The Complainant reported that the following articles of clothing were taken from her bedroom closet:

One (1) red, sleeveless, knee-length dress, size 10	$32.00
One (1) yellow, short-sleeve, slipover sweater, medium size	15.00
One (1) pair of light-blue dress slacks, size 10	24.00
One (1) navy blue, short-sleeve shirt, medium size	12.00
One (1) shell-pink, short-sleeve blouse, size 36	11.00
One (1) blue, sleeveless, long evening gown, size 10	53.00
TOTAL	$147.00

The above values are those given by the Complainant.

ADDITIONAL INFORMATION

ELIOT gave the following description of DONNE's car: Dodge Swinger, 1973 model, baby blue, small dent in the front passenger door, and one "Call of the Wild" sticker on the back bumper.

Officer will contact Mr. VOMISA at 8:00 a.m., Friday, May 21.

STATUS OF CASE

Open, pending further investigation.

Signed:

Terri SPEARS

COMMENT:

Terri basically follows the formulaic pattern in the first section. However, the "while on patrol" is unnecessary; if you are assigned to a patrol car, you had better be "on patrol" when not out of service or on a run.

Her Investigation section is excellent. Her organization of the content gives the reader a complete picture of the incident and investigation. Terri's use of the subheading Further Investigation is optional. As she is still in the Investigation section, a reader may safely assume that investigative action follows. However, following a lengthy interview, this subheading may be a helpful signal to the reader. Terri has wisely withheld a description of the suspect's car in the Investigation section. At this point it is of little importance whether the car is a new Cadillac or an old Volkswagen.

Given the investigative results, Terri's Reconstruction section is logical. She may be wrong, but she has carefully begun her *inference* by indicating that *it is an inference.*

In the Stolen Property section, she has failed to record the brand names of the various articles of clothing. But frequently such information is simply unavailable.

2

INITIAL INFORMATION

At 0905 hrs., Wednesday, June 16, 1976, Deputies KENDZIORSKI and KINSINGER (Car 2), southbound on Second at Tawas, received a radio run: J&M Sport Shop, B&E report.

INVESTIGATION

Upon arrival at the above address (0920 hrs.), deputies were met by Complainant. Complainant states someone had broken the back door and stolen several pairs of new skis. Deputy KENDZIORSKI then made a search of the scene and the area around the back of the building. He found pry marks around the lock on the outside of the back door. There were also pry marks on the frame next to the lock. KENDZIORSKI photographed and measured the marks for evidence.

Interview with Complainant: While KENDZIORSKI made a physical search of the scene, Deputy KINSINGER interviewed the owner of the store, Jack SHIELDS. Mr. SHIELDS stated that he had locked the store the previous evening (June 15) at 1800 hrs., and reopened the store at 0900 hrs. (this date) by coming through the front entrance. Shortly thereafter he noticed that five (5) pairs of Alpine skis were missing; nothing else had been touched. The stolen skis were still in their shipping cartons and had just been delivered the day before. Mr. SHIELDS then turned the doorknob of the back door and found it was unlocked and that there were pry marks around the door and frame. Mr. SHIELDS stated that while he had no idea who had broken in, Mr. B. BAND who lives across the alley from the shop might have seen something. SHIELDS stated Mr. BAND is a bartender and returns home early in the morning.

Interview with Witness: At 0955 hrs. deputies interviewed B. BAND at 2233 Sands. BAND stated that on the previous evening (June 15), he had arrived home around 0310 hrs. and noticed an old black van parked behind the sporting goods store. Mr. BAND said he saw no one, however; nor could he add to his description of the van.

RECONSTRUCTION

Based on the above, deputies believe that between 1800 hrs., June 15, 1976, and 0900 hrs., June 16, 1976, Suspect(s) gained entrance to the sporting goods store by prying open the rear door. Suspect(s) removed five (5) pairs of Alpine skis and then left through the rear door. Suspect(s) may have used an old-model black van in the theft.

EVIDENCE

The following photographs, taken by Deputy KENDZIORSKI, are attached to this report:

Photo 1: Pry mark, 1½ inches long, ¾ inch wide, ¼ inch deep, top of outside door lock

Photo 2: Pry mark, 3 inches long, ¾ inch wide, ¼ inch deep, bottom of outside door lock

Photo 3: Pry mark, 2 inches long, ¾ inch wide, ⅜ inch deep, next to the lock on the outside of the door frame

STOLEN PROPERTY

The Complainant reported the following items missing:

One (1) pair skis: K-2, "Winter Heat," 185 centimeters	$195.00
One (1) pair skis: Head, "Competition," 180 centimeters	195.00
Three (3) pair skis: Hart, "Javelin," 170 centimeters @ $150.00 ea.	450.00
Total Value	$840.00

Above values are those listed on Complainant's invoice.

All skis were in individual brown-cardboard shipping cartons bearing the manufacturers' and Complainant's names and addresses.

STATUS

Open, pending further investigation.

Signed:

Matt KINSINGER

COMMENT:

By reporting the events in their natural order, Matt gives the reader an overall view of the incident as revealed by the investigation. Students should note that deputies took the time to follow the rather improbable lead furnished by the complainant. Although it was doubtful that the bartender had seen much, they interviewed him anyway. The direct results were predictably slim; however, the public relations benefits may have been substantial.

Matt was not misled to attach too great a significance to the van. It remains only a *possibility*, and he has noted this in the Reconstruction section. In the same section, he has cut down on the number of words by using the word *Suspect(s)*. By adding the *s* in parentheses, he indicates that more than one person may have been involved without resorting to the customary "person or persons unknown."

3

INITIAL INFORMATION

At 1453 hrs., Sunday, May 23, 1976, Officers KENDZIORSKI and KINSINGER (Sct. 201), westbound on Grand Traverse at Saginaw, received a radio run: Pasadena and Industrial, larceny from auto.

INVESTIGATION

Upon arrival (1459 hrs.), officers were met by Complainant, Miss Lottie LAWSON. Complainant stated someone had stolen the CB radio and antenna from her pickup truck while she was at work. Officer KINSINGER investigated and discovered that the vent window, driver's side, was open. KINSINGER could detect no visible signs of force used on either the window or the frame. Nor could he find any tool that could have been used. Inside the vehicle was a bracket for a portable CB radio. The radio was gone. KINSINGER also found the hood closed but unlatched; there were numerous fingerprints visible in the dust on the hood.

Interview with Complainant: While Officer KINSINGER was conducting the physical search, Officer KENDZIORSKI interviewed the Complainant. Complainant stated that she had parked her truck at approximately 0620 hrs., this date, and then walked to her job at the Buick factory. When she returned from work at 1430 hrs., she saw that the antenna had been removed from the truck. She then looked inside and saw that the radio was missing. At this time, she called the police. When informed of the dirty fingerprints on the hood, Complainant stated she had not opened the hood for "some time," and the vehicle had not been serviced for at least a week.

Officer KINSINGER photographed the latch area of the vehicle hood. He then lifted several prints from the hood.

KINSINGER also dusted the inside door handle, driver's side, and the bracket for the CB radio. Only smudged, unusable prints were obtained.

RECONSTRUCTION

Based on the above, it appears Suspect(s) broke into the truck by force between 0620 and 1430 hrs., this date. The Suspect(s) apparently gained entry by prying open the vent window on the driver's door, reaching in, and opening the door. Suspect(s) then removed the CB radio and antenna. Suspect(s) also opened the hood to remove wiring for the CB unit.

EVIDENCE

Photographs of lifted prints are attached to this report. Lifted prints were turned over to Sgt. Denise PARK, Identification Bureau, at 1630 hrs., May 23, 1976.

STOLEN PROPERTY

The Complainant reported the following items missing:

One (1) "Realistic" twenty-three-channel CB radio—model TRC124 $160.00

One (1) CB antenna   37.00

TOTAL VALUE $197.00

Above values given by Complainant.

STATUS

Open, pending investigation.

Signed:

Mel KENDZIORSKI

COMMENT:

Mel's report deals with a common police problem: larceny from an auto. The increased number of vehicles equipped with easily removable CB radios and tapedecks has increased the opportunities for the alert thief. It has also increased the number of headaches for the police. But Mel has handled the report efficiently. In this instance, his location upon receiving the run adds little, for the theft could have occurred eight hours before police were notified. However, it is still a good practice and requires little time, especially as the patterning becomes more automatic.

His Investigation and Reconstruction sections are clear and compact. He notes each step in the investigative sequence so that the reader always knows what was done and why. He has little repetition. Since he has clearly indicated in the Investigation section which officers did the photographing and lifting of prints, he omits this information from the Evidence section.

APPLICATIONS

Exercise 1:

Write a complete report on the incident described below. Supply any details needed. We have already grouped the information under the appropriate headings.

Initial Information

You are alone in a radio unit, working in a rural/resort area. At 4:00 p.m., July 3, 1976, a Saturday, you receive a radio run to investigate a reported breaking and entering at 1200 Deer Lake Road.

Investigation

You are met at the above address, a lakefront cottage, by the complainant, Mr. Tom Snow. Snow tells you someone broke into his cabin through the front door and then removed assorted items.

You investigate and find the glass broken from the window in the front door. The glass fragments are lying on the floor inside the cottage. You also discover several dresser drawers and their contents spread around. All other doors and windows to the cottage are secure.

Interview with complainant: Complainant tells you he arrived at approximately 3:00 p.m., reporting date. Upon approaching the cottage, he noticed the glass broken from the front door. He states that he then entered "to look around" and saw the dresser drawers scattered on the floor with their contents dumped out. Complainant also informs you that Mr. Robert Sharp, 1250 Deer Lake Road (across the road from complainant's cottage) keeps an eye on the place for him. Complainant then lists and describes the missing articles (in the Missing Property section).

Interview with Witness: You cross the street to 1250 Deer Lake Road and interview Mr. Robert Sharp. Sharp tells you he last checked the complainant's cottage at about 8:00 a.m., Thursday. He tells you the cottage "looked all right" then. Sharp also tells you that he saw fresh tire tracks in the sandy driveway about 3:00 p.m., Friday, but merely thought the owner had returned for the weekend.

Reconstruction

Use the above information to complete this section.

Missing Property

The complainant reports several small articles missing from the cabin. Make your own list, keeping the total value at less than $50.

Status

For comparison purposes, we have included below Tom Laracey's report on the same incident.

INITIAL INFORMATION

At 1600 hrs., Saturday, July 3, 1976, Officer LARACEY (62-626) received a radio run: breaking and entering report, 1200 Deer Lake Road.

INVESTIGATION

Upon arrival (1615 hrs.) Officer LARACEY was met by the Complainant, Mr. Tom SNOW. Complainant stated someone had broken in the front door of his cabin and removed several articles.

Officer LARACEY then conducted a physical investigation of the premises. The search revealed a broken window in the front door with the glass on the floor in the cabin. Officer LARACEY also observed several dresser drawers dumped out onto the floor.

Interview with the Complainant: The Complainant stated that he arrived at 1300 hrs., and upon approaching the cabin, noticed the glass broken out of the door. The Complainant then entered the cabin and observed several drawers and their articles on the floor. The Complainant also stated that Robert SHARP, who lives across the road, watches the cabin for him.

Interview with Witness: Witness stated that he had checked the cabin at 0800 hrs., Thursday, July 1, 1976, and everything was in order. Witness then stated that he observed fresh tire tracks in the driveway at 1500 hrs., Friday, July 2, 1976, but thought the owner had arrived for the weekend.

RECONSTRUCTION

Based on the above, officer believes that between 0800 hrs., Thursday, July 1, 1976, and 1300 hrs., Saturday, July 3, 1976, Suspect(s) broke into the Complainant's cabin by breaking out a 12 by 24 inch window in the front door and reaching in and unlocking the door. It appears that Suspect(s) ransacked the cabin and then left through the front door with assorted items.

STOLEN PROPERTY

Complainant reported the following items missing:

One (1) spotlight: chrome, hand-held, plugs into cigarette lighter $10.00

Six (6) boxes of cartridges: "Super X," .22 caliber long rifle shells @ $2 each.   12.00

One (1) compass: pocket type, flat black, sighting slot, locking directional device.   6.00

One (1) BB gun: "Daisy," lever action, brown plastic stock,
    very old.   8.00
                            Total Value $36.00

No serial numbers are available.

All values are those assigned by Complainant.

STATUS

Open.

                                                Signed:

                                        Tom LARACEY

COMMENT:

Tom has written a good report. In theory, officers should photograph the suspect point of entry, the interior of the cottage, and visible tire impressions. They should also attempt to lift prints. In practice, however, such actions are often impossible. First, many patrol units simply lack the necessary equipment. Second, while the break-in is serious to the complainant, it is routine to police in a resort area. Unless the incident is connected with others, follow-up investigations by detectives are highly unlikely.

Usually departmental policy will dictate the procedure. In the absence of such policy, officers must exercise their own judgment, taking into consideration all factors discussed in this chapter.

Exercise 2

In this and each of the following exercises, use the given information as the basis for a complete report. Supply any details needed.

You are working alone in a residential area. At 9:00 a.m., Monday, August 9, 1976, you receive a radio run to investigate a larceny at 1688 Orange Street.

You are met by the complainant, Mr. Buck Brummel, who tells you three bicycles were stolen from his front porch during the weekend. You check the unenclosed, roofed porch but find nothing.

Complainant states that the family had gone away for the weekend, leaving at approximately 6:00 p.m., Friday, August 6. The bicycles were on the porch when they left. When they returned at 9:00 p.m., Sunday, August 8, the bicycles were gone. All three bicycles are 26-inch Schwinn girls 10-speed bicycles. Two are blue and the other green. All are licensed with the police department, although complainant does not know the tag numbers nor the stamped identification numbers.

You talk to various neighbors who were home over the weekend. One reports seeing a yellow pickup truck with a green top over the box parked in front of the complainant's house around 10:00 p.m., Saturday. He saw no one in the truck and assumed it belonged to a guest/visitor in the neighborhood.

You return to the station and get the tag numbers and stamped identification numbers.

NOTE: This is a routine Larceny Report which involves little active investigation. Nearly all information is obtained from the complainant. Therefore, as the reader has little to put together, the Reconstruction section is optional.

Exercise 3

You are working alone in a radio unit on Saturday, June 12, 1976. At 4:00 p.m. you receive a radio run to investigate a B&E at the Lovelace Building. When you arrive, you are met in the lobby by the complainant, Ms Louise Mason. She informs you that someone had broken into her second-floor office and stolen some petty cash.

You investigate and find pry marks on the door and jamb. A search of the office reveals nothing. You then check the other offices—all unoccupied—in the second floor of the two-story building and find them locked.

The complainant states she had left the building at 2:45 p.m. to do some errands. Upon her return, as she took out her office key, she saw the marks on the door. She then entered and discovered that $10 to $15 in small bills and change was missing from a petty cash box which was on a table against the far wall. The complainant also tells you that upon her return, she had met a man walking down the outside steps away from the building. She also gives you a sketchy description of the man.

You interview two persons working in the only occupied first-floor office. They saw nothing.

Exercise 4

You are alone in a radio car working in a small city. Your unit is the only one on the road. At 4:30 p.m., Saturday, December 18, 1976, you are dispatched to Dante's Department Store to investigate a reported shoplifting.

You arrive at the store and are met at the curb by the store security guard, Earl Pembroke. Pembroke tells you that he saw the suspect pick up a packaged sweater. The suspect then slipped the sweater under her jacket and walked past the cashier before the guard could catch her. Pembroke stated he ran outside after the suspect but lost her in the crowd. Pembroke then returned to the store to call the police.

You get descriptions of the suspect and the stolen sweater. You then check the area for several minutes but come up empty.

NOTE: A Reconstruction section is optional in this incident.

Exercise 5

You are in a two-officer unit. At 2:30 p.m., Thursday, July 15, 1976, you are dispatched to 1575 Raisin Street to investigate a reported B&E.

Upon arrival you are met by the complainant, Miss Michele Nagelkick, 419 Elm Street. She tells you her parents' home has been broken into and directs you to a bedroom window on the west side of the house. You see pry marks on the outer window casing apparently made when the suspect(s) pried the screen from the window. The metal-framed screen, also with marks visible on the edges, is lying on the ground beneath the window. You find no other physical evidence outside the house. Inside the house, you find a bedroom closet door open. The closet is empty. There are pry marks on the door casing, and the door's edge is splintered in the area of the lock. Since you have neither a camera nor a measuring tape in the patrol car, you are not able to photograph or measure the pry marks.

You interview the complainant, who tells you that her parents are away on vacation. She also tells you that the window (suspected point of entry) was always left partially open for ventilation. She says that she checks the house every day as she has to feed the animals left inside. She discovered the break-in when she checked the house at 1:00 p.m., this date. She had last checked the house around 9:00 p.m., the previous evening, July 14, 1976. The complainant cannot tell what, if anything, is missing. She also informs you that the closet doors are usually kept locked.

You then interview the neighbor at the house adjoining the west edge of the victim's property at 1565 Raisin Street. The resident tells you that he did not hear or see anything.

You ask the complainant to call her parents to determine what could be missing. You also tell her that she will be contacted later by detectives and that she is not to disturb anything in the house.

Exercise 6

You are alone in a radio car. At 10:00 p.m., Friday, May 14, 1976, you are dispatched to Surrey's Supermarket to investigate a reported quick-change. You are met by the owner, Susannah Surrey, who tells you a quick-change artist had cheated one of her cashiers. Miss Surrey states the crime was not discovered until the cashiers checked out at 9:30 p.m. She then takes you to the victimized cashier, Edmund Walton.

Walton tells you that he is ten dollars short in his cash balance. He says that he suspects he was fooled by a customer at approximately 4:15 p.m. when he had been extremely busy. Walton gives the following account of the exchange: A man purchased a six-pack of beer costing two dollars. The suspect paid Walton with a twenty-dollar bill and received a ten, a five, and three ones in change. The man then added two more ones to the five and the three ones and asked for a ten-dollar bill in exchange. Walton took a ten from the register to make the exchange. Withdrawing the five and the ones, the suspect quickly handed Walton a ten and asked for his twenty-dollar bill back. Walton gave him the twenty.

Walton states he thought "there was something wrong"; but with the two tens in his hands, he felt he must owe the man a twenty. Walton adds that there was a long line of customers at the counter and the man had kept up a steady stream of distracting patter while making the exchange. Walton is unable to recall what the man was talking about but remembers the suspect had a "Southern accent." He then provides a sketchy description of the suspect.

Exercise 7

You are working with another officer in a radio car. At 4:30 p.m., September 27, 1976, a Monday, you are dispatched to 81 Hadrian Street, Apartment B-103, to investigate a breaking and entering.

Upon arrival you are met in the lobby of the large, multistory apartment building by the complainant, Mr. Andrew Oakes. He tells you he is a student at the local university and while he was gone over the weekend, someone entered his apartment and stole a number of items.

You go to the apartment, a second-story studio apartment with access only through the hallway door, and investigate. You find pry marks clearly visible on the door and the jamb. Inside the apartment you discover the latch retainer on the floor, where it had apparently fallen when the door was forced open. You discover clean areas on the carpeting, indicating spots where furniture had stood. You measure and photograph the pry marks on the door and jamb. You unsuccessfully attempt to lift prints from the door and various other areas.

The complainant tells you he left for a weekend at home at about 3:30 p.m., Friday, September 24. He returned to the city at 10:00 a.m., this date, but went directly to class; consequently, he did not discover the break-in until 3:00 p.m., this date. The complainant states he saw the marks on the door jamb as he was about to insert his key in the lock. He then opened the door, looked in, saw his television set and other articles missing, and then went to the manager's office to call the police. The complainant also tells you that several times during the past week he had received phone calls from parties refusing to identify themselves. The complainant said the caller would either pretend to have a wrong number or hang up. The complainant examines his apartment and then itemizes and describes the missing property.

You then check with the available residents of neighboring apartments. One tells you he saw two men, both white, in their mid-twenties, wearing blue coveralls with "Marcus's Moving" lettered in white on the back, carrying a console television set down the hallway about 2:30 Saturday afternoon. He tells you that he didn't pay much attention since "someone is always moving in or out." The other residents saw nothing or were away themselves over the weekend. All residents interviewed, however, said they also had received several anonymous phone calls from people who would immediately hang up.

You go to the manager's office and find out that no one was scheduled to move in or out during the past weekend. But the manager adds, "They don't always tell me when they're moving out." However, he saw nothing suspicious.

Chapter 6
Incidents against Persons and Miscellaneous Field Reports

INCIDENTS AGAINST PERSONS:
BOX INFORMATION

Offenses against persons are an ever-increasing problem to line officers. As a result, more and more reporting time must be devoted to these cases. Dealing with victims who have often suffered severe injury or nervous strain places even greater emphasis on the need for accurate and comprehensive reports. A bungled Burglary Report may make the departmental brass somewhat annoyed at the officer; it may make the victim fume at police incompetence; and it may draw criticism from insurance representatives. But since only property is involved, the consequences are rarely harsh. When people are involved, the consequences can be.

In reports involving incidents against persons, well-planned reporting forms are helpful. Although so far we have focused on the narrative part of the report—the area that normally causes the most difficulty—we do not mean to belittle the value of these forms. We recognize that they can provide useful guidelines for reporting officers as long as the officers recognize that such "box" items are not the answer to all their reporting problems. These items provide a place to insert essential information, much the same as the supplementary headings do. In fact, where there are no boxes provided for such data as the victim's name, the complainant's address, etc., officers are advised to insert this information under an appropriately titled supplementary heading.

What kind of box information will an officer find in a police report? It varies with departments. Some have a single report form for *all* offenses; these reports usually contain only brief box formats and rely nearly entirely on the narrative. Other departments have developed extensive reporting forms for separate offenses. These forms usually have many "check-off" spaces. Other departments strike a middle ground; they allow the officers space for information always required but do not try to anticipate and to provide for every possible circumstance. Generally, the box guidelines available will consist of the following:

Information about the Victim or Complainant: Victim's Name and Date of Birth. Write the victim's last name first, followed by the first name and then the middle name or initial. Many departments require reporting officers to use capital letters for the entire last name. Some forms allow space for more than one victim. If you have several victims and the space is not sufficient, insert the needed names at the head of the narrative space. Use an appropriate label, for example, "Victims (cont.)."

If the victim is a business, write the full name of the business in the space provided. It may appear peculiar to have a "business" as the victim in an incident against persons complaint. However, in some instances, this may be the case. For example, a bank messenger may be held up. The victim is the bank. In fact, many jurisdictions would regard the crime as an incident against property, arguing that the cash or bonds are the object of the holdup. But other jurisdictions would consider it an incident against person since there is a threat to personal safety. You will, of course, follow your departmental policies. As far as the narrative is concerned, the issue is of little importance: the format we have presented throughout the book will also serve, with some slight changes, for incidents against persons.

Victim's Address. Simply insert the victim's residential address. If no provision has been made for the victim's business address, place this information, if applicable, in the Additional Information section.

Victim's Telephone Number. Insert the victim's phone number. Whenever available, add the victim's *business* phone number also. Indicate at which number the victim may be reached during the day. Doing so will make any follow-up investigation easier.

Victim's Occupation. Write in the victim's occupation. If you have not already put down the victim's place of employment (business address), do so. This may appear unnecessary; however, a victim's occupation can often provide important leads to an investigator. Often an incident against a person stems directly from some aspect of the victim's occupation, for example, assaults may stem from professional jealousy; robberies may result from the victim's displaying large sums of money while at work; rapes may occur because the attacker is near the victim on the job. In addition, the victim's coworkers may provide useful leads.

Victim's Condition. Here you will describe the victim's condition at the time the crime occurred, i.e., under the influence of alcohol, drugs, etc. Few reporting forms provide enough space for this important information. If this is the case, we recommend that officers include a supplementary section for this information. We will discuss this information in more detail later.

> Victim was under physician's care for hypertension. Victim had taken two capsules (5 milligrams each) of Valium approximately twenty minutes before the incident. He spoke slowly and slurred some words.

Nature of Incident.   Identify the actual crime by statute name: Murder, Assault with a Deadly Weapon, Rape, etc.

Time, Day, and Date of Occurrence.   Enter the exact time, day, and date the crime occurred. If the exact time is unknown, indicate the range. Some departmental reports provide for this latter possibility. Others lack the space necessary for indicating a range in time. We suggest, therefore, that you get in the habit of including this information in the Reconstruction section of your narrative.

Time and Date Reported to Police.   Enter the *exact* time the crime was reported to the department. Departments vary on this point. Some departments give the responding officers this information upon dispatch. Some will require the officers to check the station log. And others will simply have officers record the time they received the run as the time reported. As usual, you will follow departmental policy. In any event, we stress once more the necessity of your recording in the Initial Information section the *exact* time you were made aware of the incident. This avoids any of the problems that can occur if the narrative begins with the traditional "At the above time and date. . . . "

Location of Occurrence.   Enter the exact location at which the incident occurred. If you cannot find a specific address, use intersecting roadways, block numbers, or, if necessary, measurements from some fixed point.

> *EXAMPLES:*
> Alley at the rear of 1313 Lochinvar Boulevard
> Northeast corner of York and Lancaster
> On Rose Road, approximately 1¹/₂ miles south of the county line

Type of Premises.   Describe the type of premises at which the crime occurred. Often this can be a double description: for example, *alley, apartment complex; street, small business/residential;* or *vehicle, county roadway*.

Witnesses' Names, Addresses, Phone Numbers.   Write in the names, addresses, and phone numbers of all witnesses. Use the same system you used for the victim: give last name first in capital letters, indicate where the witness can be reached during the day, etc. If no space has been provided for this information, place it in the Additional

Information section and briefly summarize what each witness can testify to. Personal data such as date of birth or age should also be included when available:

W-1 HEOROT, Harvey W. 5/26/36, 409 Hrothgar Street
  Residence Phone: 999-9999
  Business Phone: 999-0001 (day)

W-2 HEARDRED, Harold K. 6/26/46, 411 Hygd Street
  Residence Phone: 000-9999
  Business Phone: 000-1111 (day)

Suspects. List the names of any known suspects, last name first. Include all available personal data, addresses, phone numbers, and aliases or nicknames. If not enough space is provided, insert a Suspects section in the narrative space *before* you begin the narrative. Some reports have a special section for an alias or nickname; others do not. If no space has been provided, add the letters A/K/A (also/known/as) followed by the alias or nickname.

If there is no place to put the suspect's description, repeat the suspect's name and write the description in a supplementary section. Also note the *source* of your description, i.e., the victim, witnesses, complainant, etc. This can be troublesome. Often you will have several different descriptions of the same suspect; yet there may only be enough space for one description. Your fellow officers would be forgiven for doubting your credibility if you were to broadcast: "Suspect is a white male or black male, either 6 feet 2 inches or 5 feet 7 inches, slim or heavyset, wearing blue jeans or navy blue trousers, a white or gray shirt, etc." Therefore, you must use your judgment and give the single best available description.

Departmental policy will help, but policies vary. Some departments will insist that the reporting officer record the description given by the person considered the most reliable by the officer. Other departments suggest that the officer try for a composite picture, i.e., that the officer include descriptive details upon which there is agreement. For example, the victim in an assault case may state the assailant had blond hair. Yet several witnesses describe the suspect as having brown hair, graying at the temples. If the witnesses were in a position to see this, the officer will record their description instead of the victim's.

Still other departments will require a composite description based on the officer's assessment of a witness's competence in a specific area. The officer will, for instance, record the suspect's clothing description as given by the best-dressed witness on the theory that this witness would be clothes-conscious and more likely to notice details of apparel. Overweight witnesses usually make the most accurate guesses about weight, very tall or short people about height, and so on.

You will follow departmental policy. If the last two methods described above apply to your department, you will probably receive training in making these decisions. Regardless of which policy you use to get your description, you should also include all other descriptions and their sources in the Additional Information section.

Suspect: EDWARDS, Cotton M., A/K/A "Pete PURITAN,"
W/M/26, DOB 6/26/50, 1117 Jonathan Avenue.

Suspect: Unknown, W/M/25–30, 6 feet 3 inches, 180 pounds, brown hair, slim build, wearing gray pants, white short-sleeved shirt, black vest sweater with red piping around neck.

Identifying Characteristics of Suspect. List any noticeable characteristics of the suspect: scars, voice, vocabulary, movements, etc. You would note, for example, if the suspect limped, if he had an accent, if she continually ran her hand through her hair, etc. This is not the same as the MO (modus operandi); the MO indicates *how* the crime was committed; identifying characteristics (or trademarks) include any actions by the criminal that can distinguish him or her from others.

Weapon or Force Used. Describe as accurately as possible the weapon or force used to commit the crime, e.g., "blue-steel revolver, long-barreled, probably .38 caliber." Many report forms will have no space for this information. If this is the case, include the description of the weapon or force under a supplementary heading. Do *not* bury it in the middle of a narrative passage.

Vehicle Driven. Describe the suspect's vehicle, if any, as accurately as possible. Include the year, make, model, body style, color(s), license number, and any other information helpful for identification.

1973 Chevrolet Vega station wagon, red/white, Michigan 1973 registration AAA 001. Damage to left front. Ferris State College student sticker in rear window, lower right corner.

The above items, along with other information such as complaint numbers, LEIN or Teletype numbers, etc., make up the box information most often found on reporting forms. Some departmental forms will include all of these and more (Apparent Motive, Notification, and so on); others will omit many. But all the information is pertinent. You must include it in the spaces provided or insert it into an appropriately titled supplementary section.

HOMICIDE: INITIAL INFORMATION SECTION

Among the most serious offenses handled by officers is the homicide complaint. Officers should begin the report routinely with the Initial Information section as in all other incidents. The guidelines for this section have already been presented (Chapter 3); therefore, we will only give an example here:

INITIAL INFORMATION

At 1120 hrs., Friday, September 10, 1976, Officers LEAR and REGAN (Sct. 9-4), northbound on First at Avenue A, received a radio run: 111 Burr, shooting, ambulance on the way.

Because of the serious nature of this complaint, officers must be extremely careful in recording the information discussed in this section. The segments dealing with time, location of officers, and reported nature of the incident are especially important, for often a seemingly routine run can turn out to be a homicide. Consequently, officers failing to note this information, or noting it inaccurately, may face some rather severe questioning by command officers, investigators, and attorneys.

HOMICIDE: INVESTIGATION SECTION

In the Investigation section the reporting officer faces a very difficult task. It is here that the "story" of the incident must be told. Several basic guidelines have already been studied: selecting and organizing material; placing details not essential for under-standing the overall incident in appropriate supplementary sections; maintaining objectivity; and using the basic principles of paragraphing. An officer who uses these guidelines and lets the report follow the *natural order* of events will have few difficulties in writing this section even in such a serious incident.

Usually the responding line officers will just write up the *preliminary investigation*, for, in most departments, follow-up investigation will be conducted by detectives and specially trained technicians. This does not mean that the line officers' investigation is not important; frequently, the success or failure of the entire investigation depends on how well the responding officers handled the preliminary investigation and on how well they reported their activities.

The investigative actions performed by line officers will vary somewhat depending on the particular incident. But their responsibilities will generally include the following activities in roughly the order presented:

Prompt response to the incident. This is essential in all incidents against persons—it may well prevent an assault from becoming a homicide. Prompt response is also important in preventing physical evidence from being destroyed by witnesses, onlookers, or natural forces such as wind, rain, or snow. Often only the quick action of responding officers can keep evidence from becoming lost forever; footprints or other impressions in snow or mud, for example, can be either protected or measured, recorded, and photographed before they disappear.

Promptness also keeps witnesses from slipping away or discussing the incident. As witnesses become increasingly aware of their involvement, they may simply fade from the scene before the officers arrive and identify them. In addition, elapsed time lets the witnesses "compare" accounts; as a result, some distortion may creep into subsequent interviews as one witness reflects the influence of another or as witnesses friendly to a possible suspect construct an alibi for him.

Notation of anything relevant while en route to the scene. We have already discussed this in Chapter 3. Officers should take note of anything observed that may be pertinent, e.g., the license number of a vehicle coming from the direction of the scene.

Approach to the actual scene. Officers must use caution in their approach for two reasons: personal safety and preservation of evidence. Careless officers have, for instance, trampled over a suspect's footprints, making them useless. Tire marks have been obliterated by a carelessly positioned patrol unit. Fingerprints have become smudged, obliterated, or become unreadable. Important items of evidence—weapons, spent bullets, etc.—have been moved from their original position and then later replaced elsewhere, thus either making them worthless in court or confusing follow-up investigators in their efforts to reconstruct the crime.*

Note: This is *standard police procedure:* officers are trained to approach with caution and to avoid damaging the evidence; therefore, officers need *not* detail each step of their approach in the report. Instead, they should note the *general* path taken and specify any evidence *inadvertently* contaminated despite their care.

On occasion, circumstances force officers to disregard the preservation of external evidence. If, for example, officers approaching the scene can hear the victim screaming or see the victim in immediate danger, it would be absurd for

*The skeptic should read *Helter-Skelter* and note the problems in that preliminary investigation.

them to be concerned with preserving evidence at the cost of further injury or death to the victim. After all, the victim's welfare is of greatest importance.

Rapid but thorough assessment of the situation. If officers are admitted by a witness or reporting party, they should immediately obtain a brief account of the incident before proceeding. They should also carefully survey the immediate scene of the crime before going further. Too often, officers simply burst into a room; consequently, they cannot reconstruct the situation accurately. They are unable to recall the seemingly insignificant details that later become important, e.g., the original position of an item of evidence that was later moved or the odor of cigar smoke when the victim was a nonsmoker.

Care of the victim. In homicide cases, of course, the officer will check for vital signs to determine whether death has occurred. Officers must take care not to disturb the position of the victim's body until all necessary photographs, sketches, and measurements have been completed. Officers should also check for signs of post-mortem lividity or other signs useful in determining the time of death.

Identification and interviewing of witnesses. This should be a preliminary interview designed to obtain quickly any information available for broadcast. Witnesses should also be separated from one another and removed from the immediate scene to prevent discussion and avoid further contamination of the scene.

Broadcast of essential information. Descriptions of suspects or suspect vehicles should be broadcast to other units as soon as possible.

Request for appropriate assistance. In some departments the detectives may be dispatched at the same time as the responding line officers. In other departments, follow-up investigators are not sent until the line officers have confirmed the incident and requested assistance.

Preservation of the scene and evidence. Officers must carefully preserve the scene and protect any evidence. This care must extend beyond the immediate scene to include fringe areas; e.g., other rooms in a house; the hallways of apartment buildings; the lawns, drives, or walks that may have been used by the suspect.

Continuing interviews of witnesses. After securing the scene, officers may continue interviewing witnesses. This quick follow-up interview can be useful. Often witnesses are talkative at first but then become less and less willing to talk as they become aware of their prospective involvement.

Assistance to follow-up investigators. This assistance will vary from department to department. It can even vary from incident to incident within a department, depending on the personnel available. In large departments, the line officers' responsibilities frequently stop after they turn the crime scene over to the detectives and technicians.

In addition, the line officers may be required to perform various other duties: conduct an immediate search of the area, assist detectives in further searches, photograph the scene and items of evidence, or dust for fingerprints. If so, officers should note the precise method of search used (point-to-point, sector, strip, concentric) and the *exact* location of any evidence discovered. The evidence should not be collected, however, until it has been photographed, located precisely, and evaluated by follow-up investigators. While officers will follow departmental guidelines in taking photographs, we suggest that the responding officers take several photographs of the scene *from eye level at the point of entry.* This will help them establish the exact conditions they found when they arrived and will enable them to inform detectives if something seems wrong.

But all these actions will be of little value if the officers fail their final responsibility: reporting the incident accurately and completely. This responsibility can be met by following the prescribed guidelines and organizing the report according to the natural sequence of the investigation.

Officers should study the following sample Investigation section.

INVESTIGATION

Upon arrival at the scene (1127 hrs.), officers parked the unit in front of 113 Burr and approached, using the front walk. Officers identified themselves and were admitted by Miss Gertrude GAWAIN, the reporting party. Miss GAWAIN identified the Victim and stated that he was dead, lying on the kitchen floor. Officers noted that all drapes in the front of the house were drawn closed; there was no light in the entryway or the living room. A light was visible in the kitchen.

Officers entered the kitchen through the hall entryway. They saw the Victim lying on his face and stomach between the kitchen table and the rear (east) door. Large amounts of blood were on the floor, on the table, and on an overturned chair next to the Victim. A table setting was on the table in front of the overturned chair. Some portions of food remained on the plate; this food was also covered with blood. The overhead light was on, and the curtains were drawn closed.

The rear door was open a few inches. There were also two holes visible in the surface of the wooden table between the table setting and the far (west) edge of the table. A sketch of the scene with measurements is attached to this report.

Officer LEAR checked the Victim for vital signs but could detect none. Officer GARCIA, escorted Miss GAWAIN to the patrol unit and radioed for investigative assistance and the medical examiner (1132 hrs.) while Officer LEAR conducted a point-to-point search of the immediate crime scene.

LEAR found the rear (east) door unlocked. There were no signs of forced entry on the door or the windows. Under the table, LEAR found two spent bullets. There were also two holes in the table: one was $17^1/_2$ inches from the east edge and $31^1/_4$ inches from the south edge; the other was $18^1/_2$ inches from the east edge and 27 inches from the south edge. Each hole measured $^3/_8$ of an inch in diameter and was smooth on the table top with splinters projecting downward.

LEAR could find no visible evidence of theft: no appliances appeared to be missing; the Victim's wallet containing $47 was clearly visible on the kitchen counter to the left of the sink; and nothing appeared to have been disturbed by the Suspect(s). Checking the Victim, LEAR found three holes visible in the Victim's back; LEAR did not move the body to see if there were any signs of the bullets' exit. LEAR could detect no evidence of rigor mortis or post-mortem discoloration at this point.

LEAR then left the kitchen, using the same path that he used when he entered, and checked the sides and the rear of the residence. He found no signs of footprints or unusual impressions on the walk or the lawn. He also noted the rear screen door was unlatched and had no lock. LEAR then retraced his steps and entered to preserve the scene for investigators.

Interview with Reporting Party: While Officer LEAR conducted the physical search, Officer GARCIA interviewed Miss

GAWAIN. Miss GAWAIN gave the following account. She stated that she had been sitting alone in her living room (115 Burr Street: 35 feet from the southern wall of Victim's residence) when she heard what sounded like gunshots next door. She gave this time as approximately 11:05 a.m., "as the 'Galloping Gourmet' had just started." She stated that she first thought the sounds came from the Victim's television set, but when she went to her window, she could not hear any other sounds from the Victim's house. Miss GAWAIN said she then hesitated for a "few minutes" before trying to telephone the Victim. When she received no answer, she went to the Victim's rear door and knocked. She reported that when she got no response, she tried the door, which was closed, and found it unlocked. Miss GAWAIN stated that she then pushed the door open and saw the Victim lying on the floor. She then ran through the kitchen into the living room and used the phone there to call the police.

Miss GAWAIN stated that she saw no one near the Victim's house at any time. Nor could she remember exactly how many shots she had heard, declaring, "It sounded like three or four."

At 1145 hrs. Det. Sgt. Robert BAYER and Det. Willie WIGLAF arrived and took charge of the investigation.

Sgt. BAYER then asked officers LEAR and GARCIA to make a sector search. This yielded nothing beyond what LEAR had uncovered in his original search.

Officer LEAR then photographed the body and the crime scene in accordance with departmental regulations while officer GARCIA assisted in sketching and measuring the scene. LEAR positioned, photographed, and then collected the two spent bullets to be preserved as evidence. LEAR also took several photographs of the scene at eye level from the hallway entry into the kitchen.

At 1205 hrs. the coroner, Dr. Felix WOLF, arrived. After a preliminary examination, Dr. WOLF stated the Victim had apparently died of three gunshot wounds in the back. Dr. WOLF added that two bullets had apparently passed through the body and a third had lodged against the Victim's lower ribs.

At 1230 hrs. Officers LEAR and GARCIA began a house-to-house canvass of the area in an effort to uncover any witnesses. Canvass was completed at 1315 hrs. with negative results (Ref.: Additional Information).

At 1320 hrs. Sgt. BAYER cleared Officers LEAR and GARCIA for further assignment.

This section gives all the pertinent information found during the preliminary investigation. The events are described in the order in which they took place and the account gives the reader an overall, complete view of the incident. Only descriptive data that will appear elsewhere in the report have been omitted: for example, the precise location of the spent bullets. But some seemingly unnecessary details have been included: those details that re-create the scene as first observed by the responding officers. They may or may not prove significant. The drapes being pulled closed, for instance, may have nothing to do with the crime; yet the fact may give investigators some insight into the victim's character or background. Perhaps the shooting was not an indiscriminate killing; the closed drapes at midday may indicate mortal fear on the victim's part. This in turn suggests a motive hidden somewhere in the victim's background.

THE VICTIM'S CONDITION SECTION

Officers should include all available information about the victim's state *prior to* the incident. They should attempt, for example, to determine if the victim had been drinking heavily immediately before the incident; this could suggest a possible drunken altercation as the cause of the death. Knowledge that the victim was a drug user can help detectives in their subsequent investigation. If the victim had been under a physician's care for an ailment that required numerous prescriptions, this, too, should be noted. The suspect(s) may have noticed him having the prescriptions filled and decided a lone person presented an easier target than a crowded pharmacy.

Investigators, of course, will always check the victim's background; but this information in the line officer's report may greatly reduce the number of expensive investigative hours.

In homicide cases officers should also add an exact description of the victim's wounds that resulted in death. If this information is available from the coroner at the time of the report, officers should use the coroner's statement. If not, officers should record their own observations and the coroner's preliminary opinions.

In a continuation of the report begun above, this section could read:

VICTIM'S CONDITION

Miss GAWAIN said that the Victim had complained of "money problems" in the recent past and that he appeared "nervous and depressed."

Victim was dead upon officers' arrival. The coroner stated death probably resulted from three gunshot wounds inflicted by person(s) unknown.

The information that the Victim was nervous and depressed, coupled with the seemingly unimportant detail of the closed drapes at midday, strongly suggests premeditation and provides detectives with a possible line of investigation.

THE RECONSTRUCTION SECTION

In the Reconstruction section, the responding officers should attempt to re-create the actual incident. Officers must rely on facts and inferences in this section. The Reconstruction segment for the report begun above, for example, could read as follows:

RECONSTRUCTION

Based on the above, it appears that at approximately 1105 hrs., Friday, September 10, 1976, Suspect(s) opened the rear door of the Victim's residence and fired three bullets into his back. Victim was apparently seated at the table, eating, with his back to the door when he was struck. It further appears that two rounds passed through the Victim's body and then through the table top, indicating the shots were fired from behind and above the Victim. After the shooting, Suspect(s) fled the scene; direction and means of escape are unknown.

THE EVIDENCE SECTION

The line officers' responsibility for physical evidence depends on departmental policy. Generally, it will be limited since the follow-up investigators and technicians are usually responsible for collecting, recording, and handling evidence. In many departments, however, line officers are responsible for all the physical evidence that they discover. In the report above, for instance, the line officers would be responsible for the two spent bullets found under the kitchen table but *not* for the third bullet, which was still in the victim's body. This bullet would become the responsibility of the follow-up investigators. In other departments, of course, the follow-up investigators would control *all* physical evidence to avoid any accidental omission.

In writing this section officers should follow the guidelines already studied. Continuing the sample report, officers would note:

EVIDENCE

Officer LEAR placed the following items in separate, uncontaminated evidence envelopes, sealed the envelopes, wrote ERL across the seal, tagged the envelopes, and then turned them over to Det. Sgt. Robert BAYER at 1225 hrs. (receipt attached to this report):

One (1) pellet: Lead, misshapen, believed to be spent .38 caliber bullet, flecked with tiny red spots believed to be blood. Found by Officer LEAR under the kitchen table 14 feet 3 inches from the rear (east) door and 11 feet 4 inches from the north kitchen wall. Tagged EL-101.

One (1) pellet: Lead, same description as above. Found by Officer LEAR 14 feet 7 inches from the rear door and 11 feet 8 inches from the north wall.

Twenty-four (24) photographs of the scene, taken by Officer LEAR, are individually identified according to departmental procedure and attached to this report.

THE NOTIFICATIONS MADE SECTION

In the Notifications Made section, officers should follow the directions already studied. In the above report, the officers would record their request for assistance and the coroner:

NOTIFICATIONS MADE

By Officer GARCIA:

Dispatch. Requested detectives, crime laboratory technicians, and the coroner. 1132 hrs.

THE ADDITIONAL INFORMATION SECTION

Officers should use the Additional Information section for all miscellaneous items not already recorded. In the above report, for instance, officers should record in the Additional Information segment the names of all persons interviewed in the canvass for possible witnesses. Since no significant results were obtained from the interviews, it would be pointless to include all the names and addresses in the narrative. Yet this information is necessary, for a prospective witness may have unknowingly seen or heard something important but have left home before the officers canvassed the area. Follow-up investigators can then use the "no-response" addresses as a starting point in their continuing investigation.

Therefore, in the example report, the Additional Information section could appear:

ADDITIONAL INFORMATION

Officer LEAR interviewed the following with negative results:

Haeth E. CYNN, 114 Burr Street

Gary I. BAIDI, 119 Burr Street

Wilma WEALTHEOW, 125 Burr Street

Sidney BRUCE, 149 Burr Street

Jack L. PINE, 150 Hamilton Street

Charlotte COHEN, 144 Hamilton Street

Annette C. ADAMS, 110 Hamilton Street

Officer LEAR received no response at the following addresses:

133 Burr Street

136 Hamilton Street

130 Hamilton Street

120 Hamilton Street

Officer GARCIA interviewed the following with negative results:

Geoffrey C. DONNE, 105 Burr Street

Eliot T. JOHNSON, 101 Burr Street

Emily D. BIERCE, 100 Hamilton Street

Shirley J. RUSSELL, 104 Hamilton Street

Officer GARCIA received no response at the following addresses:

109 Burr Street

108 Hamilton Street

OTHER HEADINGS

Depending on the specific case, officers may need other supplementary headings. If officers arrive in time to exchange gunfire with a suspect who later escapes, the report will need a Shots Fired section. If injuries were sustained by officers or onlookers, these would be recorded in a Persons Injured section. Most departments in such instances will require separate reports on these incidents; therefore, officers will also need to include cross-references to these reports. Again we urge officers to make up any supplemental headings that may be helpful. And again we emphasize that judgment must be used: too many headings distract and confuse.

INCIDENTS AGAINST PERSONS: ASSAULTS

Officers investigating assault cases have one distinct advantage over officers investigating a homicide: the victim is alive and can frequently give valuable information—descriptions, names, etc.—that will lead to the apprehension of the suspect(s). The preliminary investigation and the report will normally reflect this advantage. Otherwise, both the investigation and the report will correspond closely to the pattern discussed above. There will, of course, be the added responsibility of rendering aid to the victim if any is required. This may involve first aid and transportation and, on occasion, the request for professional medical assistance at the scene.

Officers responding to an assault will usually follow these procedures:

Arrive promptly
Assess the situation
Treat the victim
Determine that an assault has, in fact, been committed
Identify and interview the victim
Search the scene
Identify and interview witnesses
Broadcast information
Conduct a subsequent investigation: follow up interviews; canvass the area for possible leads or witnesses; track down leads suggested by the interviews and the physical evidence.

The order, of course, may vary somewhat depending on the particular incident. In some cases, for example, the victim will require no immediate attention and will be able to give officers a ready and accurate description of the assailant. If too much time has not passed and the victim's story is credible, the officers may broadcast information before continuing the investigation.

The report will then begin as always with the Initial Information section. Next officers will write the Investigation section. In this unit, the responding officers should:

Describe their approach and arrival.

Describe the situation as it appeared to them.

Note treatment of the victim. (The details of the treatment and the exact description of the victim's injuries should be put in the Persons Injured section.)

Record the victim's initial statement. [The first interview should be kept short to avoid unduly taxing the victim and to get a quick overview of the incident along with any names or description of the assailant(s).]

Note the broadcasting of any information. (Again, the details need not be included.) The officer should simply note that a description of the assailant or the vehicle was broadcast. The details of the description will appear either in the block spaces provided for the suspect's description or in a unit entitled Suspect's Description.

Record the statements of witnesses, if any.

Note the results of a physical search of the scene.

Indicate further actions taken and the results of these actions.

Officers should use the supplementary headings that are appropriate to their situation. These headings have already been discussed; however, in assault cases, officers should take care not to confuse the heading Victim's Condition with Persons Injured. The Victim's Condition segment refers to the victim's state *before* the incident; in the Persons Injured section the officer records those injuries apparently sustained *during* the incident or resulting *from* the incident. Officers who find this distinction confusing can simply attach an Extent of Injuries subheading to the Victim's Condition.

The following student report illustrates these principles.

INITIAL INFORMATION

At 0130 hrs., Thursday, July 1, 1976, Officers DOWLING and DOGG (Car 74), northbound on U.S. 23 at Pogi Crossing, received a radio run: Happy Acres Bar, U.S. 23, cutting.

INVESTIGATION

Upon approaching the scene (0140 hrs.), officers could observe no signs of a disturbance. Officers entered the bar and were met by Miss Sue PAPER, the reporting party. Miss PAPER said that a fight had occurred in the tavern parking lot but that the participants had left prior to the officers' arrival. She stated the injured Victims had been transported to the hospital and the assailants had fled. She identified the assailants as a Peter GLENN and Charles LEER, frequent patrons at the bar. She added that the assailants had come up and insulted the Victims in the bar before the fight broke out.

Officers then checked the parking lot where the alleged fight had taken place. They found no blood nor any weapons in the area.

Officers then went to the Alpenhut General Hospital to interview the Victims, arriving at 0205 hrs.

Interview with Victim No. 1: At 0210 hrs. Officer DOWLING interviewed Sloan MELLY (Victim No. 1) in the hospital lounge. MELLY stated that he and a friend, Kurtis JON, were sitting at the bar when a group of "four or five" men began to harass them and asked them to "step outside and fight."

MELLY stated he and his friend went but did "not provoke the fight."

MELLY stated that when they got outside, Kurtis JON (Victim No. 2) removed his belt and was wrapping it around his hand when one of the men attacked and cut JON with a jackknife. MELLY said he then struck the assailant several times and knocked the knife from the assailant's hand before he in turn was attacked by the others. A fight began in which MELLY was also injured.

MELLY stated the assailants then got into a black van and drove away north on U.S. 23. MELLY said he was able to rip off the van's rear license plate as it left the lot. The plate was turned over to Officer DOWLING. MELLY said that he did not know the assailants but that he could recognize them.

Interview with Victim No. 2: At 0210 hrs. Officer DOGG interviewed Victim No. 2, Kurtis JON, in the cafeteria of the Alpenhut Hospital. JON stated that he and a friend (MELLY) were at the bar when challenged by the assailants to "step outside and fight." JON said he and his friend attempted to avoid a fight but finally walked out into the lot. He said he was attacked as he was "tightening his belt" and suffered cuts on his arm. He stated that a general fight broke out. Shortly afterward, the assailants escaped north on U.S. 23 in an old black van. He added that MELLY had the rear license plate of the van. JON declared he had never seen the assailants before but that he could recognize them if he saw them again.

Interview with Witness No. 1: After interviewing MELLY, Officer DOWLING interviewed Witness No. 1, Diane BROWN, in the hospital lounge. Miss BROWN, an employee at the bar, had transported the Victims to the hospital. Miss BROWN stated that she had seen the two groups of men walk outside and then had seen one assailant strike JON. She stated that she then yelled at the man to drop the knife, which he did. She said the men then drove away in a black van, direction unknown. Miss BROWN added that she went outside and used JON's belt as a tourniquet for his arm, which was bleeding severely. She then took both Victims to the hospital in her automobile.

Miss BROWN declared she could not identify the assailants by name although she had seen them in the bar on other occasions.

Officer DOWLING then checked the telephone directory for the addresses of Peter GLENN and Charles LEER. He found that both men lived at 133 Selt Street, Pogi.

At 0300 hrs. officers arrived at Suspects' address just as Suspects were stepping from their auto, a sports car. Both Suspects were dressed in clean clothes and presented an orderly appearance. Neither showed any signs of having been in a fight.

When questioned, both men denied any knowledge of a fight at the Happy Acres Bar. Both admitted being there and leaving shortly before closing. Both further stated that after leaving the bar they had stopped at the Northern Restaurant for coffee and had then driven straight home.

Officer DOWLING ran a LEIN check on the plate allegedly taken from the assailants' vehicle (Ref.: <u>Evidence</u>). Both men disclaimed any knowledge or relationship with the reported owner, a William JOSEPH, 1999 Nineteenth Street, Practical, Michigan.

Officers could not continue the investigation immediately as the van's owner lived too far from their district.

RECONSTRUCTION

Based on the above it appears that at approximately 0130 hrs., this date, the Victims were attacked when they responded to an invitation to step outside and fight. One Victim was stabbed and the other beaten by unknown Suspects who drove off in a black van.

PERSONS INJURED

JON, Kurtis (Victim No. 2), received a puncture wound in his outer left forearm. He also suffered several scrapes and bruises on his body.

Victim transported to Alpenhut Hospital by Miss BROWN. Arrival 0150 hrs. (approximately). Puncture wound bandaged and abrasions cleaned and sterilized by Dr. I. FRENCH. Released at 0205 hrs.

MELLY, Sloan (Victim No. 1), suffered from minor bruises. No treatment given at the hospital.

EVIDENCE

One (1) Michigan 1975 registration plate 1776 USA, registered to William JOSEPH, 1999 Nineteenth Street, Practical, Michigan, on a 1965 Ford Van, VIN 1111111, was tagged and secured in the evidence locker. Tag No. 1.

NOTIFICATIONS MADE

By Officer DOWLING:

Trooper Major MONROE, MSP Post No. 999, informed of incident and requested to check Mr. William JOSEPH. 0310 hrs.

STATUS

Open, pending further investigation.

James DOWLING

INCIDENTS AGAINST PERSONS: ARMED ROBBERY

Many jurisdictions consider armed robbery a crime against property. Officials base this description on the criminal's object: money or other valuables. However, since armed robbery presents an actual danger to the people involved, we have chosen to present a discussion of armed robbery here.

Moreover, the preliminary investigative procedures are similar. Officers responding to an armed robbery call, for example, must be careful in approaching the scene and upon their arrival. They must assess the situation before bursting in. Often, there are injured victims who need treatment. Victims and witnesses must be identified and interviewed. Important information must be broadcast to other units as soon as possible. As can readily be seen, the responding officers' duties are similar to their duties in assault cases. This is to be expected since *assault* is an element of armed robbery.

The reporting officers begin their robbery reports as they do all other reports, with the Initial Information section. In the Investigation section they will follow the same principles already studied. The Reconstruction section comes next, then any supplementary sections that are needed. As in an Incident against Property Report, a Stolen Property unit will be necessary, provided, of course, the bandit was successful.

Officers should study the student report below, which is typical.

INITIAL INFORMATION

At 16:45 hrs., Thursday, March 11, 1976, Officers DUFF and STEVENS (Sct. 9-7), northbound in the 1300 block of Kendrick, were hailed by an unidentified man who reported seeing two men carrying shotguns enter the Lycidas Lounge, 1340 Kendrick, a few minutes before.

INVESTIGATION

Officer DUFF immediately relayed the information to Dispatch. He then went on foot to the front of the lounge while Officer STEVENS drove to the alley in the rear.

When Officer STEVENS was in position at the rear, Officer DUFF entered through the front door. He found four men at the lounge bar, all talking loudly. Officer DUFF could also see another man, apparently the bartender, lying on the floor, behind the bar. The bartender appeared to be unconscious, and there was blood on his head. The cash register drawer was open.

The men at the bar told Officer DUFF that two holdup men, armed with shotguns, had slugged the bartender, taken the money from the cash register, and escaped through the rear exit. Officer DUFF called for Officer STEVENS to enter and render aid to the bartender; then DUFF radioed for an ambulance.

Officer DUFF then obtained a description of the bandits from the witnesses and at 1651 hrs. broadcast their description to all units.

At 1652 hrs. Scout 9-9 (Officers FRANK and GEORGE) arrived to assist.

At 1655 hrs. the ambulance arrived to transport the still unconscious bartender to the hospital.

Officer DUFF then told witnesses and other officers not to touch the cash register or the interior handle of the rear door. Officer DUFF used the bar phone to inform the owner of the Lycidas Lounge of the situation. The owner, Larry LYCIDAS, said he would come to the lounge immediately.

Interview with Witness No. 1: Officer DUFF interviewed Mr. Clifford SILVERWOOD (W-1). Mr. SILVERWOOD stated he had been standing at the bar when two men burst into the lounge through the front door, brandishing shotguns. He said that the Suspects motioned the patrons to the bar by waving their shotguns. Mr. SILVERWOOD stated that when the patrons obeyed, Suspect No. 1 motioned the bartender toward the cash register with the barrel of his shotgun. SILVERWOOD stated that when the bartender appeared to hesitate, Suspect No. 1 leaned over the bar and hit the bartender with the stock of the shotgun swung in a sweeping upward arc. He said it appeared that the lower edge of the stock struck the bartender above the left eye.

Mr. SILVERWOOD said that Suspect No. 2 then said something but that he was "too damned scared to remember." He reported that after striking the bartender, Suspect No. 1 then opened the register and removed the contents. He said both men then immediately ran through the back door without another word. Mr. SILVERWOOD described the Suspects and declared that he would be able to recognize them.

Interview with Witness No. 2: Officer STEVENS interviewed Mr. Branch MARLETTE (W-2). Mr. MARLETTE declared all he could remember was that "two big bastards came in waving cannons." He stated that he remembered Suspect No. 2's speaking but could not recall what was said. Mr. MARLETTE said he did not see the bartender being struck as he had focused his eyes on Suspect No. 2. Mr. MARLETTE could not, however, describe either Suspect. He also stated that he would not recognize them again.

Interview with Witness No. 3: Officer FRANK interviewed Mr. Dewitt BRANCH (W-3). Mr. BRANCH stated he had been seated at a table in the corner when two men openly carrying shotguns entered. He stated the two men pointed the guns at him and waved him to the bar with the gun barrels. Mr. BRANCH complied. He said that Suspect No. 1 placed his shotgun on the bar, holding it with two hands—the right hand on the stock and trigger and the left on the barrel—and then suddenly, for no apparent reason, clubbed the bartender. Mr. BRANCH said the Suspect struck the bartender by raising the stock with his right hand and swinging the gun in an upward arc. He then demonstrated the motion for Officer FRANK.

Mr. BRANCH also recalled that Suspect No. 2 spoke after the bartender had been hit, but could not remember what was said. He said that Suspect No. 1 then opened the register, removed the money, and stuffed it into his jacket pockets; both Suspects then fled through the rear door.

Mr. BRANCH gave descriptions corresponding to those given by Witness No. 1. He also said he could recognize the Suspects if he saw them again.

Interview with Witness No. 4: Officer DUFF interviewed Mr. John LARRY (W-4). Mr. LARRY gave substantially the same account as the other witnesses gave.

Mr. LARRY, however, stated that he remembered Suspect No. 2's exact words: "Goddamn it all; grab the bread and let's cut out." Mr. LARRY said the Suspect seemed to slur all the words together. He could detect no particular accent, however. Mr. LARRY also stated that he could recognize the Suspects.

Further investigation: Officer GEORGE attempted to lift fingerprints from the cash register and the rear door handle. She was unsuccessful.

Officer DUFF informed the witnesses that detectives would call them in later.

At 1745 hrs., the owner arrived. He stated that he could not determine the exact amount of money missing but estimated the loss at $200 to $300.

At 1755 hrs., the officers were cleared from the scene. Officers FRANK and GEORGE resumed normal activities while Officers DUFF and STEVENS drove to the hospital. At the hospital Dr. W. W. CHAN told officers that the bartender had suffered a severe concussion and had not yet regained consciousness.

RECONSTRUCTION

Based on the above, it appears that two Suspects, armed with shotguns, entered the Lycidas Lounge at approximately 1635 hrs., March 11, 1976. They struck the bartender and escaped with the contents of the cash register.

INJURED PERSON

Mr. Michael MIRABEL, the bartender at the Lycidas Lounge, was transported to the Lady of Mercy Hospital by Mercy Ambulance (Attendants: WULFGAR and SMITH). MIRABEL suffered a deep gash over his left eye and was still unconscious at the time of this report.

PROPERTY TAKEN

Mr. Larry LYCIDAS, owner of the establishment, estimates the loss at between $200 and $300 in cash.

ADDITIONAL INFORMATION

Officers FRANK and GEORGE (Sct. 9-9) assisted.

STATUS

Open, pending further investigation.

Respectfully submitted:

Steven B. DUFF

Shield No. 487

MISCELLANEOUS INCIDENTS

Police officers deal with a variety of incidents. We have studied the reporting problems of many of them: arrest situations, crimes against property, and crimes against persons. But some incidents do not fit any of the above categories. Therefore, many departments have developed a Miscellaneous Incident reporting form. The word "miscellaneous" itself can be misleading in police usage: many departments, for example, use this Miscellaneous Incident report for homicides, assaults, and rapes. However, we shall use the term to mean those various incidents that are neither crimes against persons nor crimes against property. Among these, for example, are accidental or natural deaths requiring police reports, assistance and service runs, and animal bites.

In the narrative, officers will use the same format as in all other incidents:

Initial Information
Investigation
Reconstruction
Supplementary headings as required.

The previously discussed guidelines for each section still apply.

Officers must be careful in completing these reports, for the one certain thing in police work is that nothing is certain. In accidental or natural deaths, for instance, officers should investigate and report according to the rigid procedures established for homicides. They must never assume that a death was accidental or natural; instead, they should assume, for investigative purposes, that it was not. Consequently, the investigation and report for such incidents will correspond closely to the Incidents against Persons Report.

Assistance and service runs may or may not require a report, depending on departmental policy. In many departments, an entry in the officer's daily log is enough; in others, a formal report may be necessary. Such incidents are many and varied: escorting a social worker, probation officer, building inspector, tax assessor, or some other official in areas where a police officer's presence is considered necessary; transporting personnel or material; transporting a physician to the scene of a crime or accident; transporting injured persons in emergency situations when no ambulance is available—if department policy permits; providing services to a citizen (in many communities, it is the police officer, not the friendly fire fighter, who removes children from tight places, chipmunks from dryers, squirrels and bats from homes, boa constrictors from the plumbing, and so on).

If a report is needed in these and other situations, officers can follow the principles already studied. When applicable, officers should include in their report an exact reference to the report number used by the agency assisted. They should also add a supplementary section specifically noting the assistance or service rendered. In such instances the format will appear as follows:

Initial Information
Investigation
Service Rendered
Supplementary sections as required

We suggest that officers retain the Investigation section for the description of the situation and the actions taken. In this way, the officers do not have to use too many different headings, since too many headings usually result in a lack of consistency and in less efficient reporting.

Animal bites are another area of police concern. Occasionally, they become a crime against person. When the owner of a dog has deliberately encouraged the animal to attack someone, for instance, the officers will take a Crime against Person Report. Or if someone introduces a poisonous snake to an area where another person is likely to be bitten, a Crime against Person Report would be in order. Frequently, however, animal bites involve the family owning the animal or close neighbors of the family owning the animal. A child, for example, pulls the ear of a sleeping family dog—normally a gentle animal—and is bitten. If the incident is reported, most departments will require a report. In many areas, this type of incident occurs so often that a special check-off reporting form and cards have been developed for it. When such a form is not available, officers will probably need a standard police report.

The above examples are only an indication of the various incidents that may be classified "miscellaneous." For reporting purposes, officers should study the following student reports.

INITIAL INFORMATION

At 1312 hrs., Thursday, May 20, 1976, Deputies KINSINGER and KENT (Car 1), northbound on U.S. 99, at Unferth, received a radio run: 333 Pacific, possible death investigation, ambulance en route.

INVESTIGATION

Upon arrival (1320 hrs.), deputies were admitted by the reporting party, Miss Anna ATLANTIC. Miss ATLANTIC stated her aunt was in a bedroom, apparently dead.

Deputies could detect no signs of disorder or struggle in the front room. Deputies then went to the bedroom, where they found the Victim lying in bed. Deputies noted that the drapes were not closed; one screened window (east exposure) was open about 4 inches; nothing appeared out of order.

Deputy KINSINGER checked the Victim for vital signs but found none. Deputy KINSINGER noted that rigor mortis had not yet set in, nor was there any indication of post-mortem lividity.

At 1330 hrs. the ambulance arrived. Attendants also checked the Victim for vital signs but found none.

At 1331 hrs. Deputy KINSINGER told the county medical examiner about the situation. The medical examiner directed deputies to have the Victim transported to the Alpenhut Hospital for examination. At 1335 hrs. ambulance attendants removed the Victim's body to the Alpenhut General Hospital.

Deputy KINSINGER then conducted a thorough sector search of the house and the immediate area but could detect no evidence of foul play.

Interview with Reporting Party: While Deputy KINSINGER searched the area, Deputy KENT interviewed Miss ATLANTIC. Miss ATLANTIC stated she had been visiting her aunt—the Victim—for the past week. She said that she had been talking to the Victim, who was lying in bed, when the Victim suddenly started up and then slumped down in the bed. Miss ATLANTIC said she checked the Victim's pulse but could detect none. She then called the police.

Miss ATLANTIC added that her aunt had been in declining health for the past few months.

RECONSTRUCTION

Based on the above, it appears that at about 1300 hrs., May 20, 1976, the Victim died of natural causes.

VICTIM'S CONDITION

Victim's niece, Miss ATLANTIC, reported the Victim had suffered a severe heart attack in January of this year. She stated that the victim was under medication prescribed by Dr. Andrew JOHNSON, Pogi, Michigan. She also stated her aunt was not depressed and accepted her illness calmly.

Victim was dead on officers' arrival.

NOTIFICATIONS MADE

By Deputy KINSINGER:

Dr. Omar WELLES, Medical Examiner, Alpenhut County. 1331 hrs.

Deputy KINSINGER attempted to call Dr. JOHNSON, the Victim's physician, at 1350 hrs. with negative results. A message was left with Dr. JOHNSON's service.

ADDITIONAL INFORMATION

Victim's body transported by Alpenhut Ambulance Service, Attendants HOWE and JONES.

STATUS

Open, pending report by the county medical examiner.

Matt KINSINGER

INITIAL INFORMATION

At 10:25 p.m., Monday, August 2, 1976, Deputy SHARP (Unit 67-2), southbound on Hersey at 23 Mile, received a radio run: Falcon Boys' Camp, runaway.

INVESTIGATION

Upon arrival (10:50 p.m.) Deputy SHARP was met by the Complainant, Tom ENGLEBERT, a counselor at the camp. Complainant reported that the runaway, Tom FINN, had been missing from a work assignment since 10:00 a.m. this date and provided a description.

Deputy SHARP and the Complainant searched the entire grounds but could find no trace of the missing boy. Deputy SHARP, accompanied by the Complainant, checked FINN's room. They found the missing boy had apparently taken none of his personal possessions nor any clothing other than what he was wearing.

Interview with Complainant: Complainant reported FINN had been at the camp for three months and had apparently adjusted well. He stated FINN had never run away before. Complainant reported FINN's home was in Smithville, Michigan.

At 11:15 p.m. Deputy SHARP broadcast all pertinent information and placed it in the LEIN.

RECONSTRUCTION

Based on the above, it appears that the Subject, Tom FINN, ran away from a work assignment at 10:00 a.m., August 2, 1976.

NOTIFICATIONS MADE

By Deputy SHARP:

> Dispatcher Deputy FLYNN. Requested local area broadcast and information placed in LEIN. 11:15 p.m.

ADDITIONAL INFORMATION

At 11:20 p.m., this date, the Michigan State Police, Pogi Post, reported they had FINN in custody and were returning him to the camp.

STATUS

Closed. LEIN and area broadcast canceled.

James SHARP

INITIAL INFORMATION

At 10:45 a.m., Sunday, July 4, 1976, Officer RODEMEYER, northbound on U.S. 27 at Spruce, received a radio run: Old U.S. 27, southbound lanes, a man trying to stop cars.

INVESTIGATION

Upon arrival (11:00 a.m.) Officer RODEMEYER was met by the Complainant, Edward BLACK, who reported the Subject was a patient at the Pinecrest Care Facility. Officer RODEMEYER could see the Subject standing along the roadside, shouting, and talking to himself. Subject had a beer bottle in one hand (right) and a beer can in the other. Officer saw the Subject flag down a southbound auto. When the auto stopped, the Subject ran toward it, shouting obscenities. As the driver immediately accelerated to leave the scene, the Subject threw the beer bottle at the auto but missed by several yards.

Officer RODEMEYER then approached the Subject, who began to curse at him. Subject also became violent and threw the remaining beer can at Officer RODEMEYER, missing by several feet. Officer RODEMEYER then subdued and handcuffed the Subject.

Interview with Complainant: Complainant informed Officer RODEMEYER that the Subject had earlier struck an older resident at the facility and then kicked several holes in the walls. Complainant stated the Subject had often exhibited violent tendencies and become destructive. Complainant also stated the Subject had formerly been a patient at the Cherry City Mental Care Facility.

Officer RODEMEYER secured the Subject in the rear seat of the patrol car. Officer then spoke to John TELL, w/m, 86, Pinecrest Care Facility. Mr. TELL was the man earlier struck by the Subject. Mr. TELL stated the blow had not been severe and he did not want to lodge a complaint. Officer RODEMEYER also observed four holes, approximately 3 inches in diameter and 6 inches from the floor, which the Subject had apparently made by kicking the walls of the facility recreation room.

At 12:25 p.m., Officer RODEMEYER transported the Subject to the Cherry City Mental Care Facility, arrival time 1:45 p.m. Subject was then turned over to Dr. I. FISHER and admitted as an involuntary patient.

SERVICE RENDERED

Michael J. BUSH, mental patient, was returned to the Cherry City Mental Care Facility.

EXCEPTIONAL OCCURRENCES

Subject threw a beer can at reporting officer but missed. Officer got an armlock on the Subject and then handcuffed him. Subject sustained no injuries.

ADDITIONAL INFORMATION

The Complainant, Edward BLACK, can testify to the Subject's behavior at the Pinecrest Care Facility and at the scene.

STATUS

Closed.

Mark RODEMEYER

APPLICATIONS

Exercise 1

Using the given information, write the following report. Supply additional details as needed.

The Initial Information Section

You and your partner are in a radio unit. At 11:25 a.m., you are dispatched to 925 Apple Lane, Apartment No. 1, to "see the lady." It's Monday, July 26, 1976.

The Investigation Section

You arrive at the scene and are met by Miss Hilda Hygd, the reporting party and manager of the apartment building. She tells you that George Grendel, the tenant in Apartment No. 13, did not leave for work as he usually does at 9:30 a.m. Miss Hygd says that he always has coffee with her in the morning; consequently, when he did not show up, she went to his apartment. She tells you that she knocked on the door but received no answer.

Miss Hygd tells you that she is concerned because Grendel's car is still in its parking place and because she had heard noises that sounded like gunshots during the night. She says the sounds awakened her at about 3:00 a.m. and seemed to come from the direction of Grendel's apartment. She adds that she tried to raise Grendel again at about 10:00 but again was unsuccessful. Then she called the police.

You go to the apartment and knock but receive no response. You try the door and discover that it is unlocked. You identify yourself, push the door open, and immediately see the victim lying with his head in a bloodstained area beside a sofa. The apartment is a one-room studio apartment. There are apparent signs of a struggle: lamps and chairs overturned, furniture moved from the original position, etc. You also note several empty beer bottles lying about the floor in various places. The only blood immediately visible is on the floor around the victim's head and shoulders and on the victim's body around the neck and upper body. No one else is in the apartment; nor do you see any weapon.

You check the victim and find him dead. You detect signs of advanced rigor mortis; you also note that post-mortem discoloration indicates the victim's body had not been moved. You find an apparent bullet wound in the victim's throat but can locate no point of exit for the bullet.

You use the apartment manager's phone to request assistance and the medical examiner.

You then conduct a point-to-point search. You find two holes that appear to have been made by bullets in the east wall of the room. You find no trace of a weapon; nor do you find any signs of forcible entry on the lone door or window.

Det. Sgt. Sam Seafarer arrives and takes command of the scene. He asks you to photograph the scene and the body. He also directs you and your partner to make all necessary measurements and sketches. Sgt. Seafarer dusts for prints.

You next conduct another search under Sgt. Seafarer's direction. You probe the holes in the wall, already photographed, and remove an expanded small-caliber bullet from each hole. (The collection, identification, and preservation of the evidence will be detailed in the Evidence section).

The medical examiner, Dr. Oberon Thomas, arrives and examines the victim. Dr. Thomas reports that her preliminary examination indicates the victim died from a small-caliber bullet in the throat. The bullet is still in the Victim. Dr. Thomas estimates the time of death as "eight or ten hours ago." Dr. Thomas then directs the removal of the body by ambulance attendants.

Det. Sgt. Seafarer states he will assume responsibility for securing the scene and asks you to continue your interview with Miss Hygd.

You then interview the apartment manager again. She tells you that she saw Grendel's girl friend, Terry Trell, enter the apartment building at about 10:00 p.m. the previous evening. She did not see Miss Trell leave. She can add nothing further to her earlier account of being awakened by gunshots; nor can she state how many shots she heard although she "guesses" that it was probably "four or five."

You then check all the apartments on the first and second floors of the building but find no one at home in any apartment.

After obtaining the address from the telephone directory, you go to Miss Trell's residence, which is only three blocks from the scene. Upon arrival you are admitted by Miss Trell. When she sees your uniform, she immediately breaks into tears and cries, "I didn't think he would do it."

Miss Trell then gives you the following account of the incident. She was with Grendel all evening. At about 2:30 a.m. he began to insist that she stay the night with him. She refused. He became angry and a fight ensued. Some furniture was knocked about during the struggle, and she was slightly injured. She further states that Grendel became "furious," took a gun from a bureau drawer, and threatened to kill both her and himself. She says he then fired two shots into the wall to prove the gun was loaded. Then he held the gun to his throat, fired again, and fell to the floor. She states that she then panicked, grabbed the gun, and ran from the apartment. Once outside, she threw the gun in a front yard near the apartment building. She says that she then ran all the way home and has since been trying to decide what to do. She adds that Grendel had been drinking heavily all evening.

Your partner immediately radios Dispatch the information about the weapon.

You note that Miss Trell has a discolored bruise above her left eye and that her upper lip is swollen. There is also dried blood visible in her nostrils. She pulls back her hair to reveal a small lump over her right ear. She says that she received these injuries during the struggle.

You request that Miss Trell accompany you to the station to make a formal statement; she agrees. She also asks that she be given a "lie detector" test.

You escort Miss Trell to the station. Upon arrival you are met by Officers Baker and Franco, who report finding the weapon on the front lawn of 975 Apple Lane. They state the gun was turned over to Det. Sgt. Seafarer at the scene.

You arrange for the final statement and schedule a polygraph examination.

The Reconstruction Section

You reconstruct the incident as it probably occurred. Remember, at this point, Miss Trell's statement has been neither proved nor disproved.

The Victim's Condition Section

You have been told by Miss Trell that the victim had been drinking heavily prior to the incident. You also have the medical examiner's report of his post-mortem examination. You should also include here the name of the ambulance service, the names of the attendants, and the hospital to which the body was taken.

The Evidence Section

You are responsible for the bullets that you extracted from the wall. You are also responsible for photographs, measurements, and sketches.

The Notifications Made Section

You should include here all notifications made by you and your partner: technical assistance, medical examiner, Dispatch relative to the weapon, and the polygraph operator.

The Additional Information Section

You list the names of all officers involved and their areas of possible testimony.

Exercise 2

Write the following report. Supply any details not given.

You are in the station when three subjects arrive and report a possible drowning. It is 12:02 a.m. on a Tuesday, June 15, 1976.

The complainant tells you that he and the victim, a girl, had been swimming in Bottom's gravel pit earlier, that they could not now locate her, and that they are afraid she has drowned.

Accompanied by the three subjects and your partner, you go to Bottom's gravel pit. You do not allow the subjects to leave the patrol car, which you park some distance from the gravel pit. You carefully check the area but can find neither evidence of a struggle nor any signs of the victim.

You request assistance from the state police divers, and a team is sent.

You then interview each of the three subjects. The complainant tells you that at about 9:00 p.m., the previous evening, he was seated at the bar in Duffy's Bar with the two witnesses when the victim entered. He says that after a few drinks the victim suggested that they should all go swimming. He states that all four persons then left the bar and arrived at the gravel pit at about 10:30 p.m. Complainant says that all four then entered the water, wearing their underclothes, but that he and the two witnesses decided the water was too cold. He reports that he and the two witnesses then left the water and returned to their auto but that the victim resisted their calls to come out of the water. He tells you that after about fifteen minutes they went to the edge of the pit to call her once more but received no answer. They then drove to the police station, a distance of 10 miles, and reported the incident.

Both witnesses, interviewed separately, give substantially the same account of the incident.

The state police diving team arrives at 1:30 a.m. At 2:05 a.m., the divers recover the victim's body clad in bra and panties. The divers report that the body was found on the bottom, face down, in approximately 30 feet of water, 20 feet from the south bank and 80 feet from the east bank.

The body shows no sign of foul play. There are no bruises or lacerations.

At 2:07 a.m. you notify the medical examiner, who tells you to take the body to the Alpenhut Hospital for later examination.

You request an ambulance to transport the body.

You notify the next of kin.

Exercise 3

Write the following report using the given information. Supply details as required.

You and your partner are in a radio unit working in a small community. You are dispatched to 714 Friday Street, Apartment No. 5, to "see a man." The call is received at 4:40 a.m., on January 19, 1976, a Monday. You are at Arthur and Bleeker when dispatched.

Upon arriving at the scene, a small apartment building, you are met by the reporting party, George Glendower. Glendower tells you that he saw one of the occupants of Apartment No. 3, across the hallway, strike the other occupant with a club. Glendower says the assault occurred in the hallway in front of Apartment No. 3 shortly before he called the police. He said the assailant, whom he identifies as Michael Mowbray, then dragged the screaming victim, whom he identifies as Harold Howell, into Apartment No. 3. Glendower says that the two men live together in the apartment and are considered "queers." He reports that the tenants call Howell "Hornet."

You check the hallway but find no signs of blood stains or other indications of an assault.

You knock on the door of Apartment No. 3, and are met by the assailant. You ask to see the reported victim but Mowbray just shouts, "Get a warrant, you blue-coated bastard."

You then have your partner stand by in front of Apartment No. 3 while you interview the other occupants on the floor. Two occupants report they heard screaming at the time indicated by the reporting party.

You then use Glendower's phone to call the desk officer, requesting that she have the prosecutor get a warrant as soon as possible.

At 5:30 p.m., the desk officer reports that the local magistrate signed the warrant and that the state police will deliver it to you.

At 5:45 p.m. the state police arrive with the warrant. Accompanied by the troopers, you again request to be admitted to Apartment No. 3. Mowbray answers the door, does not acknowledge the warrant, but does invite you in.

You enter and find the victim lying in bed. He has contusions on his forehead, and his left eye is discolored and swollen shut. His lower lip is also cut and swollen. The victim is wearing a pink nightgown and has apparently applied makeup to his face.

Victim states that there was no fight. He insists that he and Mowbray simply had a quarrel.

Exercise 4

Using the given information, write the following report. Supply details as needed.

You and your partner are in a two-officer radio unit when you are dispatched to meet a military police team at Collins and Ord. You are at Stoneman and Parris when dispatched. It is 10:30 p.m., July 13, 1976, a Tuesday.

You arrive, and the military police officer informs you that they require assistance in apprehending an AWOL suspect believed to be in the residence at 1313 Selfridge.

You accompany the MPs to the door while your partner covers the rear of the house.

You knock on the door, which is answered by the AWOL subject's mother. She tells you the AWOL is in the living room and has been expecting the military police. She invites you in. The AWOL subject surrenders to the military police without struggle.

Exercise 5

Using the given information, write the following report. Supply details as needed.

You and your partner are in a radio unit. At 2135 hrs. you receive a radio run to investigate an assault on Sunset Strip at River Road. You are at Sunset and Grant at the time. It is a Thursday, June 17, 1976.

You are met by the two victims. Neither one has injuries that require any treatment. One victim states he and his friend were bicycling on River Road when a vehicle behind them sounded its horn. He says they both moved off the road but that the car followed them onto the shoulder, nearly striking them. He adds that the car then stopped and the driver came back and struck him several times with his fist. When his friend (the second victim) tried to help, another man got out of the car and attacked the second victim, striking him several times with his fists.

The first victim adds that he believes the assailants had been drinking. He also states there were other persons of both sexes in the car. He then gives you the license number of the assailant's auto.

The second victim corroborates the first victim's statement. He also says that they did nothing to start the fight.

Both victims state they could identify the assailants and give you descriptions.

You go to the address of the auto's registered owner. You interview the owner, a girl. She declares that the victims had refused to move off the road and had shouted obscenities at the occupants of the car. She refuses to identify the occupants of her car at the time of the assault.

Exercise 6

Using the given information, write the following report. Supply any details needed.

You are working alone in a radio car, patrolling a rural area. At 8:06 p.m., July 4, 1976, a Sunday, you are westbound on M 99 at M 199 when you are dispatched to investigate a possible assault at Mike's Bar in Pogi, Michigan. An ambulance is on its way.

Upon arrival you find the victim lying on the ground in the parking lot. A crowd has gathered about the apparently injured victim, but no one is giving first aid. You see a twelve-pack of Pabst beer beside the victim.

You go to the victim and discover he has bleeding gashes on his forehead. The victim also complains of pain in his lower back and abdomen. You give first aid.

Before the ambulance arrives, the victim tells you that he was attacked by a man and a woman in the parking lot after he had refused to trade the beer for some marijuana. Victim said the woman knocked him to the ground and the man kicked him several times before both fled in an auto that had been parked nearby. Victim gives you a rough description of the couple but says he did not see the car clearly.

You then locate two witnesses to the assault, and after a brief interview, broadcast the names and descriptions of the assailants as given by these witnesses.

The ambulance arrives and takes the victim to the hospital.

You conduct follow-up interviews with the two witnesses.

The first witness tells you that he was in the parking lot and saw the assailants strike and kick the victim. He reports that they appeared to be arguing before the attack. The witness cannot identify the assailants' auto although he saw it move out of the unlighted portion of the lot.

The second witness gives substantially the same account. She reports that it was she who ran into the bar and asked the bartender to call the police after the assault. The witness does not know the assailants by name but provides the same physical description received from the victim and the first witness.

You go to the hospital and receive a report on the victim's injuries and treatment. You interview him further, but he can add nothing to his previous statement. He does say that he will sign a complaint.

You locate the addresses of the assailants, go there, but find no one at home.

Chapter 7
The Elements
of Crime:
A Brief Reference
Guide

This guide to the elements of crime serves an instructional purpose: it provides law enforcement students with a quick, handy reference to the usual statutory requirements of various crimes. It is not intended to be a legal manual, nor is it intended to be a replacement for the legal training professional police officers need, particularly since statutes differ from state to state. While the elements of the offenses included in this survey are basically the same, the wording of the statutes and the names of the offenses may differ from area to area. For example, what one state calls Breaking and Entering, another may call Burglary; what one calls Larceny, another may call Theft.

Moreover, statutes by their very nature are often changed. In Michigan, for example, the old statutes dealing with sex offenses—Rape, Statutory Rape, etc.—have been replaced by the new Criminal Sexual Conduct statute. Therefore, we urge officers to study the applicable statutes in their jurisdictions and make changes in this guide as needed.

Our listing is necessarily not complete. We cannot, because of limitations of space, treat many lesser offenses in detail, e.g., Illegal Entry, Entry without Permission, Entering without Breaking, etc. Other offenses, such as Embezzlement, Larceny by Conversion, and Conspiracy, which generally are handled by specific investigative units, have been omitted. We have, instead, concentrated on offenses that are normally dealt with by the line officer.

One final note: Students and officers alike must remember that, regardless of the elements present, it is the prosecutor who has the *exclusive* right to determine the specific charges that will be brought against a suspect.

ASSAULT AND BATTERY

Assault is

*an *intended violence*
*to the person of another
*with the *present ability* to carry out the intent.

Battery is

*the *willful touching*
*of one person by another
*or by *some article set in motion* by such other.

Officers should note that *threats alone* do not constitute Assault; *violence* must be *actually offered* and *within such distance* that injury may result if the assailant is not stopped. Nor must the intended injury be severe: a simple attempt to stop another person, for instance, may be Assault.

EXAMPLES:
In an argument, one person draws back his fist to strike his opponent. Bystanders intervene before the blow is struck. This is Assault, for present ability *existed. Had the assailant landed the blow,* battery *would be complete. (*Note: *In court,. of course, the quarrelsome disposition of the complaining witness as well as that of the assailant would be at issue. However, this is a matter for the court, not the police.)*

During a barroom dispute, a drunken patron takes a bottle from the bar, apparently intending to strike her opponent. As she picks up the bottle, she passes out. In this case officers would be well advised to question the patron's present ability.

FELONIOUS ASSAULT

The elements of Felonious Assault are

*an *assault*
*with a *dangerous weapon*.

The requirements of Assault are fundamentally the same as outlined under Assault and Battery. Some instruments such as guns, knives, and brass knuckles are in themselves dangerous weapons. Whether other instruments are dangerous weapons must be decided by a jury. Criteria for such a decision often include whether the particular instrument was used as a weapon, and when so used, whether it was dangerous. Various instruments held to be dangerous weapons in specific instances by juries include beer bottles, automobiles, and flashlights.

> *EXAMPLE:*
> *A subject breaks a bottle on a table and strikes at the complainant with the jagged edge. The basic elements of Felonious Assault are present, although, of course, the final decision must be made by the court.*

ASSAULT—GREAT BODILY HARM LESS THAN MURDER

The elements of Assault with the Intent to Do Great Bodily Harm Less than Murder include

*the *attempt* with *force* or *violence*
*to do *corporal* harm to another
*with the *intent* of doing *serious injury.*

Intent is usually a key element. It may be shown by words or conduct. However, the simple fact that an injury was inflicted does not supply intent.

> *EXAMPLES:*
> *A farmer, angry at hunters trespassing on his land, deliberately shoots one hunter in the leg. The act constitutes Intent to Do Great Bodily Harm.*
>
> *Two people are negotiating the sale of a shotgun. The prospective buyer, thinking the gun is unloaded, pulls the trigger and shoots the seller in the forearm. The seller calls the police, charging the shooting was deliberate. In this instance, the injury in itself would not sustain an Intent to Do Great Bodily Harm charge. In such a situation, an officer would do well to treat the injured, conduct a thorough investigation, write the report—and let the prosecutor worry about issuing a warrant. If the circumstances require an immediate arrest, the officer could effect the arrest on any of various charges: Felonious Assault, Assault—Great Bodily Harm, or Assault—Intent to Commit Murder, allowing the prosecutor to evaluate the incident and determine the charge later if need be.*

ASSAULT—INTENT TO COMMIT MURDER

There are two basic elements to this crime:

*assault
*with the *intent* to commit murder.

For the fundamental elements of *assault*, see Assault and Battery. Basically the crime consists of the unjustified and unexcused *intention to kill* when committing an assault. Again, *intent* is critical, and this is a question of fact for a jury to decide. Such factors as statements prior to the assault, displaying or brandishing a weapon, or threats—even those uttered several months before the assault—are usually admissible in court.

EXAMPLE:

Assailant, in the company of reputable witnesses, states: "One of these days I'm going to blow his damned head off." Later she fires at the complaining witness with a .22 rifle at close range, severely wounding him. The threatening statement would lend substance to a charge of Assault—Intent to Commit Murder.

BREAKING AND ENTERING (Burglary)

The elements of Breaking and Entering are

*breaking
*and *entering* into a structure or place specified by statute
*with the specific *intent*
*to commit a larceny or any felony.

Only the slightest amount of force is necessary to constitute breaking, usually regarded as breaking the "seal," e.g., pushing open a closed door. It is not necessary for entry to be followed by an illegal act; if the *intent* was present at the time of entry, the crime is complete when entry is made. Moreover, actual entry by the perpetrator's body is also not essential; the perpetrator may, for example, use a magnet or other device connected to a rod to take property from a room, thus never inserting any part of the body into the structure.

Officers should consult the statutes of their own state for the definition of "structure." Generally it refers to any roofed, enclosed area: houses, apartments, and business buildings are obvious examples. In some jurisdictions, animal shelters and locked vehicles are considered structures. In the broadest sense, a structure is any artificially constructed piece of work whose parts join together in some definite manner.

For the purpose of determining penalties, distinctions are also made between the breaking and entering of dwellings and the breaking and entering of other structures. Further distinction may be made between occupied dwellings and unoccupied dwellings, with the breaking and entering of occupied dwellings carrying the most severe penalty.

EXAMPLE:

Officers, responding to a silent alarm at a jewelry store, apprehend the armed suspect in the building. Officers discover that the protective bars have been removed from a window and that the window glass is broken above the sash lock.

Some of the merchandise is scattered about, and some is found on the suspect. This evidence, coupled with the suspect's inability to explain her presence in the store, establishes the elements of Breaking and Entering.

CARRYING CONCEALED WEAPON

The elements are

  *the carrying of a dagger, dirk, stiletto, or other dangerous weapon
  *concealed *on* or *about one's person*
  *or concealed or otherwise in any vehicle *operated* or *occupied* by that person.

Hunting knives carried as such are not included. Additionally, the statute does not apply in a person's dwelling or place of business or on any other land owned by the person. The phrase "other dangerous weapon" is restricted to stabbing weapons only; rifles, shotguns, clubs, or other "dangerous weapons" are not included. Officers must charge these under Carrying Dangerous Weapon with Unlawful Intent.

Specific wording will differ from state to state. Some elements listed here under CCW may be listed elsewhere under Carrying Dangerous Weapon. The opposite is also true. Officers should consult the statutes in their jurisdictions and make any necessary notations here.

Concealment is a question for the jury. Generally, complete invisibility is not necessary; concealment is sufficient if the weapon cannot be seen by ordinary or casual observation.

EXAMPLE:
Officers stop a vehicle and see a pistol butt sticking out from under a sweater lying on the back seat. The driver, the lone occupant of the auto, may be charged under this statute.

See also: *Carrying Dangerous Weapon*

CARRYING DANGEROUS WEAPON

The elements are

  *the carrying of a pistol or other firearm, dagger, dirk, stiletto, or knife having a
  blade over 3 inches in length,
  *or any other dangerous weapon or instrument,
  *with the *intent* to use the same unlawfully *against* the *person of another.*

Note that a jackknife or razor is not in itself a dangerous weapon if the blade is more than 3 inches in length. Officers must be able to establish that such an instrument was carried for assault or defense. Whether the instrument carried was in fact a dangerous weapon and the reason for possible use are questions for the jury.

> *EXAMPLE:*
> *Following a neighborhood quarrel, one party returns home and gets his rifle. He then starts back to the scene of the dispute, carrying the rifle. The man is in violation of the Carrying Dangerous Weapon statute, although the ultimate question of his intent is a matter for the jury.*

Refer: *Carrying Concealed Weapon*

CONTROLLED SUBSTANCES

Statutes dealing with the illegal possession of controlled substances vary widely throughout the United States. The distinctions made between misdemeanor and felony counts on such possession also vary. Therefore, officers should consult the statutes in their jurisdictions and make corrections here accordingly. Generally, however, to convict a person of illegal possession of a controlled substance, an officer must establish the presence of the following elements:

*that the suspect exercised control over the controlled substance or had authority to control,
*that the suspect knew the substance was present,
*that the suspect *knew the substance was proscribed*,
*and that the substance existed in a usable amount or was a remnant of a usable amount.

DRIVING UNDER THE INFLUENCE OF LIQUOR OR NARCOTICS (DUIL and Impaired)

The elements of this offense are

*driving a motor vehicle
*on a public roadway, parking lot, or place open to the general public,
*while under the influence of liquor or narcotic drugs.

The laws dealing with this offense normally apply to *all* public places—i.e., non-private property—even though such places may not be roadways. States may provide separate statutes for each offense. One statute will treat Driving under the Influence of Intoxicating Liquor (variously called DML, Drunk Motorist Law; DWI—Driving while Intoxicated; etc.) and the other Driving under the Influence of Narcotic Drugs, Barbitol, or any Derivative of Barbitol. Unless complaining witnesses are available, it is usually necessary that the officers themselves observe the suspect driving the motor vehicle.

EXAMPLE:
An officer discovers an automobile parked beside the roadway with its motor running. Investigation reveals that the person sitting at the wheel is intoxicated. In Michigan, the officer could seize the keys to the vehicle if it were obvious that the person was unable to drive; but in the absence of any witnesses who saw the person drive the automobile, the officer could not effect an arrest for DUIL.

EXTORTION

The elements of this crime are

threatening injury to the person or property of mother, father, husband, wife, or children of another
*or *threatening* to *accuse another* of any crime or offense
*with the *intent* to exact money, acquire some financial advantage, or force the victim to comply as directed.

While the threats may be either oral or written, they must not be vague. Usually they must be such as would reasonably cause fear in an ordinary person. How specific a threat must be varies from state to state. Officers should make changes here using the statutes applicable in their jurisdictions.

EXAMPLES:
A business person receives an anonymous letter telling him to leave a paper sack containing $50 at a specific location; the letter further indicates that if he does not do this, his business establishments will be burned. This is Extortion.

A victim receives a phone call from a woman to whom he owes money. The woman threatens to run the victim off the road if he doesn't pay the debt. This may be Extortion. Although the debt is a valid one, such threats are not permissible since there are other, legal means of collection.

LARCENY—GENERAL

The elements of General Larceny are

*the actual or constructive taking
  and carrying away
*of another's property
*without his consent and against his will
*with a felonious intent to deprive permanently.

It must be clearly demonstrated that someone's criminal act caused the property to become lost; the simple fact that the property is missing is not sufficient.
  The value of the property may be essential in classifying an offense as a felony or a

misdemeanor. (In Michigan, the critical level is $100.) Usually, the value placed on the property is the market price when taken, not the special value to the owner; however, the owner's testimony may be sufficient to take a question of value to the jury.

LARCENY FROM PERSON

The elements of Larceny from Person are

*the actual or constructive taking and carrying away
*of another's property
*from the person of another
*without consent and against his or her will
*with the intent to deprive permanently.

"From the person of another" means in the "immediate presence" as well as in one's possession.

EXAMPLES:
A woman riding a bus places her purse on the seat beside her. A man snatches the purse as the bus comes to a halt and runs off.

At a bus station a pickpocket, attempting to lift the victim's wallet, jostles the victim, reaches into the victim's coat pocket, but finds the pocket empty. An officer in plainclothes observes the activity. Although the pickpocket attempted to pick an empty pocket, the Larceny from Person is complete.

LARCENY FROM MOTOR VEHICLE

The elements are

*unlawful *taking*
*of parts or property
*from the *outside*
*of another's motor vehicle
*or the inside of an unlocked vehicle.

Larceny from Motor Vehicle includes the unlawful removal of wheels, tires, hubcaps, heater, radio, or any other part of the vehicle. Some jurisdictions also consider *breaking* and *entering* a motor vehicle with the *intent to carry away* the property of another as Larceny from Motor Vehicle. Other specific restrictions may be in force [in Michigan, for instance, other qualifications are (1) the property must have a value of $5 or more *unless* (2) actual damage is done to the auto, e.g., the breaking of glass, the tearing of upholstery, etc.]. There may also be differences in labeling this act. Some jurisdictions may list this offense as Burglary and others as Breaking and Entering.

EXAMPLES:
You are on patrol and observe a suspect stripping an auto of its hubcaps. You have Larceny from Motor Vehicle.

You see a suspect smash a car window with a brick; he then reaches in, opens the door, and removes a citizens band radio. Depending on the prevailing statutes in your state, you have either Larceny from Motor Vehicle or Burglary (Breaking and Entering).

LARCENY IN A BUILDING

The elements are

*those applicable under General Larceny
*and that the place of occurrence was a dwelling house, office, building, etc.

Shoplifting would be under this statute in Michigan. In other states, a distinction may be made between Burglary Shoplifting (offenses where there was a *specific intent* to commit theft *at the time of entry*, usually established by the suspect's possession of burglary equipment, e.g., "booster" pockets, false packages, etc.) and Theft Shoplifting (offenses where the *intent* was *present* at *the time of the theft*.)

EXAMPLES:
A clerk in a clothing store saw a lady remove two blouses from a rack and then slide them under her skirt. Asportation was complete upon her concealing the blouses.

A store security officer observed a man pick up three sweaters from a shelf. The man then concealed the sweaters under his coat and walked past the cashier toward the exit. The security officer moved toward the man to intercept him. The man, seeing the security officer approaching, turned, ran back to the shelves, and replaced the sweaters. The larceny was still complete.

MALICIOUS DESTRUCTION OF PROPERTY

Malicious Destruction of Property may be either a felony or a misdemeanor. The offense encompasses personal property and buildings. The elements of this offense are

*to cause destruction of or injury to
*the personal property or buildings (house, garage, barn, or appurtenances) of another,
*willfully and maliciously.

EXAMPLE:
Some youths deliberately break several windows in the school they attend. They also spray paint on the exterior brick and mortar. Since the statute is not limited to the property of individuals, the elements of Malicious Destruction of Property are present.

MANSLAUGHTER

Manslaughter is the unlawful killing of another *without premeditation* or *malice* under any of the following conditions:

*during the *intentional* commission of an unlawful act *less than a felony* and *not naturally tending to result in death* or *great bodily harm*;
*through *gross negligence*, during the performance of some act *that is in itself lawful*;
*or through negligence, by the *failure to perform a legal duty*.

Although the specific statute may not make distinction, courts often distinguish between two types of manslaughter: voluntary and involuntary. Generally, voluntary manslaughter is any intentional killing of another which would be murder *if it were not committed in the heat of passion and with sufficient provocation*. Sufficient provocation may be considered those *circumstances under which reasonable people of ordinary dispositions would be likely to react without reflection, governed by passion rather than reason*. Sufficient provocation may, *depending upon the specific circumstances*, result from a number of causes: assault, battery, vile acts perpetrated on a loved one, trespass, etc.

In addition, there must be *no reasonable cooling period between the provocation and the act* such as would allow a reasonably prudent person time to reconsider. Whether or not a *reasonable* cooling time has elapsed may very well be a question of fact for the jury.

The basic difference between voluntary and involuntary manslaughter lies in the *former's* requirement of the *intent* to kill or do great bodily harm.

EXAMPLES:
A rural resident, gathering firewood at his woodpile shortly after dark, hears a car speeding down his drive. He looks in time to see the car, driven by "deer-shiners," strike his son, who was walking down the drive. Enraged, he seizes a length of firewood, rushes over, and hurls the wood at the driver. The wood strikes the driver on the temple and the car crashes. The medical examiner later determines that the initial blow on the head was the proximate cause of death. This could be voluntary manslaughter if the malice were judged to be negated by the provocation.

A speeding driver runs a red light and is then pursued by police. During the chase, the driver runs several more red lights at high speed and finally crashes into another car, killing two of its occupants. Probably, we have Manslaughter.

A drunken woman, waving off the objections of friends, insists on driving her auto. She then strikes a pedestrian with her auto, killing the pedestrian. She may be found guilty of Involuntary Manslaughter. (In Michigan, the charge in this situation could also be Negligent Homicide.)

MURDER—FIRST DEGREE

The fundamental elements of Murder—First Degree are

*the *willful*,
deliberate,
premeditated
killing of a *human being*
*under circumstances that do not excuse, justify, or mitigate the degree of the offense to second-degree murder or manslaughter.

Premeditated is a key word. Since one cannot instantaneously "premeditate" a murder, murder in the first degree must be deliberate with a time lapse sufficient to give the suspect a chance to reflect. Such a time lapse may be seconds, minutes, or hours, depending on the circumstances surrounding the killing.

Officers will usually make the arrest on an open charge of murder. The specific charge of Murder—First Degree must, of course, be made by the prosecutor. As an executive officer of the government, the prosecutor has the exclusive right of determining the exact charge to be brought against a defendant. To conduct a proper investigation, however, officers must be aware of the various elements.

EXAMPLE:
The suspect lies in wait for his victim. He forces the victim at gunpoint to accompany him to a secluded area. Upon arrival, the suspect ties the victim to a tree. He then beats the victim repeatedly with a length of two-by-four, ultimately causing death. The elements of Murder—First Degree are present.

See also: *Murder—Second Degree*, *Murder—Felony*, and *Manslaughter*.

MURDER—SECOND DEGREE

The elements of Murder—Second Degree are

*the willful killing of a human being
without deliberation or *premeditation*
*under circumstances that do not constitute excuse, justification, or mitigation of the offense to Manslaughter or Negligent Homicide.

This offense would include *unplanned* or *impulsive* homicides committed in the heat of passion but intentionally and with malice aforethought.

> *EXAMPLE:*
> *In the midst of a family argument, a man suddenly seizes a poker and strikes his wife on the head, killing her. In such an instance, the intent to kill was formed upon a sudden provocation immediately prior to and accompanying the action. This may be Murder—Second Degree, or a jury may determine the provocation was such as to warrant reducing the charge to Manslaughter.*

See also: *Murder—First Degree, Murder—Felony,* and *Manslaughter.*

MURDER—FELONY

Felony Murder is

*the killing of a human being
during the *commission* or *attempted commission* of a felony, i.e.:
    arson
    burglary
    extortion
    kidnapping
    larceny
    rape
    robbery

The commission of the felony crimes listed above or others (refer to applicable state statutes) often results in death. Therefore, homicides committed during the commission of such crimes constitute murder. The corpus delicti of Felony Murder is twofold: the evidence of death with a criminal agency as its cause *and* the evidence of the felony committed.

> *EXAMPLE:*
> *Three suspects attempt an armed robbery. Officers intervene, and gunfire is exchanged. During the exchange one suspect and one police officer are killed. Although the police officer was mortally wounded by a fellow officer, the remaining suspects may be charged with Felony Murder.*

See also: *Murder—First Degree, Murder—Second Degree,* and *Manslaughter.*

NEGLIGENT HOMICIDE

The elements of Negligent Homicide are

*the negligent operating of a motor vehicle on a public roadway,
*thus causing an accident
*that resulted in the inflicting of fatal injuries.

In Michigan this is a lesser charge than Manslaughter. Only *ordinary*, not *gross*, negligence is required.

EXAMPLE:
A person, late for an appointment, is driving too fast to stop at a stop sign. The auto skids into the intersection into the path of another vehicle, which has the legal right-of-way. The driver of the second auto suffers fatal injuries. The driver at fault could be charged with Negligent Homicide.
See also: *Manslaughter.*

POSSESSION OF BURGLAR'S TOOLS

The elements of this offense are

*the knowing possession
*of any explosive, tool, chemical, or implement,
*designed or adapted for cutting, burning, or breaking open,
*with the knowledge that it is so adapted,
*and with the intent to use it for breaking to steal property.

Some states may include possession of devices adapted or designed for shoplifting (hooks in undergarments, false packages, "booster" pockets, etc.) under their statutes. In Michigan the essential element of this offense is the *intent* to use for the purpose of *breaking* and *entering*. The words "designed or adapted" also mean that the equipment must be *specifically designed* for the purpose of breaking; common household instruments (butter knives, spits, etc.) that could be used for breaking and entering are generally not included.

EXAMPLE:
Responding to a prowler call at 2:30 a.m. in a residential neighborhood, officers stop a suspect in the immediate area. A search shows that the suspect is carrying a glass cutter, electrical tape, pliers, and a wire coat hanger twisted out of shape with a loop at the end. The suspect does not live in the area. The officers may reasonably assume the suspect was carrying burglary tools.

RAPE

The basic elements of Rape are

*sexual intercourse with a female not one's wife
*with penetration of the female's vaginal tract by the male penis,
*effected by the use of force or without the consent of the victim.

Emission is not necessary; penetration, no matter how slight, is sufficient.

Certain persons are regarded as incapable of giving consent: those who are unconscious; those who are mentally unsound; those who are highly intoxicated; and those who are under the legal age of consent. The legal age of consent varies from state to state; therefore, officers should consult the appropriate statutes in their jurisdiction. Some states have a specific statute dealing with statutory rape—those offenses involving females who have not reached the age of consent.

In Michigan the rape and statutory rape statutes have been replaced (April 1, 1975) with the Criminal Sexual Conduct statute. Briefly, this statute breaks sex offenses into four degrees as follows:

*First degree deals with sexual penetration by either male or female of another person's private parts. The statute specifies what offenses are included, such as penetration during the commission of a felony, penetration as a result of a felony, causing personal injury to the victim, and other offenses.

*Second degree deals with the same type of misconduct as does first degree *except* that in second degree penetration is not necessary; sexual contact is sufficient.

*Third degree also deals with sexual penetration. However, the difference between first-degree misconduct and third-degree misconduct is that third degree does *not* include:
   1. Crimes of penetration where the victim was less than thirteen years of age (a first-degree offense)
   2. Crimes of penetration that occurred during the commission of a felony (a first-degree offense)
   3. Crimes of sexual assault resulting in an injury to the victim

*Fourth degree deals with those who engage in sexual misconduct with others. The *fourth degree* differs from the *second degree* as the *third* does from the *first*. The *fourth degree* does *not* include:
   1. Sexual misconduct with a victim who is less than thirteen years of age
   2. Sexual misconduct during the commission of a felony
   3. Sexual misconduct when the victim has been injured

In addition, this statute provides for the prosecution of a person who sexually assaults his *legal spouse if the couple are living apart and one of them has filed for separate maintenance or divorce*.

The statute is complex, and we have only touched on some of the more important points here. Michigan officers are urged to study the statute thoroughly and make notes here as needed.

RESISTING AND OBSTRUCTING

The elements of Resisting and Obstructing are

*the knowing and willful
*obstructing, resisting, opposing, assaulting, or wounding
*of an authorized officer
*while such officer was lawfully performing his duty.

Generally, actual physical interference is not essential; the threat of interference is sufficient if it is coupled with the present apparent ability to carry out such a threat. *Note:* If the arrest itself is *illegal*, resistance could be considered justifiable.

EXAMPLE:

Officers arrest a man in a bar for Felonious Assault. The arrested man's wife leaps on a chair and tells the other patrons to keep "the pigs" from taking her husband. The other patrons respond by closing in on the officers, who finally require assistance to control the crowd. The woman may be charged with Resisting and Obstructing although she did not physically come between the officers and her husband.

ROBBERY—ARMED

The elements of Armed Robbery are

*the assault of another
*to rob and take feloniously
*from the person of such other or in the other's presence
*money or other property that is the subject of larceny
*while armed with a dangerous weapon or an article used or fashioned in such a
  manner as to lead to a reasonable belief that a dangerous weapon exists.

If the assailant causes a reasonable belief in the victim that a dangerous weapon exists and that he or she might suffer harm, actual proof that an assailant was armed is not always necessary. An assailant may, for example, use one hand and a covering so as to resemble a gun, thus causing the victim to believe that there was a dangerous weapon and that he or she could be injured. Even if the assailant uses a realistic-looking toy pistol, he could be charged with Armed Robbery.

EXAMPLES:

An assailant approaches his victim from the rear, places his arm around the victim's neck, holds a flat metal object to the victim's throat with the other hand, and says "Drop your purse or I'll cut your throat." Whether or not the assailant actually held a knife (rather than a screwdriver, pen, metal rod, etc.), upon his taking of the purse, he had committed Armed Robbery, for the victim could reasonably believe that the assailant did have a knife and that she was in danger.

A woman enters a loan office and asks to discuss a loan. While seated in the office with the loan officer, she tells him that she has a bomb in her purse and demands a sum of money. The act constitutes Armed Robbery.

ROBBERY—UNARMED

The elements of Unarmed Robbery are

*the felonious taking of money or property subject to larceny
*from the presence or person of another
*through force, violence, assault, or placing in fear
*but *without being armed with a dangerous weapon*.

EXAMPLE:
A large, muscular man enters an all-night diner. He orders the lone waitress to open the cash register and deliver its contents or suffer a beating. Out of fear, she gives him the money. Unarmed Robbery has been committed.

UNLAWFULLY DRIVING AWAY AUTOMOBILE (GRAND THEFT: AUTO)

The elements of this offense are

*the taking or driving away
*of a motor vehicle
*willfully and without authority.

This offense is usually regarded as a felony regardless of the actual value of the stolen auto at the time of the theft. If there is no *intent* to deprive permanently, taking a motor vehicle without permission may constitute the lesser offense of joyriding.

EXAMPLE:
Officers find a suspect in a used-car lot early in the morning. He is standing beside an auto with its engine running and no key in the ignition. He is not an employee and cannot explain his presence in the lot. Officers have sufficient circumstantial evidence to hold the suspect.

Chapter 8
A Glossary of Police
Diction and Usage

A, AN

A is used before a consonant or before the sound of *y* or *w*.

A *revolver*, a *suspect*, a *uniformed officer*, a *one-way street*.

An is used before a vowel or a silent *h*.

an *officer*, an *assault*, an *investigation*, an *unidentified man*, an *hourly check*.

ABBREVIATION

Follow departmental procedures (for example, *V.* for victim, *C.* or *Comp.* for complainant, and so on). In addition, the following guidelines may be helpful:

1. Abbreviate common titles that precede proper names:

    Lt. Sidney Scroop, Dr. Christopher Lane
    Mr. Phillip Raleigh
    Ms. Stella Astrophel

2. Abbreviate the names of some agencies, organizations, and institutions:

    FBI   ACLU   HEW
    LEAA   FSC   NEA

3. Abbreviate some technical terms, trade names, and scientific words:

    AM-FM   rpm   AMC
    mph   LEIN

4. Abbreviate ante meridiem (midnight to noon) and post meridiem (noon to midnight):

    > *6:30 a.m. (or 6:30 A.M.)*
    > *4:30 p.m. (or 4:30 P.M.)*

    Both are clear indications of time. Do not add "in the morning," "in the afternoon," or "o'clock."

Note: Do not abbreviate titles used without names.

Original	Revision
The Lt. advised booking	The lieutenant advised booking.

ACCEPT, EXCEPT

These words are often confused because as commonly pronounced they sound much alike. *Accept* (verb) means *to receive. Except* (verb) means *to exclude. Except* (preposition) means *but.*

He refused to accept *the bribe.*

The captain excepted *her from the sergeants' list.*

Everyone except *Ike was in uniform.*

ACTIVE VOICE

In active construction the simple subject is the *doer* of the action. In your reports, use the active voice whenever possible. It is more direct than the passive voice, and its use may help you avoid serious omissions. See *Passive Construction* also.

Officer Lear searched *and* handcuffed *the suspect. [Lear is the subject. He performed the search, and he handcuffed the suspect. Using the passive voice, an officer would write:* The suspect was searched and handcuffed by Officer Lear. *However, in the passive construction, officers sometimes* fail *to record the agent (in this case, Officer Lear), creating problems in later testimony.]*

*Officer Regan fired three shots at the fleeing auto. (*Compare: *Three shots were fired at the fleeing auto by Officer Regan.)*

Note: Do not change from active voice to passive voice in the same sentence without good reason.

*Officer Malach returned to patrol when he finished the report. (*Not: *Officer Malach returned to patrol when the report was finished by him.)*

ADJECTIVE

A word used to modify (describe or limit) a noun or pronoun.

The suspect ran into the dead-end *alley.*
Four *witnesses heard the gunshots.*

The officers were exhausted. *(*Exhausted *is a predicate adjective describing officers.)*

ADVERB

A word used to modify a verb, an adjective, or another adverb.

The suspect turned quickly. *(*Quickly *modifies the verb* turned.*)*

The suspect appeared extremely *agile. (*Extremely *modifies the predicate adjective* agile.*)*

Officer Lear drove very *slowly. (*Very *modifies the adverb* slowly.*)*

ADVISE

Use this verb for *give advice.* It is overused in police reports to mean *say, declare, state.*

Officer Lear advised the suspect of her right to remain silent.

Officer Regan advised the complainant to see the prosecutor on Monday.

But:

The suspect stated *that he had intended to pay for the merchandise but had forgotten. (The suspect is merely making a statement; he is not giving advice.)*

The witness told *the officers that they were too late to save the bleeding victim. (*Not: advised. *Perhaps you are too late, but you would do well to ignore the witness's "advice" and check the victim yourself.)*

Officer Oswald reported she had lost the suspect in the 1300 block of Donalbain. (This is a report on the situation, not advice on what to do about it.)

AFFECT, EFFECT

These words are commonly confused because they sound similar. *Affect,* as a verb, means *to influence* or *to assume. Effect,* as a verb, means *to bring about, to cause.* As a noun, *effect* means *result.*

The witness's lie will affect *the jury.*

The witness affected *a casual manner on the stand.*

The officers effected *their entrance through the front door.*

The defendant's tears produced the desired effect.

AGREEMENT: SUBJECT-VERB

A verb agrees with its subject in person and number.

1. A singular subject takes a singular verb; a plural subject takes a plural verb:

    The traffic safety officer investigates *all accidents. (Singular subject* officer *takes the singular verb* investigates.*)*

    The detectives investigate *robberies. (Plural subject* detectives *takes the plural verb* investigate.*)*

Note: In the present tense, only the third-person singular of regular verbs changes by adding an *s* or *es* to the root form:

Person	Singular	Plural
First	*I write*	*We write*
Second	*You write*	*You write*
Third	*He* writes	*They write*

2. Two or more subjects joined by *and* usually take a plural verb.

    Officers Lear *and* Regan appear *unconcerned.*

    The inspector *and his* driver are *in the street.*

3. When subjects are joined by or, nor, either . . . or, *or* neither . . . nor, *the verb will agree with the nearer subject:*

    Either the witnesses or the complainant is lying.

    Neither the complainant nor the witnesses are lying.

4. The indefinite pronouns *either, each, neither, anyone, anybody, everybody, everyone, someone, somebody, no one,* and *nobody* require singular verbs:

    Each *of the officers* is *responsible for her own scout car.*

    Everyone sells *field-day tickets.*

    Neither *of the officers in Scout 9-4* speaks *to the inspector.*

5.   *Who*, *which*, and *that* (relative pronouns) take the same number as their antecedents (an antecedent is the word to which the pronoun refers):

Officers who drive *recklessly are transferred to the motor traffic bureau.*

[Who *refers to* officers *(the antecedent); therefore,* who *is plural and takes the plural verb* drive.]

An officer who drives *carelessly will be disciplined. (*Who *refers to* officer; *therefore,* who *is singular and takes the singular verb* drives.)

She drives a patrol car that leaks *oil. (*That *refers to car; therefore,* that *is singular and takes the singular verb* leaks.)

Problems in Agreement:

1.   Do not be misled by words that separate a subject from its verb:

Original	Revision
A *description* of the two suspects *were given* to the dispatcher. (The singular noun *description* takes a singular verb. *Of the two suspects* is simply a phrase modifying *description* and does not influence the verb.)	A *description* of the two suspects *was* given to dispatcher. (*Or: Descriptions* of the two suspects *were* given to the dispatcher.)

2.   Do not be confused by the *there-verb-subject* pattern. In such constructions, where the subject follows the verb, the verb still agrees with the subject:

Original	Revision
There *was* two *suspects* in the vehicle. (*Suspects*, the subject of the sentence, is plural and requires the plural verb.)	There *were* two *suspects* in the vehicle.

AGREEMENT: PRONOUN—ANTECEDENT

A pronoun agrees with its antecedent (the word to which it refers) in person, number, and gender.

I *lost* my *nightstick at roll call.*

We *shall take* our *car to the city garage.*

You *can complete* your *report when you are off duty.*

Officer Messer *joined* her *partner and said* she *would drive.*

Officers Lear *and* Regan *will finish* their *tour in an hour.*

Note: Words like *each*, *every*, *everyone*, *either*, *neither*, and *nobody* are followed by singular pronouns.

Neither *of the officers brought* his *ticket book.*

Every *officer knows* she *will make sergeant.*

Everybody *has completed* her *tour of duty.*

Does anyone *know what* he *is doing?*

Do not use a singular pronoun to refer to a plural antecedent or a plural pronoun to refer to a singular antecedent:

Original	Revision
Officers observed that the *women* had blood on *her* clothes. [*Women* (the antecedent) is plural; *her* (the pronoun) is singular. Perhaps *women* is a misspelling.]	Officers observed that the *women* had blood on *their* clothes. (*Or:* Officers observed that the *woman* had blood on *her* clothes.)

ALLUDE, ELUDE

These words are confused with one another, because when they are pronounced, they sound much alike. *Allude* means *to refer indirectly*; *elude* means *to escape, evade*. (Clearly, officers will use elude more often.)

The witness alluded *to the victim's profession.*

How could the suspect elude *six officers?*

ALL READY, ALREADY

All ready means *everything* or *everyone* is ready. *Already* means *previously* or *by this time*.

The platoon commander reported that the officers were all ready *for their tour of duty.*

The officers searched the building, but the suspect had already *gone.*

ALL TOGETHER, ALTOGETHER

All together means *everything* or *everybody* in one place. *Altogether* means *wholly, completely*.

The lieutenant had his platoon all together *for the last time.*

The defendant appeared altogether *confident of her testimony.*

AMBIGUOUS

Ambiguous means having *two or more possible meanings.*

Officer Jones alone *can capture the suspect. (Does it mean that* only *Officer Jones can capture the suspect, or that other officers aren't needed?)*

The lieutenant has ordered all officers to stop drinking in the park. *(Who has been doing the drinking?)*

The suspect broke the bottle on the end table, striking the victim in the eye. *(Did the suspect break the bottle and then strike the victim? Or did the victim get hit by glass fragments when the bottle hit the table?)*

No one was killed because the semitruck struck an unoccupied parked auto. *(Was someone killed for another reason? Did the accident prevent any deaths? Or is the car's being unoccupied the only reason there were no deaths? Try a comma after* killed.*)*

AMOUNT, NUMBER

Amount refers to things in mass. *Number* refers to items that can be counted.

Officers found a large amount *of heroin under the dashboard.*

The reduction in the budget has decreased the number *of officers on patrol.*

Note: The common error in police reports is to use *amount* for *number*:

Original	Revision
Officers were stopped at the door by the large *amount* of people standing in the entryway.	Officers were stopped at the door by the large *number* of people standing in the entryway.

AN

See *A*

APOSTROPHE

Use the apostrophe to show possession; to form the plural of numbers, letters, and symbols; and to indicate omissions in contractions.

1. Possession. Show possession by adding an apostrophe or an apostrophe and the letter *s*. Generally, add only an apostrophe if the word already ends in *s*:

Singular	Plural
The *officer's* baton	The *officers'* batons
The *suspect's* shoes	The *suspects'* shoes
The *child's* mother	The *children's* mothers
Captain *Jones'* orders	Captain and Sergeant *Joneses'* orders

2. Plural of *numbers, letters*, and *symbols*. Form these plurals by adding an apostrophe and the letter *s*:

> *The officers found four* 38's *in the glove compartment.*

> *Officers discovered five swastikas (卐's) painted on the refrigerator door.*

3. Contractions. Use an apostrophe to indicate missing letters or numbers:

> *I* can't *see the target.*

> *Suspect was arrested three times in* '73

Note: In police reports the most common misuse of the apostrophe is the *unnecessary apostrophe.* Do *not* use an apostrophe when you simply need the plural:

Original	Revision
Officer's Lear and Regan investigated.	*Officers* Lear and Regan investigated.
Complainant informed *officers'* that. . . .	Complainant informed *officers* that. . . .

APPRAISE, APPRISE

Appraise means *to estimate the value. Apprise* means to *notify.*

Although the officer reported serious damage to both cars, the insurance adjustor appraised *the repair costs at less than $75 for each car.*

Dispatch apprised *officers that the suspect was armed.*

BREAK, BRAKE

Do not confuse these words. The device used to stop or slow a machine or vehicle is a *brake.*

The driver stated he was unable to brake *in time to avoid the accident.*

BREAKDOWN

In standard English, *breakdown* means *collapse.* Bureaucrats use it to mean *classification, itemization,* or *analyses.* This use is well established, and officers can adopt it; however, consider the following:

We have a complete breakdown *of traffic enforcement on the West Side.*

What's the breakdown *on officers available for riot duty?*

The breakdown *of prisoners in the outlying precincts shows a need for new jails.*

BUSTED, BURSTED

Both are often incorrectly used for *burst*:

Original	Revision
The officers *busted* (or *bursted*) into the room.	The officers *burst* into the room.

CAPITAL LETTERS

Use capital (uppercase) letters as required by conventional usage.

1. Capitalize *proper nouns and proper adjectives* (nouns that distinguish unique persons, places, or things):

   Major Malvolio *commands Post 12.*

   Many agencies want officers who speak Spanish.

   The French *restaurant catered to off-duty officers.*

2. Capitalize *common nouns* used in conjunction with a proper noun:

   Officers discovered an open door at 1313 Walton Street*, the Walton Elementary* School.

   Captain Clink graduated from Ferris State College.

   But:

   The officers were unable to locate the correct street *although they had both attended* schools *in the area before going to* college.

3. Capitalize *names* of *races* and *ethnic groups*:

   Indian, Negro, Caucasian, Eskimo, Chicano

   Note: Do *not* capitalize *black* or *white*:

   Officers arrested eight blacks *and eight* whites *for disturbing the peace.*

4. Capitalize *points of the compass when they refer to specific geographical locations*:

    Many of the local residents formerly lived in the South.

    Wanted posters have been sent to all agencies in the Middle West.

    But do *not* capitalize compass points when they refer to *direction*:

    Officer Regan pursued the suspect south *on Lee Boulevard.*

    Suspect turned left (east).

5. Capitalize *titles that precede names*:

    When Officer *Lincoln stopped the speeding vehicle, she discovered the driver was* Governor *Grinch.*

6. Capitalize the *first word of a direct quotation*:

    The witness asked: "Where are you cops when somebody needs you?"

7. Capitalize *brand names* and *registered trademarks*:

    Suspect was wearing faded Levis; *she had a can of* Stroh's *in one hand and a* Colt *in the other.*

8. Capitalize the *days of the week*, the *names of the months, holy days, holidays,* and *festivals*:

    On Tuesday, December 25, *all officers attended the precinct* Christmas *party.*

Note: In addition to these standard practices, we suggest officers capitalize *Suspect*, *Witness*, *Victim*, and *Complainant* in their reports when these words refer to specific persons:

Officers apprehended the Suspect *as he left the scene.*

The Witness *could not identify the* Victim.

The Complainant *reported her auto was stolen during the afternoon.*

Some agencies also require the use of capital letters for the entire family name:

Complainant, Felicia A. FALSTAFF, *stated she was robbed while walking home.*

This lets the reader find and extract information more easily.

CAPITAL, CAPITOL

Capitol refers to the *building*; everything else is *capital*:

The capitol *is in Lansing, the* capital *of Michigan.*

Murder is a capital *crime.*

Some jurists are opposed to capital *punishment.*

CITE, SIGHT, SITE

Cite means *to quote, to refer to*, or *to summon. Sight* means *a thing seen.* A *site* is a *building location*:

Officer Lear cited *from Section III, Paragraph A, of the Motor Vehicle Code to substantiate his charge.*

After eight hours of patrol, officers viewed the barn as a welcome sight.

The old Ninth Precinct formerly stood on this site.

COLLISION

A *collision* should involve at least two *moving* objects:

The fire truck, going east on York, collided *with the police car, which was going south on Lancaster.*

The suspect's vehicle struck *the lamppost and stopped. (It did* not collide *with the lamppost.)*

COLON

Use the colon (:), following a main clause, to introduce an *explanation*, a *formal quotation*, or a *list*:

The officers disliked the inspector for one reason: he had never worked on the street.

The complainant stated: "I was walking down the sidewalk when suddenly I felt something hit the side of my head."

The complainant reported the following items missing:

One (1) refrigerator: "Hotpoint," 17 cubic feet, frostless, coppertone with chrome trim. Taken from the basement.

Value $379.00

One (1) cooking stove: "Tappan," electric, 30 inch, four burners, self-cleaning oven, coppertone. Taken from the kitchen.

Value $250.00

Note: Do not use a colon in the middle of a clause:

Original	Revision
On riot duty were: Scroop, Peters, Bardolph, and Bronson. (The colon is used incorrectly in the middle of the clause.)	On riot duty were Scroop, Peters, Bardolph, and Bronson. (*Or:* The following officers were on riot duty: Scroop, Peters, Bardolph, and Bronson.)

COMMA

A comma is the most frequently used punctuation mark. It usually indicates a slight pause; thus, you should use your "ear" to help in placing commas. Essentially, commas have two functions: they *separate* sentence elements, and they *enclose* sentence elements.

1. Use commas *to separate two independent clauses joined by a coordinating conjunction.* Independent clauses are clauses that can stand alone. The coordinating conjunctions are *and*, *or*, *for*, *but*, and *nor*:

   The officers searched the building, but *they were unable to find the escaped rattlesnake. (*The . . . building *is one independent clause;* they . . . rattlesnake *is the other.)*

   *Officers Lear and Regan covered the front entrance, and Officers Cord and Granger took their positions at the rear. (*Officers . . . entrance *is one independent clause;* and Officers . . . rear *is the other. Note how the comma indicates the break in the sentence; otherwise, the three* ands *in one sentence would momentarily confuse a reader.)*

2. Use commas *to separate items in a series:*

   Officers Stangl, Randolf, *and* Antonio *assisted at the scene of the accident. (Words in a series.)*

   The inspector wants all officers to polish their shoes, shine their leather, *and* clean their service revolvers *before being inspected by the superintendent. (Phrases in a series.)*

   The mayor realizes that you are fine officers, that you are dedicated, *and* that you are committed to enforcing laws impartially; *nevertheless,* she *would still like to discuss her son's arrest. (Clauses in a series.)*

3.   Use commas *to separate items in addresses and dates*:

> *The suspect stated that he lives at* The Hookery, 13 Restoration Road, Pogi, Michigan.

> *One* Saturday, January 10, 1976, *only three patrol cars were in service.*

4.   Use commas *to separate introductory elements* from the rest of the sentence:

> (*a*)   *Verbal phrases.* Verbals are simply verb forms used as adjectives, nouns, or adverbs. There are three: *participles*, *gerunds*, and *infinitives*. A *participle* is a verbal *adjective*. It may be either the *present participle* (*root* + *ing*: *singing*, *shooting*, *crying*) or the *past participle (sung, shot, cried)*. A *gerund* is the present participle used as a *noun*. An *infinitive* is the root form usually preceded by the word *to*. Normally, you will not need to distinguish between these forms, but you should put commas after them to avoid confusing your reader:

Original	Revision
Before shooting the officer cried, "Halt!" (For a moment, it appears that the officer was shot.)	Before shooting, the officer cried, "Halt!" (The pause marked by the comma prevents confusion.)
To succeed the inspector drove his officers relentlessly.	*To succeed*, the inspector drove his officers relentlessly.

> (*b*)   *Dependent clauses.* Dependent clauses cannot stand alone:

Original	Revision
After you finish your report will be sent to the detectives.	*After you finish*, your report will be sent to the detectives.

> (*c*)   *Long or transitional phrases.* A series of phrases forming a long construction may require a comma. A comma is also necessary for a *transitional* phrase.

> To the left of the table in the center of the kitchen, *officers found several patches of blood. (A long series of phrases.)*

> *Thirty-six officers were sent directly to the disturbance;* in addition, *forty officers were placed on alert. (A transitional phrase.)*

> (*d*)   *Confusing elements.* Commas may be required to prevent misreading:

Original	Revision
Only a few moments before Officer Lear backed into the inspector's private auto. (For a moment, this ap-	*Only a few moments before*, Officer Lear backed into the inspector's private auto.

pears to be a sentence fragment raising this question: what happened before Lear backed into the inspector's car?)

Inside Officer Regan interviewed a witness.	Inside, Officer Regan interviewed a witness.

5. Use commas *to enclose nonrestrictive elements*. Nonrestrictive elements are words, phrases, or clauses that simply *add more information* but are *not essential* to the meaning of a sentence:

> *Mrs. Wiggs,* the complainant, *declared that only a scoundrel would steal a lady's dictionary. (*The complainant *simply adds information about a person already identified by name.)*

> *Officers Lear and Regan,* no longer needed at the scene, *were cleared for another assignment. (Their being* cleared *for another assignment suggests they are no longer needed; therefore, the phrase is not essential.)*

> *Officer Regan,* who likes loud noises, *turned on the siren. (One would hope the officer had another reason for turning on the siren.)*

Note: Do *not* enclose *restrictive* elements with commas. These elements are words, phrases, or clauses that are *essential* to the meaning of a sentence:

> *The complainant identified the officer* who had allegedly struck her with his baton. *(The clause* who . . . baton *restricts the meaning of* officer; *it points out* which officer *was identified. It is, therefore, essential.)*

COMMA FAULT

Do not join independent clauses with a comma only.

Original	Revision
The driver of the suspect vehicle accelerated and turned down Wilbert Street, upon turning the corner, the suspect's car collided head-on with another vehicle. (The *comma fault* occurs between *Street* and *upon*.)	The driver of the suspect vehicle accelerated and turned down Wilbert Street. Upon turning the corner, the suspect's car collided head-on with another vehicle.

There are several ways to correct a comma fault:

1. *Use a coordinating conjunction with the comma:*

Original	Revision
At Shires and Ende Officers Friar and Knight directed traffic, Officer Clarke operated the traffic signal.	At Shires and Ende Officers Friar and Knight directed traffic, *and* Officer Clarke operated the traffic signal.

2. *Make one clause dependent.*

Original	Revision
Officers carefully sifted through the debris left by the explosion, they found no evidence. (Both clauses are independent.)	*Although* officers carefully sifted through the debris left by the explosion, they found no evidence. (The first clause is now dependent, and so the comma fault has been removed.)

3. *Use a semicolon or a period:*

Original	Revision
Officers pursued the suspect south into the alley, however, they lost sight of him between the houses at 1313 and 1319 Manciple Street.	Officers pursued the suspect south into the alley; however, they lost sight. . . . (*Or*: Officers pursued the suspect south into the alley. However, they. . . .)

Note: The comma fault causes only mild confusion when the independent clauses are side by side. However, when phrases or dependent clauses come between the independent clauses, the reader may have difficulty *attaching them to the correct independent clause* :

> The officers heard the shooting, as they kicked down the door and entered, *they saw the victim lying face down under the table in the adjoining room.*

What was the correct sequence of events? Does the dependent clause, *as . . . entered*, belong with the first independent clause or the second? If the officers *first* heard the shooting and *then* kicked in the door, the sentence should read:

> The officers heard the shooting. As they kicked down the door and entered, *they saw the victim lying face down under the table in the adjoining room.*

This would indicate that some time had elapsed between the *officers' hearing the shots and their entry*.
Or does the dependent clause belong with the *first independent* clause? If the officers *heard the shooting at the same time they entered*, the sentence should read:

> The officers heard the shooting as they kicked down the door and entered. *They saw the victim lying face down under the table in the adjoining room.*

This would indicate that *all three actions*—hearing the shots, entering, and seeing the victim—occurred *at nearly the same time*.

CONSCIENCE, CONSCIOUS

Conscience is a noun meaning a *person's sense of what is right*. *Conscious*, an adjective, means *aware*.

The embezzler stated her troubled conscience *forced her to confess*.

Although the victim was conscious, *he was bleeding profusely*.

CONFUSED SENTENCES

This is a catchall label for *muddled* sentences. Often, such sentences defy analysis; consequently, there is no *one good way* to revise them. We suggest the following steps: first, rearrange the parts so that there is some kind of logical order; second, break the passage into shorter sentences; third, if all else fails, start over again.

Original	Revision
Officer Lear radioed for assistance in securing the scene at 3:15 p.m. and the need for an ambulance was required. (*At 3:15 p.m.* is ambiguous: did the officer call at 3:15 p.m., or is that when he will need assistance? Was it the *need* that was required or the *ambulance*? The writer is using *need* as both the *object* of *securing* and the *subject* of *was required*; either way, this is nonsense.)	At 3:15 p.m., Officer Lear requested assistance and an ambulance.
Upon approaching the parked vehicle, the suspect in the driver's seat turned and saw the patrol car, the driver of the suspect's vehicle accelerated and turned down Simmers Street upon turning the corner the suspect's car collides head-on with another vehicle. (Presumably, the writer means the patrol car *approached* the suspect vehicle. As written, however, the suspect is ap-	As officers approached, the driver of the suspect vehicle turned and saw the patrol car. He then accelerated, turned onto Simmers Street, and struck another vehicle head-on.

proaching a third vehicle. There is a comma fault between *patrol car* and *the driver*. The remainder of the passage is a *run-on* sentence; there are *two independent clauses* with no punctuation to indicate a separation. Consequently, the reader must infer that the phrase *upon turning the corner* belongs with the last part of the sentence, *the suspect's* car ... *vehicle*. The writer has also changed tenses from the past to the present by using *collides*.)

He was advised by this trooper that his assistance was required to complete a damage report to state property and the nature of the capture of the suspect in custody. (*Advised* is jargon. *And ... custody* is wordy, awkward, and confused. It is either an object of *to complete* or a phrase modifying *damage report*. In the first sense, it means *to complete the nature of the suspect in custody*; in the second, *to complete a damage report on the nature of the suspect in custody*.)

Trooper Puck reported the apprehension of the suspect and damage to state property.

CONTINUAL, CONTINUOUS

Continual means *recurring at intervals*; *continuous* means *uninterrupted*.

The continual *interruptions caused the detectives to postpone the interrogation.*

The suspect greeted the officers with a continuous *stream of profanity.*

COULD OF

Incorrect for *could have*. The writing error stems from the sound of the spoken contraction *could've*.

The officers could have *arrested him for drunk driving. (*Not: *could of arrested.)*

COUNCIL, COUNSEL

A *council* is a *governing* or *advisory* board. *Counsel* (noun) means *advice* or *attorney*. As a verb, *counsel* means *advise*.

The president of the Police Officers Association addressed the city council.

The defendant's counsel counseled *him to plead guilty.*

CREDIBLE, CREDULOUS

Credible means *believable*. *Credulous* means *gullible*.

The prosecutor believes officers give credible *testimony*.

Apparently, the complainant was credulous *enough to be deceived by the "pigeon drop" trick.*

DANGLING MODIFIER

See *Modifiers*.

DASH

Use dashes *to emphasize parenthetical expressions or to enclose appositional material within a sentence.*

Suspect No. 1—the one with the Thompson submachine gun—escaped through the rear door.

Three officers—Lear, Webster, and Flecknoe—were injured in the accident. (Lear . . . Flecknoe is an appositive: a word or group of words *used to* rename *or* explain *some other word in the sentence.)*

Note: Dashes *emphasize*; parentheses *de-emphasize*; and commas *enclose*.

DATA

This is the *plural* form of the Latin *datum*, "something known." Strictly speaking, it should take a plural verb. In actual practice, however, the singular *datum* is rarely used. Many writers use a *singular* verb with *data* when it means *information* (i.e., facts or figures):

These data are for the annual report.

The data *on burglary incidence in the Ninth Precinct* is *now available.*

DEPRECATE, DEPRECIATE

To deprecate means *to express disapproval (of). To depreciate* is *to lessen the value (of).*

The mayor publicly deprecated *the police department's performance during the riot.*

The city council, however, refused to depreciate *the department's role in restoring order.*

DISINTERESTED, UNINTERESTED

Disinterested means *impartial. Uninterested* means *not interested.*

Officers were unable to find a disinterested *witness.*

The complainant was uninterested *in the officer's questions.*

DIVISION OF WORDS INTO SYLLABLES

When the last word of a line must be continued on the next line, divide the word by syllables:

The officers in Scout 9-4, who are noted for their efficiency, grace and cheer-fulness, received a standing ovation at the awards ceremony. (Cheer-ful-ness is properly divided by syllables.)

Note: In police reports, you do not have to keep a straight right-hand margin. When in doubt about how to break a word, start the word in question on the next line.

DUAL, DUEL

Dual means *double. Duel* means a *formal fight with deadly weapons.*

The suspect vehicle had dual *exhausts.*

The officers arrived just as the duel *began.*

ELICIT, ILLICIT

Elicit means *to evoke, to draw forth. Illicit* means *illegal.*

The detectives could not elicit *any further information from the suspect.*

The police raid temporarily halted the illicit *traffic in drugs.*

ELUDE

See *allude*.

EMINENT, IMMINENT

Eminent means *distinguished, renowned. Imminent* means *impending, about to happen.*

The suspect informed officers that he was an eminent *member of the community.*

The officer fired, for she believed she was in imminent *danger.*

EXCEPT

See *Accept*.

EXPLICIT, IMPLICIT

Explicit means *stated directly. Implicit* means *stated indirectly, suggested.*

Sergeant Duessa gave explicit *orders to enforce parking regulations on Britomart Boulevard.*

The inspector told the officers to improve their personal appearance. Implicit *in the statement was the threat of disciplinary action if there was no improvement.*

FEEL

Use *believe* rather than *feel* in police reports. Precisely, *believe* means *think, have strong convictions about. Feel* suggests *emotion,* not *reason.* Although the common practice is to use *feel* in the sense of *believe,* you would do well to avoid the hint of emotionalism in your reports.

Officers believe *the suspect entered through the skylight. (*Not: *Officers* feel *the suspect entered through the skylight.)*

FORMALLY, FORMERLY

Formally means *in the proper manner. Formerly* means *in the past.*

The commissioner formally *presented the marksmanship trophy to the Ninth Precinct.*

Sergeant Fortinbras was formerly *in the mounted division.*

HEAR, HERE

Hear is a verb meaning *to perceive, to notice* (associate *ear* with *hear*). *Here* is usually an adverb meaning *at* or *in this place.*

The suspect insisted that he could not hear *the officer's questions.*

The accident occurred here.

ILLICIT

See *Elicit.*

IMMINENT

See *Eminent.*

IMPLICIT

See *Explicit.*

ITS, IT'S

Its is the possessive of *it*. *It's* is a contraction of *it is.*

The vehicle overturned and landed on its *side.*

It's *too late to call for assistance.*

JARGON

Do *not use jargon:* unintelligible or confused words and construction. Say what you mean as directly as you can. Use everyday, ordinary words instead of technical or "police" language. Remember, not all your readers are police officers, and not all police officers are in your department.

Original	Revision
R/O's received an *I* and *H* of a possible *10-96* at 730 Flecknoe, *L* and *S* authorized, at 1440, when their *10-20* was Archimago and Florimell. (Your readers may not know either your departmental shorthand or the ten series; therefore, they could not understand this passage.)	At 1440 hrs., . . . , Officers . . . , at Archimago and Florimell, received a radio run: 730 Flecknoe, mental patient, code three. (The *I* and *H*, meaning identify yourself and *handle*, is simply one way of finding an available unit. It is unnecessary in the report.)

Officer Dormant *blew up* the suspect with four rounds from his service revolver. (This is police slang.)

Four bullets fired by Officer Dormant *struck* and *killed* the suspect.

The *unit* arrived at the scene at 0433 hrs., parking the *squad* just north of the seed company. (What is the *unit*? Presumably, unit means the *patrol car and the officers*. If so, who—or what—parked the squad?)

Officers arrived (0433 hrs.) and parked the patrol car north of the seed company.

LEAD, LED

Led is the past tense of the verb *to lead*.

The officers led *the suspect to the car.*

LEAVE, LET

Leave in the sense of *cause to remain* and *go away from* is often confused with *let* in the sense of *allow, permit,* or *cause.*

All officers will leave *the station immediately after roll call.*

Mounted officers will not let *anyone else feed their horses.*

Let *all the officers know of the commissioner's orders.*

LOOSE, LOSE

These words are frequently confused in spelling. *Loose*, as an adjective or adverb, means *free from restraint, unconfined. Lose* is a verb meaning *to fail to keep, to suffer defeat, to misplace.*

The complainant objected to dogs running loose *in the street.*

The sergeant asked, "How could you lose *your service revolver?"*

MODIFIERS, DANGLING AND MISPLACED

A *dangling modifier* is a sentence element that does not logically modify any word in the sentence. Most frequently these modifiers appear at the beginning of a sentence. Readers tend to connect such opening modifiers with the nearest word, usually the subject. Therefore, you should make sure that the opening modifier *does modify the subject.*

Original	Revision
Activating the emergency equipment, the suspect turned left on Main. (*Activating . . . equipment* modifies the subject, *suspect*. Is the *suspect driving* the patrol car?)	*As officers activated the emergency equipment*, the suspect turned left on Main.
Upon searching the suspect, he became hostile and resisted. (*Upon . . . suspect* modifies the subject *he*. Therefore *he* must be searching the suspect; but *he is* the suspect. In this sentence, the suspect *searches himself* and *resists* the search at the same time.)	*Upon being searched*, the suspect became hostile and resisted.

The *misplaced modifier* is just what the name denotes: a modifier that loses effect because it is in the wrong place:

Original	Revision
Suspect's car was taken to the police garage to be held for the detectives *by the Triple Z Wrecker Service*. (*By . . . Service* is a prepositional phrase which apparently modifies *held*; consequently, the civilian towing service is to secure the car for the detectives.)	Suspect's car was taken to the police garage *by the Triple Z Wrecker Service* to be held for the detectives. (Now the towing company *merely towed the car*.) *Or:* The Triple Z Wrecker Service towed the suspect's car to the police garage. Officers escorted the vehicle and placed a "hold" on it for detectives.
Officer Mouse found six marijuana cigarettes outside the car *rolled with toilet paper*. (*Rolled . . . paper* apparently modifies *car*. This is a possibility; people do strange things with toilet paper, especially on Halloween. Probably, though, this writer meant the cigarettes were rolled with toilet paper.)	Outside the car, Officer Mouse found six marijuana cigarettes *rolled with toilet paper*. (*Rolled . . . paper* now modifies *cigarettes*.)
Officers observed suspect vehicle parked behind the building *with two occupants in it*. (What had *two occupants*—the car or the building?)	Officers saw suspect vehicle *with two occupants* parked behind the building.

MYSELF, YOURSELF, ETC.

Use these words as *intensifiers* or as *reflexive* pronouns. Do *not* use them as *personal* pronouns.

The commissioner, himself, *will present the awards. (*Intensifying *pronoun to* stress commissioner.)

The officer cut herself *on the broken glass. (*Reflexive *pronoun: the action of cutting is* reflected *back to the* actor, *the officer.)*

The complainant refused to speak to me. *(*Not: myself.)

NOTED, NOTORIOUS

Both mean *widely known*, but *noted* is *usually used in a favorable sense*, whereas *notorious* is *usually used in an unfavorable sense*.

The noted *criminologist Raskal Nikov addressed the graduating class at the police academy.*

The officers in Scout 999 were notorious *for "jumping" runs.*

NUMBER

See *Amount*.

OMISSIONS

Do not carelessly leave out necessary words.

Original	Revision
Suspect was described as tall, with brown, curly hair and eyes. (There are two possible ways to read this: *brown* and *curly* modify both *hair* and *eyes*; thus the suspect has *curly eyes*. Or the suspect has brown, curly hair, and he *has* eyes.	Suspect was described as tall, with brown, curly hair and *brown* eyes.
Officer Loser had six bird-shot pellets removed from his hand *and then wrapped*. (Did the officer have the pellets wrapped for evidence? Or was it the officer's *hand* that was wrapped?)	Officer Loser had six bird-shot pellets removed from his hand and then *had his hand* wrapped.

Officer Lear accompanied the suspect vehicle to the police garage and *was turned over* to Officer Edmund. (For some reason, *Officer Lear was turned over* to Officer Edmund.)

Officer Lear escorted the suspect vehicle to the police garage where *it was turned over* to Officer Edmund.

In order to use fewer words, some officers leave out the subject. This can create confusion.

Officer Lear arrived at the scene at 1430 hrs. Knocked and was admitted. Interviewed the complainant. Stated that someone had broken in through the rear window during the night. *(Who stated someone . . . night? If Officer Lear is the understood subject in the preceding sentences, he must be the subject in this one.)*

PARALLEL STRUCTURE

Use the *same grammatical form* for each item in a series.

Original

Backup officers *arrived* and *assisting* in controlling the suspect. (*Arrived* is past tense; *assisting* is the present participle.)

Revision

Backup officers *arrived* and *assisted* in controlling the suspect.

At 2:30 a.m., the suspect was *handcuffed, searched,* and *two more switchblade knives were found.* (The comma between *handcuffed* and *searched* indicates a continuation of the series of *past participles.* Instead, an *independent clause* follows.)

At 2:30 a.m., the suspect was handcuffed and searched. *Two* more switchblade knives were found.

Sgt. Smith *initialed* the evidence, *logged* it in the evidence book, and, in the presence of Officer Lear, was *locked up* in the evidence room. (The writer uses the *active voice* for the first two verbs in the series and then changes to the *passive voice.* Result: *Sgt. Smith was locked up,* not the evidence.)

Sgt. Smith *initialed* the evidence, logged it in the evidence book, and, in the presence of Officer Lear, *locked it up* in the evidence room.

Mrs. Monk's lip was bloody; her right eye was *swollen and bruised arms.* (Do *swollen* and *bruised* modify *eye*

Mrs. Monk's lip was bloody; her right eye was swollen; and her *arms were bruised.*

or *arms* or *both*? The confusion stems from breaking the series of independent clauses.)

PARENTHESES

Commas, dashes, and *parentheses* are all used to separate parenthetical elements. Of these, *parentheses* give the *least emphasis.* Use parentheses for references, for figures introducing items in a list, and for *information you may need later.*

The suspect vehicle (Ref.: <u>Sec. 26A</u>*) struck the lamppost and continued south. (The parenthetical element* refers *the reader to the section containing a description of the suspect vehicle.)*

Officers applying for a transfer must comply with this procedure: (1) submit a written request in triplicate on Departmental Form 99/13 to your immediate supervisor; (2) hand-carry the approved original and copy one to division; (3) hand-carry the approved original to the head of personnel at police headquarters.

At 1420 hrs., Scout 9-4 (Officers Segal and O'Brien) arrived at the scene to assist; however, help was not needed. (Since these officers were not involved in the incident, the reader does not need their names. Yet, if complications arise, you *may need them to back up your testimony.)*

PASSED, PAST

Both are past participles of the word *pass*, but their usage differs. Study the following:

Regan has passed *the sergeants' examination.*

Troopers passed *fourteen mileposts before overtaking the suspect.*

Officer Lear passed *his flashlight to Regan.*

Officers drove slowly past *the deserted lumberyard.*

In the past, *officers worked extra duty without compensation.*

Some past *practices remain practical.*

PASSIVE CONSTRUCTION

Many police officers are overly fond of passive constructions, or subject-verb combinations in which the *subject is acted upon* by an agent that may or may not be identified. Such constructions are usually wordy and can be confusing.

Original	Revision
It was ascertained that the suspect was not injured and *was* at that time placed under arrest on a charge of theft attempt. (*Who* ascertained the Suspect was uninjured? Note how the passive construction leads the student into further difficulty. What is the subject of the third *was*? Either *it* is the subject, meaning *it* was arrested, which is absurd; or the sentence means that *it was ascertained that the suspect was placed under arrest.* If so, *who* arrested him?)	Officers determined that the suspect was not injured. They then arrested him for theft attempt.
When the officers approached the suspect vehicle, *it was noted by the officers* that the driver was slumped over the steering wheel. (This is wordy.)	Upon approaching the suspect vehicle, *officers noted* that the driver was slumped over the steering wheel.
A hunting knife *was found* on the suspect during the search. (The danger here lies in the possibility of leaving out the name of the officer who conducted the search.)	Officer Lear *searched* the suspect and *found* a hunting knife.
As the unit *was being placed* into motion by Trooper Lear, *it was observed* by him that the suspect was running out the rear door of the building.	Driving forward, Trooper Lear *saw* the suspect running out the rear door of the building.

PERIOD

Use a period at *the end of a sentence* (declarative or imperative) and in *some abbreviations.*

The officers completed their check at 4:30 p.m. (Note that only one period is necessary after m.)

The complainant asked if the officers had found anything. Mr. Arch E. Mayes, the complainant, refused to testify.

PERSONAL, PERSONNEL

Personal is an adjective meaning *pertaining to a certain person. Personnel* is a noun meaning *persons employed in any work, job,* etc.

The suspect stated that personal *problems caused her to surrender.*

The inspector seems pleased with the personnel *in the precinct.*

PRECEDE, PROCEED

Precede means *to go before. Proceed* means *to continue, to go on. Proceed plus an infinitive* is an overused construction in police reports. Often the word *proceed* is unnecessary and can be eliminated without losing the meaning of the sentence.

Police cars will precede *all fire department units on alarms in that area.*

Officers proceeded *to question the complainant. (Proceed here is unnecessary. Write: Officers questioned the complainant.)*

PRINCIPAL, PRINCIPLE

Principal means *chief* or *foremost. Principle* means *general* or *fundamental truth.*

His principal *fault is an inability to act under pressure.*

The department needs more men and women of principle.

QUESTION MARK

Use the question mark after a *direct* question.

Complainant asked: "What are you cops going to do about all those hot rodders?"

What is the shortest route to police headquarters?

QUIET, QUITE

These can be confused if the final two letters are transposed. *Quiet* means *calm, not noisy; quite* means *completely, entirely.*

Officer Lear ordered the suspect to remain quiet.

The officers were unable to quiet *the crowd.*

The witness appeared quite *disgusted.*

QUOTATION MARKS

Use quotation marks to set off words that were actually spoken or written.

The campus officer approached the violator's car, doffed his cap, and asked the driver, an English professor: "Whither goest thou, O thou speedy one?"

As the suspect ran from the officer, she continually shouted: "Don't shoot, officer. It's just a misdemeanor!"

Note: At the end of a quoted passage, periods and commas go *inside* the quotation marks; colons and semicolons go *outside*. Question marks and exclamation points go *inside* if they apply to the quoted matter; *outside*, if they don't.

REFERENCE OF PRONOUNS

Use pronouns with clear, definite antecedents.

Original	Revision
Backup officers arrived and helped Officer Lear subdue the suspect, during *which* suspect was injured. (What is the antecedent of *which*?)	Backup officers arrived and helped Officer Lear subdue the suspect. During the *struggle*, the suspect was injured.
Suspect was transported to Patrick Hospital, *who* was then taken by officers to the prison ward. (The *hospital* was taken to the prison ward?)	Officers transported suspect to the prison ward at Patrick Hospital.
When officers arrived at the scene, *they* told *them* that *they* had already gone. (To whom do the *theys* refer?)	When officers arrived at the scene, *witnesses* told them that the *assailants* had already gone.
The complainant stated that *he* had seen the suspect as *he* entered the building but that *he* didn't recognize *him*. (Who *entered* the building? Was it the *complainant* who couldn't recognize the *suspect*? Or was the *suspect* unable to recognize the *complainant*?)	Complainant stated that as he was entering the building he saw the suspect. Complainant did not recognize the suspect. [*Or:* Complainant believed suspect did not recognize him. *Or:* Complainant stated that he saw the suspect entering the building. (Rest as above.)]

RESPECTFULLY, RESPECTIVELY

Respectfully means *with respect. Respectively* means *in order cited.*

Officer Lear respectfully *greeted the council members.*

Officers Dimitri, Regan, and Cord are assigned to Scouts 9-4, 9-6, and 9-9, respectively.

SEMICOLON

Use the semicolon *to separate independent clauses* and *elements in a series* that already has commas.

*Within three minutes of receiving the call, the officers arrived at the scene; however, the burglars had already fled. (*Within . . . scene *is one independent clause;* however . . . fled *is the other.)*

Officers were surprised when the alleged intruders turned out to be Dr. Roland R. Rosencrantz, president, Elsinore State College; Prof. George G. Guildenstern, head of the English Department; and Dr. Polly Polonius, vice president.

STATIONARY, STATIONERY

Stationary means *fixed, immobile. Stationery* means *writing materials.*

Officer Lear remained stationary *outside the rear door.*

The commissioner issued an order prohibiting the use of departmental stationery *for private correspondence.*

TENSE

Tense is the verb property that expresses *time* of action or *time* of condition. In English these divisions of time, *past, present,* and *future,* are indicated by six tenses: *present, past, future, present perfect, past perfect,* and *future perfect.* Study carefully the following comments and examples concerning the *meaning of time* in each tense. For the *formation* of each tense, study the table at the end of the section.

The Primary Tenses:

1. *Present Tense.* The present tense shows that an action is occurring *now* or that a condition exists *now.*

    That officer drives *too carelessly, but you* drive *safely. Officer Lear* is transferring *to the Motor Traffic Bureau. (Progressive.)*

    You are *right; Officer Regan* does make *a lot of arrests for sexual misconduct. (The verb* does make *is the* emphatic *form.)*

2. *Past Tense.* The past tense indicates that an action occurred or a condition existed at some definite time in the *past.*

When the officers drove *down the alley, they* noticed *an open door at the rear of 1313 Cleopatra.*

The officers were questioning *her yesterday. (Progressive.)*

The inspector did talk *to him about his unacceptably sloppy appearance. (Emphatic.)*

3. *Future Tense.* The future tense indicates that an action will take place or that a condition will exist in the *future.*

    The inspector stated, "I shall inspect *the officers at roll call this afternoon."*

    All officers will wear *ties for the precinct open house tomorrow. Some officers* will be escorting *visitors through the building. (Progressive.)*

The Compound Tenses:

4. *Present Perfect Tense.* The present perfect tense indicates that an action or condition was *begun in the past* and *has just been completed* or *is still in progress.*

    Officers Lear and Regan have finished *their report on the robbery. (The report was begun in the past, and the writing has just ended.)*

    The inspector has gone *to headquarters. (He left some time ago and has not yet returned.)*

    The detectives have been investigating *that robbery for the past three months. (The investigation, begun three months ago, continues.)*

5. *Past Perfect Tense.* The past perfect tense shows that an act was completed before some other specified act or time.

    The officers were unable to serve the warrant because the suspect *had already* fled *the state. (The suspect's flight began and succeeded before the attempt to serve the warrant. Both events occurred in the past.)*

    Officers Lear and Regan had completed *the report before they realized that they* had omitted *the evidence. (The completion of the report and the omission of the evidence occurred before the realization; all take place in the past.)*

    The inspector had commanded *the precinct for three years prior to his transfer. (The transfer, a past event, came after the command and termination of command.)*

6. *Future Perfect Tense*. The future perfect tense indicates that an action or condition already begun will be completed at some future time. (You will rarely use this tense in police reports.)

> *By two o'clock, I* shall have completed *eighteen consecutive hours on duty. (The eighteen-hour tour of duty has already begun and* will be finished *at two o'clock.)*

> *The ambulance crew* will have removed *the victims before you arrive. (The removal* has begun, is in progress, *and* will be completed *prior to a time in the future, your arrival.)*

Tense Sequence:
Be consistent in the use of tense. Do not shift needlessly from one tense to another. Generally, in your reports, use the *past* tense. However, in some instances, it may be necessary to use one of the others, e.g., the *present* to record direct quotations or the *future* to indicate proposed follow-up investigation. The biggest problem occurs in sentences with dependent clauses. In these, let the main verb guide your choice of the verb in the dependent clause. If the main verb is in the *past* or *past perfect* (the most frequently used tenses in police reports), the verb in the dependent clause may be either *past* or *past perfect*. Use the one that eliminates any possibility of misunderstanding.

Original	Revision
Officer Lear *gave* the assisting officers a description of the second suspect, who *turned* and *ran* east between the houses. (*Gave* is past tense; so are *turned* and *ran*. This usage suggests all actions—the giving of the description, the turning, and the running—happened simultaneously when, in fact, the *turning* and *running* preceded the giving of information by several minutes.)	Officer Lear *gave* the assisting officers a description of the second suspect, who *had turned* and *run* east between the houses. (The *past perfect, had turned* and *run*, indicates these actions took place *before* Officer Lear *gave* the description.)
Officer Lear *informed* the suspect that he *is* under arrest. (*Informed* is the past tense; therefore, the verb in the dependent clause should be either *past* or *past perfect*, not *present*.)	Officer Lear *informed* the suspect that he *was* under arrest. (The verbs are now consistent.)

Formation of Tenses.
For the form of the various tenses, refer to this table.

TO GO: INDICATIVE MOOD, ACTIVE VOICE

Principal Parts: go   went   gone

	Singular		Plural	
	Simple	Progressive	Simple	Progressive
Present tense				
1st person	I go	am going	we go	are going
2d person	you go	are going	you go	are going
3d person	he goes (she, it)	is going	they go	are going
Past tense				
1st person	I went	was going	we went	were going
2d person	you went	were going	you went	were going
3d person	he went	was going	they went	were going
Future tense				
1st person	I shall go	shall be going	we shall go	shall be going
2d person	you will go	will be going	you will go	will be going
3d person	he will go	will be going	they will go	will be going
Present perfect tense				
1st person	I have gone	have been going	we have gone	have been going
2d person	you have gone	have been going	you have gone	have been going
3d person	he has gone	has been going	they have gone	have been going

Past perfect tense

	Simple		Progressive	
1st person	I had gone	we had gone	had been going	had been going
2d person	you had gone	you had gone	had been going	had been going
3d person	he had gone	they had gone	had been going	had been going

Future perfect tense

	Simple		Progressive	
1st person	I shall have gone	we shall have gone	shall have been going	shall have been going
2d person	you will have gone	you will have gone	will have been going	will have been going
3d person	he will have gone	they will have gone	will have been going	will have been going

Verbals (nonfinite verb forms)

	Simple	*Progressive*
Present infinitive	to see	to be seeing
Perfect infinitive	to have seen	to have been seeing
Present participle	seeing	(none)
Past participle	seen	(none)
Perfect participle	having seen	having been seeing
Present gerund	seeing	(none)
Perfect gerund	having seen	having been seeing

THAN, THEN

Than is a *subordinate conjunction. Then* is an *adverb.*

The suspect was stronger than *the officers had thought. (*Than *is a subordinate conjunction introducing the dependent clause* than . . . thought.*)*

All officers will turn in their service revolvers; then *they will be issued new sidearms.*

THEIR, THERE, THEY'RE

Their is a *possessive pronoun. There* is an *adverb* or *expletive. They're* is a *contraction.*

Officers Lear and Regan forgot their *nightsticks.*

There *goes the inspector. (An adverb indicating* where.*)*

There *are seven patrol cars in the precinct. (*There *is an expletive, i.e., a "filler" word. The subject of the sentence is cars.)*

They're *replacing all cars that are more than six months old. (*They're *is the contracted form of* they are.*)*

THREW, THROUGH

Threw is the past tense of *throw. Through* has various meanings. Study the following:

The suspect threw *a chair at Officer Pericles.*

Officer Nelson threw *her nightstick at the auto.*

Officer Peto drove through *the area but was unable to detect any odor of smoke.*

The suspect declared he was through *with crime.*

The accident occurred when the through *train struck the slow freight train.*

TO, TOO, TWO

To is a *preposition (*to *the store) or the sign of the* infinitive (*to *shoot). Too* is an *adverb* meaning *also* or *excessively. Two* is the number.

Officer Lear is going to *testify if he can get* to *court on time.*

The officers were too *busy to write the* two *reports required by the lieutenant.*

WENT, GONE

Went is the past tense of the verb *to go. Gone* is the *past participle* of the same verb. Do *not* use *went* with an auxiliary verb.

The officers have gone *to their sectors. (Not:* have went.*)*

WERE, WHERE

Were is a *verb. Where* can be several different parts of speech.

The suspects were *in custody.*

Where *is everyone? (Interrogative adverb.)*

I do not know where *she was arrested. (Conjunction.)*

WHICH, WHO, THAT

Who refers to *people. Which* refers to *things. That* may refer to either.

There is the suspect who *attempted to run down the officer. (*Who *refers to* suspect.*)*

That is the building *in* which *he was found. (*Which *refers to* building.*)*

Where are the reports that *the inspector wants? (*That *refers to* reports.*)*

Point out the man that *(or* whom*) you scratched. (*That *refers to* man.*)*

WRONG WORD

Use the word that carries the desired meaning. Be careful when writing confusing pairs (affect, effect) and words that sound alike (sight, cite, site). When in doubt, consult a dictionary or a glossary of usage. Try not to *overwrite.* Examine the following passages.

Suspect's escape attempt was hailed *by both officers. (*Halted*? Or did the officers* applaud*?)*

Officers noticed blood on her abused *lips. (*Bruised *lips?)*

Suspect was a mental patience. (*Patient, *a person receiving care or treatment, is the desired word.)*

Mrs. Monk then attacked Officer Lear with an end table. He removed *the end table from her. (An example of overwriting. He* took *the end table* away *from her. As written, a reader might think that the officer had disarmed her by dropping the table on her and then had to lift the table from her.)*

Suspect was trying to eject *another shell into the chamber. (*Eject *means to expel. The suspect was trying to* eject *the spent round from the chamber so that he could replace it with a live cartridge.)*

The above incident stemmed *when Mrs. Polonius struck the officer. (The writer* wants *occurred* or *took place* or *happened.)*

Suspect suffered a brake *just above the left elbow. (See* Break.*)*

APPLICATIONS

Exercise 1

Select the correct word.
1. Although the suspect exceeded 80 mph, he was unable to (lose, loose) the officers.
2. Officers believed the suspect was one of the (principals, principles) in the riot.
3. Officer Cornwell (passed, past) the inspector's car in a no-passing zone.
4. The witness refused to be (quiet, quite) while officers were interviewing the complainant.
5. Officer Lear (believes, feels) the witness may have been mistaken in her description of the suspect's auto.
6. The directive read: All officers shall (precede, proceed) to their assigned areas immediately after roll call.
7. The complainant (said, advised) that the burglar had probably already left the scene.
8. Officers Lear and Regan went to (there, their) patrol car (to, too, two) see if (there, their) shotguns were (there, their).
9. The sergeants (were, where) surprised when the line officer actually enforced the jaywalking ordinance.
10. The commanding officer criticized Officer Arundel for his failure (to, too, two) use (capitol, capital) letters at the beginning of each sentence.
11. Officer Lear interviewed all the neighbors but could not find a single (disinterested, uninterested) witness to the fight.
12. Captain Bardolph knows more law (than, then) most of the assistant prosecutors.
13. The driver refused to (accept, except) the traffic summons; instead he tore it into pieces and (threw, through) them at Officer Howell.
14. The precinct kept (it's, its) dubious position at the bottom of the efficiency rating.
15. The victim was (conscious, conscience) but appeared unable to answer questions.
16. The officers have (went, gone) to the wrong address.
17. Officer Lear reported that (a, an) informant had given the information.

Exercise 2

Add capital letters and quotation marks as needed.
1. For generations, said officer glendower, it has been traditional in our family not to have children.
2. Judge Duncan admonished the witness by stating, golf is the only game that can be improved with a good lie.

Exercise 3

Add commas and periods as needed.
1. Officer Fleane handcuffed the suspect read the suspect his rights and placed him in the patrol car
2. Mr Prospero the victim asked the officers to call Dr Angelo C Roni his family physician
3. Suspect gave her address as 14 Banquo Blvd Pogi Michigan but added that she had formerly lived in Valence Ohio
4. Before cleaning your revolver should be empty
5. When the officers signaled the driver he accelerated

Exercise 4

Add colons or semicolons as needed.
1. Officer Beggan arrested three suspects Lottie Mitchell, a shoplifter, Sally Harris, a streetwalker, and Lucy Evans, a conartist.
2. Officer Lear directed traffic at Wall and Broadway Officer Martin stood by the radio.
3. The suspect stated "I was just walking down the street, minding my own business, when you cops grabbed me."

Exercise 5

Revise the following sentences (Ref.: *Modifiers*).
1. While chasing the suspect down the alley, Officer Arbuthnot's nightstick fell from his belt and tripped him.
2. The traffic controller watched the nine-car crash that happened on their closed-circuit TV control sets.
3. Officer Regan confiscated the switchblade from the suspect with a carved ivory handle.
4. Upon turning to approach the suspect vehicle, the suspect accelerated and attempted to elude officers.
5. When resisting arrest, the officers used their nightsticks to subdue the suspect.
6. Officer Lear killed the dog that attacked him with a single shot.

7. Officer Panton directed the victim: "Tell us if your dog has rabies on this stamped card."
8. After being released from the prison ward, Officer Lear transported the arrestee to the county jail.

Exercise 6

Revise the following sentences (Ref.: *Active Voice* and *Passive Construction*).
1. Cpl. Charles was informed by Officer Pangloss that the search of the scene had been conducted by the laboratory technicians.
2. It was determined by the officers that entrance was gained by the burglars through the rear door.
3. The suspect was observed by the officers to be wearing a blue coat.
4. Officers were advised by the dispatcher that the LEIN check had been made and was negative.
5. It was noted that the suspect vehicle had red paint scrapings on the dented right front fender.

Exercise 7

Revise the following sentences (Ref.: *Tense*).
1. The officers believed that the suspect escapes on foot.
2. Just as Officer Lear thought his tour was finished, he receives another run.
3. At 2:00 p.m. Officer Barbican arrived. She sees the broken window. She then asked the complainant for a statement.
4. While the officers were looking the other way, the witness runs out the side door.
5. After a thorough search of the area, Officer Voltimond failed to locate the missing person and returns to patrol.

Exercise 8

Revise the following sentences (Ref.: *Agreement*).
1. Each of his fellow officers have contributed to the memorial fund.
2. Every one of the suspects are under seventeen.
3. Neither of the witnesses are certain.
4. Among the suspects was a local pimp, a pusher, and an ex-convict.
5. Near the doorway was three expended shells.
6. There was only the suspect and the complainant in the room at the time.
7. Any one of these people are capable of shooting at the police.
8. We need more traffic officers at Bath and Bailey; is any available?

Exercise 9

Select the correct form (Ref.: *Agreement* and *Reference of Pronouns*).
1. Each of the officers was asked to list (his, their) duty preference.
2. Did either of the officers file for (her, their) compensatory time?
3. The prosecutor was certain the jury would reach (its, their) verdict quickly.
4. The city council asked Officer Ophelia, along with Officer Oberon, to give (her, their) views on the effectiveness of police decoys.
5. The city council finally made up (its, their) mind and gave the department a 20 percent pay raise.

Exercise 10

Revise the following sentences (Ref.: *Ambiguous* and *Confused Sentences*).
1. The inspector stated he wanted more specific details in the reports.
2. The sergeant told him frequently to check the doors.
3. The complainant stated officers could contact him in the afternoon between three and five o'clock in his office on Monday.
4. The riot officers wearing helmets with visors and flak jackets trying to keep the disorderly crowd from crossing the barricades to attack the speaker.
5. Trinculo gave officers U.S. Armed Forces identification of the U.S. Air Force stationed at Caliban Field and advised Trinculo that he was under arrest for Possession of Controlled Substance.

Exercise 11

Revise the following sentences (Ref.: *Reference of Pronouns*).
1. Although the holdup squad is small, they have some excellent detectives.
2. When the officer placed a "hold" on the car, they said they would release it to the owner later.
3. She was told by Officer Lear they would be in touch with her.
4. Officer Clay informed the victim that he could call his doctor if he didn't feel well.
5. Officers instructed the complainants to call the police if they saw them again or if they caused any trouble for them.

Exercise 12

Study the first report and the accompanying comment. Then evaluate the others as if you were the command officer. Nearly all the errors are explained in the Glossary. We should add that while these are actual reports, they were written by students before they took our course in police report writing.

Report	Comment
The undersigned officers' in Unit 93 while on patrol heading north on 21 Street and Main observed a light-brown over brown station wagon heading north on 21 Street and disregarded a Stop sign at 21 Street and Cooper. The incident occurred at 2:00 p.m., Sunday, on October 11, 1973.	(1) *Officers* is the simple plural; no apostrophe is required. (2) Are 21st and Main the same street? The parallel structure of *21 Street and Main* suggests this. If so, what is the cross street? (3) As written, the officers *disregarded* the stop sign, for *observed* and *disregarded* are also parallel. *Officers* is the subject of the verb *observed*; the *and* links *disregarded* with *observed* (the only other past participle in the section); therefore, the . . . *officers observed* . . . and *disregarded*. (4) The *s* in *Stop* should be lowercase. (5) The passage is wordy. The *while on patrol* is unnecessary. The reader does not need the *light-brown over brown station wagon* at this point. The repetition of 21 Street is unnecessary; if the violator is on 21st, he could hardly run a stop sign on some other street. The last sentence is an afterthought; it will simply interfere with the officer's transition into the next paragraph. Compare this version:
	At 2:00 p.m., Sunday, October 14, 1973, Officers ARUNDEL and GLENDOWER (Unit 93), northbound on 21st at Main, observed the Suspect vehicle, northbound on 21st, disregard the stop sign at Cooper.
The Suspects' vehicle, a brown over brown 1971 Ford Pinto hardtop, Michigan registration FMG 999, was observed headed north on 21st. When the Suspect disregarded the Stop sign at 21 Street and Cooper.	The passage is repetitious. The writer has already given the information. Apparently the last sentence of the paragraph above was confusing. Placing the apostrophe after the *s* in *Suspects* suggests more than one occupant in the car, which is false. The vehicle description is still not necessary; moreover, the *station wagon* has

somehow become a *hardtop*. *Stop* still does not need to be capitalized.

Upon pursuit of the Subject, it was noted by the officers' that when the overhead lights and siren were operating with the intent of pulling the Suspect over for questioning; that the Suspect turned his head around in the direction of the officers'. The Suspect than accelerated the vehicle and turned left on Leicester Lane, proceeding in a easterly direction.

The plural *Suspects* above has now become the singular *Subject*. No apostrophe is necessary with *officers* anywhere in this passage. The passive construction *it was noted by* leads the writer into all sorts of difficulty. The incorrect semicolon after *questioning* results from the writer's entanglement in these semantic difficulties. *Than* is the wrong word; it should be the adverb *then*. The *proceeding in a easterly direction* is wordy as well as incorrect: a northbound vehicle turning left will be going west, not east. Use specific directions, i.e., east, west, northeast, etc. The *easterly direction* is excessive. Few judges will insist on precise compass points if you have testified "Suspect turned east." If they do, your prosecutor can always get a recess and a road map. The *a* should have been *an* anyhow.

Wordiness adds further to the problem. When you use your emergency equipment in a traffic arrest, one assumes your intention was to halt the suspect as well as to alert the general public to possible danger. (We have disregarded the questionable use of the siren at this point in a traffic arrest. We know of no departments that advocate using the siren to halt traffic violators except under unusual circumstances.) Compare:

Officers turned on emergency equipment and pursued the Suspect vehicle. Officers saw the driver turn his head, look back at them, and then accelerate. Suspect then turned left (west) on Leicester.

Suspect then took a right on Warwick Road and proceeded north on Mortimer Street, at 2:07 p.m., assistance was requested and Dispatch was notifyed as to the nature of the complaint and location.

This is also wordy. There is a comma fault either between *street* and *at* or between *p.m.* and *assistance*. *Notifyed* is a misspelling. Did the suspect turn from Warwick onto Mortimer? Or are the names applied to the same street? Compare:

Suspect turned right (north) on Warwick. At 2:07 p.m., officers requested assistance.

The Suspect was stopped at Mortimer and 100th Streets. When the officers' approached the Suspect vehicle, it was observed by both officers that the Suspect disposed out the window on the passingers side; several small packages. At this time Officer ARUNDEL requested Suspects drivers lisence, auto registration, and proof of insurance. Officer GLENDOWER recovered three plastic Baggys full of a powdry green substance believed to be marijuana.

Again the apostrophe on *officers* is wrong. The passive construction *it was observed by both officers* once more creates problems and results in an incorrect semicolon. The sentence *When . . . packages* could be written: *As officers approached the Suspect vehicle, they saw the Suspect throw several small packages through the passenger window.* In addition, *passingers* is misspelled and needs an apostrophe. There should be an apostrophe in *suspects* and *drivers*. *Lisence, registrations, Baggys,* and *powdry* are also incorrectly spelled. Incidentally, *where* did Officer Glendower find the Baggies?

While suspect was being I.D., the backup car arrived and inquired if the situation was under control. The backup car was informed by officers that indeed the situation was under control.

I.D. is police terminology for the noun *identification*, not the verb *identified*. Neither the backup unit nor the officers are identified. The last sentence adds to the wordiness. (*Compare:* As officers identified the Suspect, Scout 111 (ALBANY and CORNWALL) arrived. Officers informed Scout 111 that no assistance was required.)

Suspect was taken back to the patrol car and given the Maranda warning. He waved his rights and advised that "some black dude who's name he

The passive construction causes the writer to leave out the name of the officer who read the warning. *Maranda* is a misspelling. *Waved* is the couldn't remember gave him real good stuff."

wrong word; the right word is *waived*. What "advice" is he giving the officers? *Who's* is also incorrect; *whose* is right.

Suspect was transported to Narcotics Detectives for questioning at 2:25 p.m. The plastic Baggys of green powder was also turned over to Narcotics Detectives for analysis.

Narcotics and *detectives* should not be capitalized. There is a lack of agreement between the subject *Baggys* (which is still misspelled) and the verb *was*. Furthermore, the writer should have noted *who* did the questioning and *who* received the plastic Baggies.

Suspect was than transported to the City Jail were he was booked for Possession of Narcotics by Sargent PEMBROKE at 3:15 p.m.

Than is the wrong word; the writer wants *then*. *Were* is also incorrect; the relative pronoun *where* is needed. *Sargent* is misspelled.

REPORT A

On Sunday, July 20, 1974, the undersigned officers were patrolling North in the alley of the 1300 Block between Cordelia Street and Pericles Plaza. This was at 1:15 p.m.

Officers' noticed a Red 1972 Plymouth Roadrunner with Michigan 1974 registration 999 parked behind one of the small business's with two people in it. They turned East and proceded to approach the patrol car.

Officer ASTARTE looked at the hot sheet and said it was the parked car, a stolen car. As they approached the parked car they sped off down the ally failing to stop at Regan Road and disregaurded the stop sign at Pericles Plaza.

Calling for assistance and Unit 93 assisted, the Suspect's vehicle then came to a halt at the intersection of Lear and Pericles. Both Suspects jumped out of the car and run. Officer ASTARTE chased the passenger Suspect East on Pericles and apprehended him in front of 111 Pericles, Caliban's Clothing Store. While placing the Suspect under arrest, the man resists and had to be subdued. After being subdued, the arrest was made.

The driver Suspect was handcuffed and searched. He was then placed in the patrol car. Officer ASTARTE returns with the passenger Suspect. This Suspect was also placed in the patrol car. Each of the Suspects were given there rights seperately.

The Suspects were then transported to the city jail. Where they were mugged, printed, and lodged for Grand Theft Auto.

Officer ASTARTE contacted George GONZAGO of 1313 Tempest Street, Pogi, Michigan, that his car had been recovered and could be picked up the following morning.

REPORT B

At the above time and date the undersigned officers were N/B on Comus at Lucidas. Haled by an unidentified citizen who reported two men with shotguns are entering Lucky's Lounge in the next block.

We immediately advised Dispatch of the two men with shotguns who were entering the lounge and requested that Dispatch send back up units. Dispatch advised that Units 97, 98, and Sargeant was on the way.

Officers proceeded to the screen. I parked the squad in front of the building just East of Lucky's Lounge (The Samson Barber Shop). Officer ALLEGRO run's to the rear of the lounge while I covered the front. At this time backup units arrive. Officer ROSS went to the rear to assist officer ALLEGRO in covering the rear exit.

The rest of us entered thru the front door. We found the Suspect had all ready fleed before we got their.

Sargent SIDNEY immediately put out an APB on the Suspects. The bartender and two patrens, the only occupants of the bar, was interviewed by Sargent SIDNEY and myself.

The bartender advised that two men walked in carrying shotguns openly. They "told me to open the register or get my damned head blowed off." The bartender did as he was advised. The two men then left out a exist at the rear without bothering the two patrens.

The bartender described Suspect No. 1, the one who talked, as being a white male, approximately 6 foot tall, wereing a blue jacket and blue jeans with dark hair and eyes. He said he had a slight Southern accent. He described the other Suspect as shorter, with light hair, wereing blue pants and a Hawain shirt. Neither of the patrens were able to add to the descriptin.

The bartender was advised by Sargent Sidney that he would be contacted by derectives later. Officers checked with other merchants in the area but none reported they saw anything suspicious.
Status: Open.

SPELLING SUGGESTIONS FOR LAW OFFICERS

We have little faith in spelling rules as such. However, we have included these common rules which may prove helpful in police report writing. In addition, we have included a list of the most frequently misspelled words in police reports.

Prefixes. A prefix consists of one or more letters that can be attached before the root word to make a new word. With prefixes do not concern yourself with single or double letters; simply *write the prefix and add the root word as it is normally spelled*. Do this and the double letters will take care of themselves. Study this chart:

Prefix	Root Word	New Word
a-	moral	amoral
un-	necessary	unnecessary
un-	usual	unusual
dis-	satisfied	dissatisfied
dis-	jointed	disjointed
mis-	spelled	misspelled
mis-	placed	misplaced

Suffixes. Suffixes are one or more syllables added after the root. Unfortunately, adding a suffix is not as simple as adding a prefix.

1. If the word ends in a *single accented vowel* and a *consonant*, *double* the consonant before a suffix beginning with a vowel. Your pattern will be:

    accented vowel + consonant + consonant + suffix = new word

   EXAMPLES:

Root Word	Suffix	New Word
be-gin + n	-ing	beginning
out-fit + t	-ing	outfitting
hand-i-cap + p	-ed	handicapped
oc-cur + r	-ed	occurred

2. If in the above sequence the root word ends in a *double* vowel and a consonant, do *not* double the consonant. Your pattern will be:

    double vowel + consonant + suffix = new word

   EXAMPLES:

Root Word	Suffix	New Word
overlook	-ing	overlooking
seek	-ing	seeking
seem	-ed	seemed
appear	-ed	appeared

3. If the word ends in a *single accented vowel* and a *consonant* and the suffix *begins* with a *consonant*, do not double the final consonant. Your pattern will be:

    accented vowel + consonant + suffix = new word

   EXAMPLES:

Root Word	Suffix	New Word
regret	-ful	regretful
man	-like	manlike

   Note: The correct suffix is *-ful*, not *-full*.

4. If the accent is *not* on the last syllable of the root word, do *not* double the final consonant. Your pattern will be:

    unaccented syllable + suffix = new word

   EXAMPLES:

Root Word	Suffix	New Word
quar-rel	-ing	quarreling
des-pot	-ic	despotic
big-ot	-ed	bigoted
cum-ber	-some	cumbersome

5. When adding *-ly* to a word ending in *-l*, retain the final *-l*. Your pattern will be:

   -l plus *-ly* (suffix) = *new word*

   EXAMPLES:

Root Word	Suffix	New Word
careful	-ly	carefully
brutal	-ly	brutally
hypothetical	-ly	hypothetically

6. When adding *-ness* to a word ending in *-n*, retain the final *-n*. Your pattern will be:

   -n plus *-ness* (suffix) = *new word*

   EXAMPLES:

Root Word	Suffix	New Word
open	-ness	openness
green	-ness	greenness
plain	-ness	plainness

7. For *most* words ending in a *silent -e, except for words ending in -ce or -ge*, drop the *-e* before a vowel suffix. Your pattern will be:

   root word minus *-e* plus *suffix* = *new word*

   EXAMPLES:

Root Word	Suffix	New Word
arrive − e	-ing	arriving
take − e	-ing	taking
drive − e	-ing	driving
berate − e	-ed	berated
note − e	-able	notable

   For words ending in *-ce* or *-ge*, consult a dictionary when you are uncertain. These words follow no consistent pattern. Examine this chart:

Root Word	Suffix	New Word
change	-able	changeable
change	-ing	changing
singe	-ing	singeing
singe	-ed	singed
place	-ed	placed
allege	-ing	alleging

8. For most words ending in one or more consonants plus a silent *-e*, retain the *-e* before a suffix beginning with a consonant. Your pattern will be:

   consonant plus *-e* plus *suffix* = *new word*

   EXAMPLES:

Root Word	Suffix	New Word
shame	-less	shameless
pure	-ly	purely
waste	-ful	wasteful
arrange	-ment	arrangement

   But when *-dg* precedes the final silent *-e*, the *-e* is usually dropped before the suffix *-ment*. Your pattern will be:

   -dge minus *-e* plus *-ment* = *new word*

   EXAMPLES:

Root Word	Suffix	New Word
acknowledg − e	-ment	acknowledgment
abridge − e	-ment	abridgment

9. With most verbs ending in *-ie*, change the *-ie* to *-y* before *-ing*. Your pattern will be:

    -ie to *-y* plus *-ing* = *new word*

EXAMPLES:	Root Word	Suffix	New Word
	lie to ly	-ing	lying
	die to dy	-ing	dying

10. Change a final *-y* to *-i* when adding all suffixes except *-ing*. Do *not* change the *-y* to *-i* if the *-y* is preceded by a vowel. Your pattern will be:

    -y to *-i*   plus *suffix* = *new word*
    -y   plus *-ing* = *new word*
    (*vowel*)*y* plus *suffix* = *new word*

EXAMPLES:	Root Word	Suffix	New Word
	study y to i	-ed	studied
	try y to i	-ed	tried
	marry y to i	-age	marriage
	controversy y to i	-al	controversial
	study	-ing	studying
	try	-ing	trying
	marry	-ing	marrying
	deploy	-ed	deployed
	valley	-s	valleys

-ie or -ei. Remember the old rhyme:
I before *E*
When pronounced as *whee*
Except after C
Or when sounded as A
As in *neighbor* and *weigh*

EXAMPLES
i before *e*:
achieve, believe, field, fierce, grief, niece, pier, pierce, relieve, retrieve, reprieve, shield, siege, wield, yield.
Except after *C*
ceiling, conceit, conceive, deceit, perceive, receive.
Exceptions:
either, neither, financier, foreign, height, weird, species.

COMMONLY MISSPELLED WORDS

Correct Spelling	Common Misspelling	Correct Spelling	Common Misspelling
abandoned	abandonded	accidentally	acciden*tly*
accelerated	*ex*celerated	acknowledged	acknowl*eg*ed
acceptable	accept*i*ble	across	ac*c*ross

Correct Spelling	Common Misspelling	Correct Spelling	Common Misspelling
acquire	aquire	forcibly	forcably
admission	admition	homicide	homocide
admonishment	admonisment	illicit	confused with *elicit*
admonition	admonision	immediately	immediatly
advice	advise	initialed	initaled
advised	adviced	initiated	iniated
against	aganst	injured	injuried
aggravated	aggrivated	institution	instatution
all right	alright	interceded	interceeded
altercation	altercasion	interior	intierior
anonymous	anonimous		
apparently	aparently	know	confused with *no*
approximately	approximatly	license	lisence
argument	arguement	lieutenant	leiutenent
argumentative	argumentive	loose	confused with *lose*
arraigned	confused with *arranged*	lose	confused with *loose*
assault	assult	maneuvered	manuvered
attacked	attackted	multiple	multapul
believe	beleive	necessary	neccessary
boisterous	boistrous	occasion	ocassion
bureau	burreau	officers	officiers
committed	comited	opinion	opinon
complainant	complaintant	opportunity	oppertunaty
complaint	complant	original	originial
controlled	controled	patience	confused with *patients*
damaged	damiged	patients	confused with *patience*
definitely	definatly		
definition	defination	performance	purformance
description	discription	personal	confused with *personnel*
disposition	desposition	personnel	confused with *personal*
disturbance	disterbance		
elicit	confused with *illicit*	persuaded	pursuaded
entrance	enterance	politely	politly
erratic	errattic	possession	posession
evidence	evedence	possible	possable
exaggerate	exaggerrate	preceded	preceeded
existent	existant	prescription	perscription
explanation	explaination	prevalent	prevelent
felonious	felonous	prison	prision
fictitious	fictious		

Correct Spelling	Common Misspelling	Correct Spelling	Common Misspelling
procedure	proceedure	sufficient	sufficent
pursue	persue	their	thier, also confused with *there*
quantity	quanity		
received	recieved	there	confused with *their*
recommend	reccommend		
referring	refering	through	thorough
registration	registeration	unconscious	unconsious
restrained	restraned	until	untill
scene	confused with *seen*	vehicle	vehical
sedative	seditive	violator	violater
seized	siezed		
separation	seperation	waved	confused with *waived*
sergeant	sargent		
shining	shinning	waived	confused with *waved*
similar	similiar		
stitches	stiches	were	confused with *where*
stomach	stomack		
struggle	strugle	where	confused with *were*
subdued	subdueed		
succession	sucession	witnessed	wittnessed

WORDS FOR FURTHER STUDY

abduction	altered	beverage	commission
abortion	analyses	bribery	commit
abrasion	analysis	bruised	committee
accepted	analyzed	burglary	comparison
excepted	answered	business	compelled
access	apparatus	caliber	complained
excess	appearance	ceiling	concealed
accessible	articles	sealing	consistent
accessory	assistance	characteristic	contribute
admissible	assumed	choose	contributing
adultery	attached	chose	contusion
affidavit	attempted	cigarette	cooperative
alcohol	attendant	citizen	coroner
alias	autopsy	civilian	corroborate
alibi	barbiturate	collision	council
alleged	battery	commenced	counsel

counselor	forgery	language	permissible
counterfeit	freight	larceny	persistent
covert	frequency	lascivious	physical
cursory	frightened	latent	preference
debt	garage	legible	presence
deceased	gradually	legitimate	previously
deceived	guarantee	length	pried
decision	guided	lewd	prima facie
defendant	guilty	liable	principal
delinquent	habitually	lien	principle
dependent	heard	liquor	prisoner
deployed	height	location	privilege
deposition	hemorrhage	loitering	probable
described	heroin	magistrate	probation
destination	hindered	maintained	prohibit
developed	horizontal	malicious	psychologist
diagnosis	hurriedly	marijuana	pursuit
disappearance	hypodermic	mileage	quarrel
disclosed	hysterical	minimum	realized
dispute	illiterate	miscellaneous	receipt
distinguishing	imagined	misdemeanor	recognized
drunken	inadequately	municipal	registered
dual	incidentally	narcotics	released
eighth	independent	neighborhood	residence
eligible	indicating	noticeable	resistance
embarrassed	infraction	notification	rigor mortis
embezzlement	inhabitant	nuisance	seizure
employee	innocence	numerous	specific
epileptic	insufficient	obscene	stationary
equipment	insured	occupant	straight
examination	intoxicated	occupied	subpoena
examined	investigation	occurrence	suicide
exceeded	involuntary	occurring	surveillance
excessive	irrelevant	occurs	suspect
extortion	jeopardize	offense	tenant
extremely	judgment	omitted	victim
facility	juvenile	organized	writing
familiar	kidnap	overt	written
fatal	kidnapped	parallel	yielded
fight	knowledge	parole	
foreign	laboratory	partial	
forfeit	laceration	particularly	

Index